George Dencil Hardman I

Ancestors and Descendants

By
Edith Sharon Hardman West

First published by 1st Books 11/28/05

ISBN: 1-4033-8005-8 (e)
ISBN: 1-4033-8006-6 (sc)

Library of Congress Control Number: 2002094743

Printed in the United States of America
Bloomington, Indiana

This book is printed on acid-free paper.

Edith Sharon Hardman West

CONTENTS

Foreword

In the summer of 1994 my friends, Ellen and Denny Stilwell whetted my appetite to fulfill a dream of my father, George D. Hardman I, to trace our family lineage. They shared with me a volume of the *Hacker's Creek Journal,* which had our Hardman ancestors beginning with Nicholas Hardman of Inglehiem-am-Rhine, Germany. And thus my work began.

As my research continued, I found that our heritage must include our paternal mother's, Bessie Maude Lowther, and maternal mother's, Hazel Bowyer Hardman, lineage. Our ancestors and descendants included Stouts, Grimes, Bowyers, McWhorters, Lowthers, Hardmans and many are we. I have included the family members of all of these families with a birth date if it was available. This is my contribution to others who are taking on the task of finding their ancestors and descendants.

As the research moved along, many interesting facts about our family was discovered. Many of our ancestors were pioneers in the religious, settlement, politics, and military ventures of the United States of America. I have included those in the early sections of the book and have shared the continuation by their descendants of them.

This effort has given me an opportunity to reacquaint myself with many of the living descendants for which I am grateful. Without their contributions this work would not have been as complete as it is. Many of these 'cousins' wanted their families included. They may be found at the end of this edition.

I am also grateful to those "cousins" I met on the internet whose research was shared with me and filled many voids in the family ancestry. As you read this work you will find all of their names in the endnotes and throughout it.

And so we begin, first with our maternal ancestors, Stout, Grimes and Bowyer and then our paternal ancestors, McWhorter, Lowther and Hardman. These lines are brought together with the marriage of George D. Hardman I and Hazel Bowyer on December 23, 1928.

Life Sketch of the

John Stout Family

My overview of the Stout Family is an excerpt of Don Norman's research.[1] Richard Stout came to America about 1640 while serving in the British Navy and was discharged at New Amsterdam, now New York. He along with thirty-nine others founded Graves End, Long Island, in 1644. Our ancestors moved westward to Harrison, Gilmer and Braxton County, West Virginia.

Richard married Penelope Van Princin who had an encounter with the Indians. She came to America with her first husband. They were ship wrecked at Sandy Hook, New Jersey where the Indians killed her husband and left her for dead. Some time later, two Indians found and took her back to their village and took care of her wounds. She lived with the Indians doing squaw's work until 1644 when some white men came to the village looking for the white woman they had heard about. Richard married her that year.

The Indian story does not end here. In 1664 and Indian came and told her there was going to be an attack on Grave's End. A battle ensued which ended with Richard's calling for a parley. After the conference they agreed to a truce and celebrated for two days. The settlers agreed to buy the land from the Indians with the date of purchase being January 25, 1664.

Penelope's father was thought to be a Puritan Baptist Separatist who had been banished from his church. In 1668, Richard and his family joined with others to form the first Baptist Church of New Jersey. Our great aunt, Effie Stout Steele, married a Baptist preacher, William Steele and served as a missionary to China.

An e-mail from a newly found 'cousin' states that our ancestor, Caleb Stout fought with the New Jersey militia during the American Revolution. Information I received online says that he served in Capt. Brealily's Co., 2nd N. J. Regiment under Col. Maxwell. In 1818 he petitioned for a pension in Harrison Co., West Virginia.[2] In addition, the nephew of our ancestor, James Stout, served with Captain William Lowther, our ancestor, in Lord Dunsmore's Ohio expedition in 1774.[3]

Life Sketch of the

Felix Grimes Family

Felix Grimes (Graham), the immigrant from Ireland, came to America in the mid-1770's when the Methodist movement was beginning. While the *History of Pocahontas County* did not reveal his religious persuasion, one of his daughters, Nancy, married Rev. Samuel C. Montgomery and several of his granddaughters married Methodist Episcopal ministers.[4] This suggests the Methodist movement influenced his family.[5]

This family contributed greatly to the settlement of our nation. Four of his daughters moved to Ohio with their bridegrooms. They settled in Maryland, Texas, Iowa, Tennessee and western Virginia, which became West Virginia. They settled in the counties of Harrison, Upshur, Webster, Pocahontas, Pendleton, and Braxton. The sons of Felix, Arthur and James, our ancestors, remained in Pocahontas.[6]

During the settling of our nation, there were many Indian stories. Arthur, our ancestor, had one with Levi Moore while out scouting for Indians on Clover Lick. They went into a house that was abandoned and fell asleep. Arthur dreamed he had been bitten by a rattlesnake and sprang out of bed. Moore was dreaming of turkeys when he was awakened. The men escaped. When they recounted the story, Moore told them that whenever he was dreaming of turkeys he would soon have trouble with Indians.[7]

There is no evidence that the Grimes Family fought in the Revolutionary War. As I stated above, the family appeared to be influenced by the Methodist Episcopal Church. During this war "John Wesley's Toryism and his writings against the revolutionary cause did not enhance the image of Methodism among many who supported independence. Furthermore, a number of Methodist preachers refused to bear arms to aid the patriots."[8]

They did join the Union Army in the Civil War. Unfortunately, in this war the fact that brother fought against brother is true of our ancestors. The four sons of our ancestor's, Arthur, David, Hugh, Zane and one grandson, Morgan were Union soldiers.[9] His son-in-law, Leonard Boyer, the husband of Nancy Grimes, fought on the Confederate side. Leonard married Catharine, our ancestor James' daughter, as his second wife. Both of them had died in Highland County, Virginia before the war started. Leonard's enlistment, capture and release papers follow.[10]

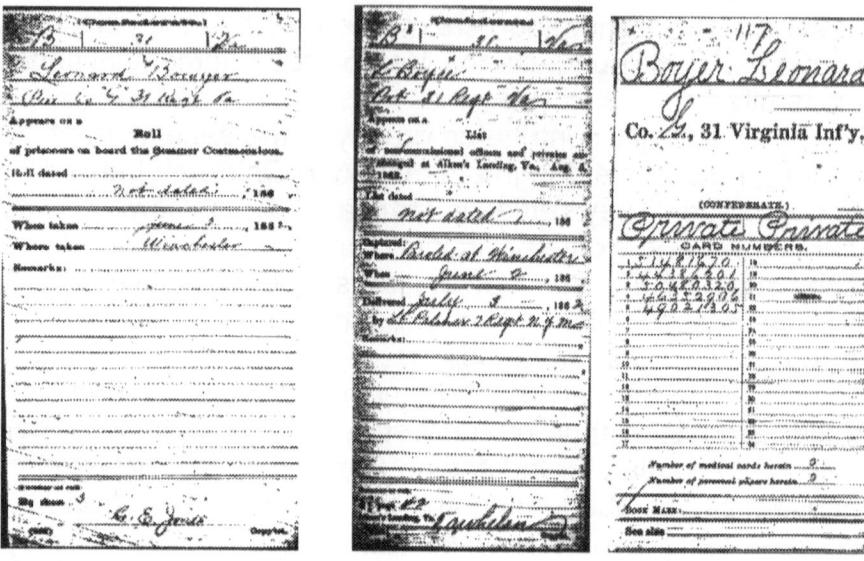

I will close the discussion of the Grimes ancestors with the last will and Testament (misspellings included) of Felix Grimes, which can be found in Bath County, Va., Will Book 2, page 34.[11]

The last and Testament of Felix Grimes being in sound mind and calling to mind the immortality of his body desires to despos of his worldly Estate in the following manner first I do beqeath to loving wife Cathine all the Household furniture except what belongs to my Daughter Nancy or is now in her name and I do likewise leave to my wife the house we now live in her lifetime except she chooses to finish the new House that is now raised & covered, and also do leave her the third of the cleared land and liberty to clear what she may need and to have the two work horses that we do now work and all the farming utincels for the use of the plantation, while she agree to live and work together and if the boys does not choose to stay and work the plantation all the property then is to be sold and divided on the price thereof equally amongst the two Boys that is Charles and James and their mother except what will pay all my just Debts and my daughter Nancy to have what horse___is in her name and as many cattle as will make her equel to what polly and Peggy got and five pound in money and one dollar to each of my other sones and son in laws as I consider I have come a full part for them and the land where I hold I leave to my sons Charles and James equally to divide or sell as may suit best but at their mothers death and my daughter Nancy is to have the same privilege as usual to live in the house with her mother while she remains single and I do leave her six head of Sheep all the stock left to her she is at liberty to dispose of or remove when ever she may think proper and I do leave James Tallman & Catherine my wife executors to my will in Witness hereof I do here unto set my hand and seal in presents of the names asined hereunto this 17th of December eighteen hundred & thirteen.

James Tallman) Some words entered   Felix Grimes
Samuel Waugh) before sined
John Connaley)
Bath County February court 1814
This last will and testament of Felix Grimes dec'd was presented in Court and proved by James Tallman, and June Court following was further proved by Samuel Waugh and ordered to be recorded. Teste
Chs. L. Tramisio? Clk
Will dated 7 Dec 1813
Will proved Feb 1814
Inventory of Estate of Felix Grimes Appraised by John Moore, Levi Moore, Samuel Waugh, John Moore, Sr.

Life Sketch of the

Leonard Bowyer I Family

My work now turns to our ancestor Leonard Boyer I.
The only resource we have for him is his will dated 1815.[12]

304

In the name of God amen I Leonard Boyers of the county of Pendleton and State of Virginia being weak in body but of sound mind and memory do make this my last will and testament in the manner and form following First of all I impower my executor as soon as convenient after my decease to sell my houses and land to the best advantage and make a right to the same likewise I allow all my personal estate to be sold except my cow her I allow to go with my two youngest children Nancy and Anthony Boyers for their use the amount of the above sales I allow my executor to discharge my just debts with and if there shall be any thing over I would allow my Executor to put it out on interest for my three children Leonard, Nancy and Anthony Boyers till they come of age when it is to be equally divided among them I also nominate and appoint Thomas Buckman Executor of this my last will and testament Revoking all former wills by me made In witness whereof I have hereunto set my hand this 11th of February 1815—

Adam Bird Junr
George Burns
John Gall Junr

Leonard Boyer

At a court held for Pendleton county the 4 day of April 181_
This last will & testament of Leonard Boyer deed was

13

In the document above he names his three children,
Leonard II, Nancy and Anthony. In the will sent to me by
Emma Snider we see the love this father had for his children in
which he specifies that "the cow her I allow to go with my two
youngest children…" Their ages at that time can be estimated
from the ages given for Leonard II and Nancy in the 1860
Highland County, Virginia census.

Book 29/71

Leonard Bonnyer }
To } Deed
Joseph Matheny }

This Deed made the 22nd day of February 1894, by and between Leonard Bonnyer party of the first part and Joseph Matheny party of the second part, Witnesseth, that for and in consideration of the sum of Two Hundred Dollars to be paid by the party of the second part, whereof the receipt is hereby acknowledged by the party of the first part and the maintenance of the said Leonard Bonnyer and Nancy Bonnyer their lifetime doth grant, bargain and convey with general warranty the following tract or parcel of land situated in Gilmer County West Virginia and lying on Lick Run of Bear Fork of Big Cove Creek and bounded as follows to-wit: Beginning at a Chestnut oak in lane gap, N 74 E 44½ poles to a maple, thence N 85½ E 44½ poles to a stone at the road, thence S 74 E 11½ poles to a stone, thence N 88 E 8¼ poles to a stone, thence S 58 E 13½ poles to a stone, thence N 32 E 16 poles to a stone, thence N 54½ W 53½ poles to a stake, thence S 36 W 27 poles to a dogwood near the road, thence S 81 W 75 poles to a hickory, thence S 29 W 15 poles to two chestnut oaks and a sassafras tree, thence S 19 E 23½ poles to the beginning, containing twenty-five acres more or less with the appurtenances thereto belonging. The party of the first part gives full possession to the party of the second part on the first day of March 1894; Witness the following signature and seal.

Witness, E. A. McCloud   Leonard his mark Bonnyer (Seal)

State of West Virginia }
County of Gilmer } I, C. F. Lane a Notary Public of said County of Gilmer do certify that Leonard Bonnyer whose name is signed to the writing within bearing date the 22nd day of February 1894, have this day acknowledged the same before me in my said County. Given under my hand this 22nd day of February 1894.

C. F. Lane N.P.

State of West Virginia;
Gilmer County Court Clerk's Office March 7th 1894. The foregoing Deed together with the certificate thereto annexed was this day duly admitted to record in said Office.

Teste Jasper N. Kee Clerk

The 1860 census does not include Anthony; there is no knowledge of him beyond the will. From other censuses and the above deed[13] Nancy lived with her brother until her death. A copy of the Bond below dated July 18, 1902, indicates Leonard died prior to that date. Nancy's date of death is unknown.

~BOND~

Know all Men by these presents:

That we, *T. M. Snider*

and *R. H. Lewis*

his surety_____, are held and firmly bound unto the State of West Virginia in the

penal sum of *Twice Hundred* _____DOLLARS,

for the true payment of which well and truly to be made we bind ourselves jointly

and severally, and each of us binds his heirs, executors and administrators firmly

by these presents. Sealed with our seals and dated this *18th* _____ day of

July 1 9 0 2_____, **.**

THE CONDITION of the above obligation is such that whereas the above bound

T. M. Snider

has been *appointed Administrator of the*

Estate of Leonard Rymer, late of Upshur

deceased

_____

_____

_____

_____

Now, therefore, if the said *T. M. Snider*_____shall

faithfully discharge the duties of said office and account for and pay over as required

by law, all money which may come into his hands by virtue of the said office or

trust, THEN SHALL THIS OBLIGATION BE VOID, otherwise to remain in full

force and virtue.

For many years no one knew where he was buried. Our second cousin, Emma Snider found his grave in her research of the family. Emma informed me that she and other descendants have set a tombstone there. Following is a copy of the field report she sent to me identifying his gravesite.

A religious affiliation is identified in a deed made by G. A. Bowyer, Leonard II's son. Emma sent me a copy of that deed which specified that a Methodist Episcopal Church was to be built on the gift of the land.

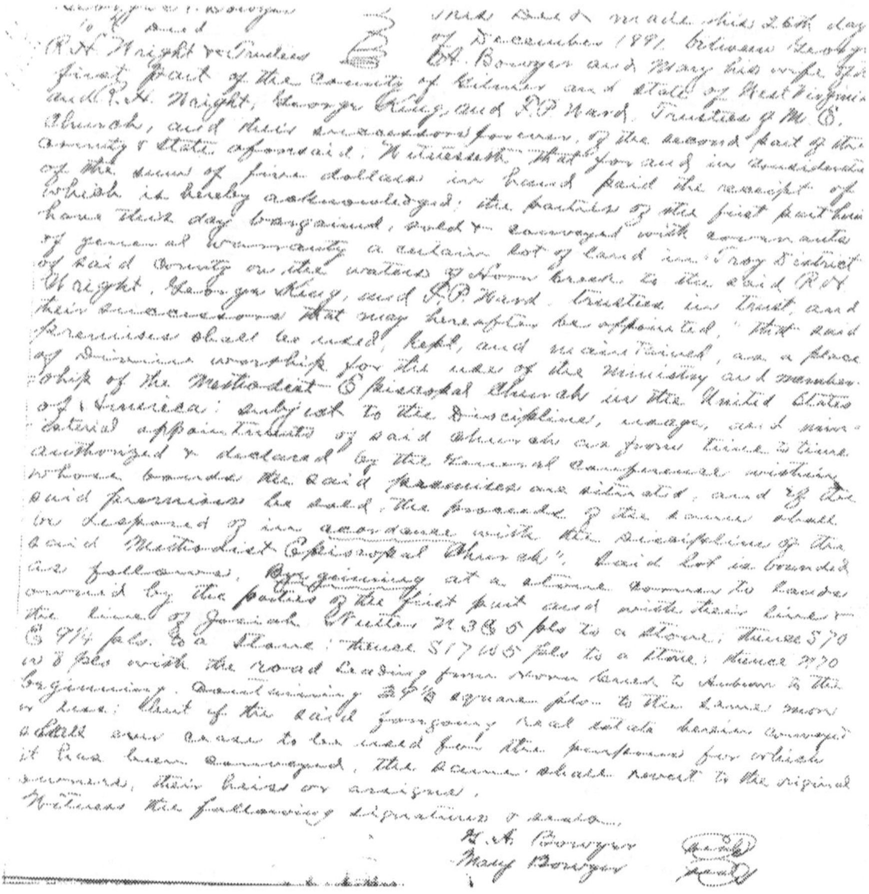

[illegible] Bowyer
to [illegible] and
R. H. Wright & Trustees

This Deed made this 26th day of December 1891 between Geo. [illegible] A. Bowyer and Mary his wife of the first part of the County of Gilmer and State of West Virginia and R. H. Wright, George King, and J. P. Ward, Trustees of M. E. Church, and their successors forever, of the second part of the county & State aforesaid, Witnesseth, that for and in consideration of the sum of five dollars in hand paid the receipt of which is hereby acknowledged; the parties of the first part have this day bargained, sold & conveyed with covenants of general warranty a certain lot of land in Troy District of said County on the waters of Horn Creek to the said R. H. Wright, George King, and J. P. Ward trustees in trust, and their successors that may hereafter be appointed, "that said premises shall be used, kept, and maintained, as a place of divine worship for the use of the ministry and membership of the Methodist Episcopal Church in the United States of America; subject to the discipline, usage, and ministerial appointments of said church as from time to time authorized & declared by the General Conference within whose bounds the said premises are situated, and if the said premises be sold, the proceeds of the same shall be disposed of in accordance with the discipline of the said Methodist Episcopal Church". Said lot is bounded as follows; Beginning at a stone corner to lands owned by the parties of the first part and with their line & the line of Josiah [illegible] N 38 E 5 ples to a stone; thence S 70 E 9 1/4 ples. to a stone; thence S 17 W 5 ples to a stone; thence N 70 W 8 ples with the road leading from Horn Creek to Auburn to the beginning. Containing 39 1/2 square ples. to the same more or less; that if the said foregoing real estate herein conveyed shall ever cease to be used for the purposes for which it has been conveyed, the same shall revert to the original owners, their heirs or assigns.

Witness the following signatures & seals.

G. A. Bowyer (Seal)
Mary Bowyer (Seal)

Charles Osbourne Bowyer, our ancestor and Leonard II's son, lived on the Bowyer home place in Gilmer county 1894 since all of his children were born on Horn Creek. He moved to Burnsville, Braxton County, West Virginia where he made his home until his death March 2, 1915. In the administration of his estate by our grandfather, Hugh Raymond Bowyer, it can be noted that he had acquired a great deal of real estate in Burnsville, West Virginia. His will and these documents are in my possession.

I, C. O. Bowyers, of the town of Burnesville, Braxton County, West Virginia, being about sixty eight years of age and being of sound and disposing mind and memory, do make, publish and declare this my last will and testament, hereby revoking and making null and void all other last wills and testaments by me made heretofore

First, my will is that all my just debts and funeral expenses including the expenses of my sickness be paid out of my estate as soon after my decease as shall be found convenient.

Second, I give, devise and bequeath unto my wife, M. C. Bowyers one third of all my personal property including bills, notes and demands of any kind whatsoever that are collectible, and the house and furnishings in which I live, situated on --------------Street in the Burnsville Industrial Company's Addition to the town of Burnsville, and marked on the plan or plat of said addition as lots . Nos.2 and 4 in Block No. 14.   This realestate she is to have and enjoy her natural lifetime, and at her decease it is my will that my executor sells this property at private or public sale as he may deem expedient, and apportion the proceeds derived from said sale among my nine children, share and share alike.

Third, The residue of my personal property and real estate I give, devise and bequeath unto my nine children to be divided among them equally, share and share alike.

Fourth, I hereby appoint and constitute my son Hugh Raymond Bowyers as the executor of my Will withou bond and I authorize and empower him to make sale of my property, both real and personal, by private or public sale as to him may seem most expedient, and when he makes sale of realestate I empower and authorize him to make deeds therefor of general warranty.

This power shall be full and complete in him, and whatsoever he may do in the premises shall be as well and fully done as if I, myself were living and transacting the business.

Witness the following signature and seal, this the 2nd. day of February, 1915.

C. O. Bowyer   (Seal).

Signed, published and declared by the above named C. O. Bowyers as for his last will and testament, in the presence of us, who in his presence and in the presence of each other, and at his request, have hereunto subscribed our names as witnesses.

M. W. HEfner   Witness
H. T. Harper   Witness.

A COPY.   Teste:---- *C. B. Adams* ----Clerk.

In the administration Charles' estate our grandfather carried out his wishes that all of the children should receive equal shares. Our great Uncle Cicero had died and grandfather divided his share equally among his three children. This document is in my possession.

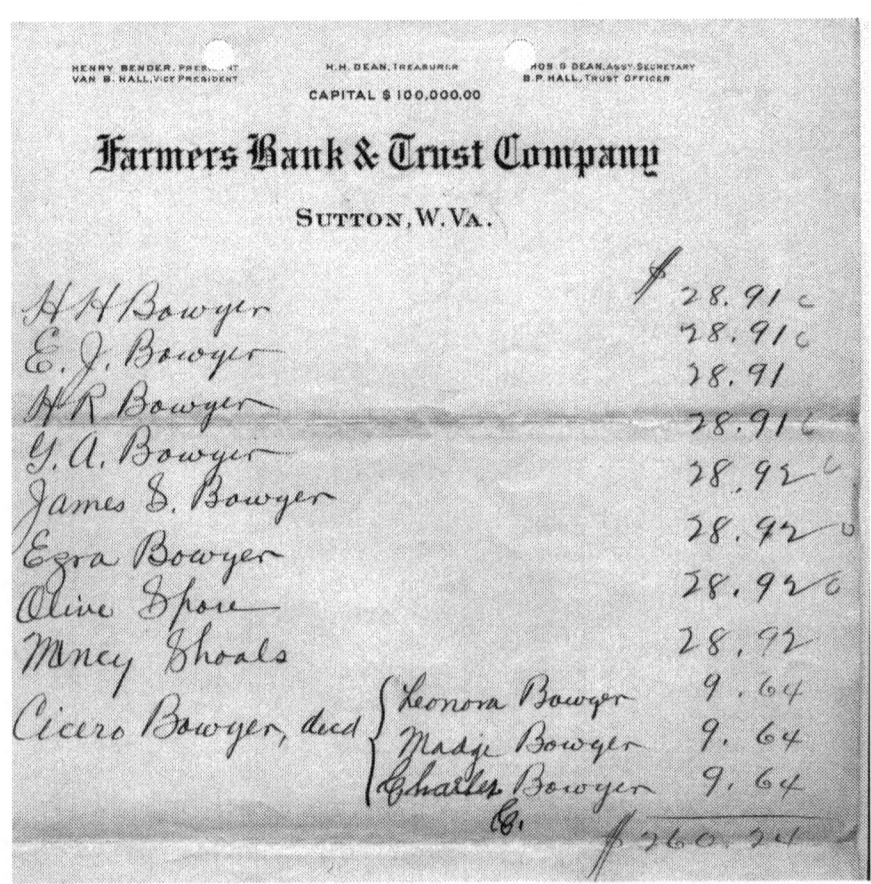

Farmers Bank & Trust Company

SUTTON, W. VA.

H H Bowyer	$ 28.91 c
E. J. Bowyer	28.91 c
H R Bowyer	28.91
Y. A. Bowyer	28.91 c
James S. Bowyer	28.92 c
Ezra Bowyer	28.92 c
Olive Spore	28.92 c
Mncy Shoals	28.92
Cicero Bowyer, decd { Leonora Bowyer	9.64
Madje Bowyer	9.64
Charles Bowyer	9.64
C.	$ 260.94

Hugh Raymond Bowyer, our grandfather, continued his father's drive to acquire real estate. During the administration of his father's property he bought the interests of his siblings documented by wills in my possession. This made it possible for him to provide a home for Catora, our grandmother, Aunt Edie and our family. Uncle Bud lived in Ohio and never returned to live in Burnsville. When my parents returned from Alexandria, Virginia they returned to the house below that would be our home in Burnsville, West Virginia. Below is a picture of it and me on the front steps.

These pictures were taken on the road beside our house. Those pictured left to right by nickname are Bessie, Billy, George I, Toots, Boots and Marge. In the background of the top pictures is the home our grandfather provided for Aunt Edie and Uncle Paul's family.

On the left is a picture of Dad and Uncle Paul, our Aunt Edith's husband, during the cellar construction. The young man bent over in the foreground is our cousin, Rex Cutright, the son of our father's sister, Aunt Lora.

Below are Hugh Raymond Bowyer's great grandchildren at his birthday celebration at his home on October 2, 1965.

Front Row from left to right: James William Roe, John Neil Roe, and Carolyn Sue Burke holding Barbara Ruth Roe.

Second Row from left to right: Robert Edward Thompson, Roberta Diane Burke and Georgia Grey Hardman holding Sherrie Anne Roe.

The Hugh Raymond Bowyer did not attend any church regularly. My mother was a member of the Women's Society of Christian Service, a Methodist organization. As a child, I attended the Methodist Protestant Church in Burnsville. My sister, Marjorie, was married in that church. My father's family had a strong relationship with the Methodist Protestant Church, which will be discussed in the Hardman life sketch as we continue through our lineage.

Life Sketch of the

Henry McWhorter Family

This brings us to the Henry McWhorter family whose granddaughter, Rebecca Celina, married the son of Col. William Lowther. Henry, our ancestor, was a member of the Methodist Church and a class leader for fifty years. Many times the services were held in his home because no church had been built at that time.[14]

The Henry McWhorter Cabin

The Neely Family had acquired the land on which the cabin set. Mrs. Neely decided to give the cabin back to the family. Minnie S. McWhorter began to acquire the funds to remove it. In 1926 she began the process of having it torn down and rebuilt. It was reconstructed at Jackson's Mill were it stands today at the entrance to the 4-H camp. On August 14, 1927 in a dedicatory ceremony it was presented and accepted by Minnie.[15]

Henry McWhorter, our ancestor, was living in Orange County, New York when he was called to service in the Revolutionary War at the age of sixteen. Thomas, his son and our ancestor, inherited a part of the home farm and lived there until his death in 1816. Sadly, Thomas's only son, Henry, was killed on January 23, 1863 at an engagement on the Greenbrier River in Pocahontas County. He was a commissary sergeant in Co. E, 3rd W. Va. Vol. Cavalry. To make matters worse, two of Thomas' grandsons saw their father killed and one was taken to Libby Prison.[16]

After the war Henry migrated to and built the cabin pictured above on the banks of Hackers' Creek in what is now Lewis County, West Virginia. Nearby he built the first mill in Lewis and Braxton County. During a shortage of food, he refused to sell the corn to buyers in Clarksburg, West Virginia and gave it to the needy settlers in exchange for labor at a rate of twenty-five cents a bushel.[17]

By 1829 a little village had grown up around the mill and home. The government honored our ancestor by naming the post office there, McWhorter's Mill and renamed Jane Lew in 1848.[18] Henry was a trustee for Weston when it was established as a town in 1818.[19]

The only Indian story involving Henry was found in his participation in the aftermath of the Indian raid. Chief Tecumseh took our Hardman ancestor, Elizabeth Waggoner, captive in this raid. He helped to carry the bodies of her massacred family to West's Fort, which was nearby.[20] More of this story will be told in the Hardman sketch of our ancestors.

Henry was the grandfather of our ancestor, Rebecca Celina Lowther, who married Elias Jackson Lowther. With her our lineage continues through their son, Granville Sharp Lowther.

Life Sketch of the

Thomas De Lowther Family

The right Hon.ble
Henry Lowther
Viscount Lonsdale

Our Lowther lineage has been researched back to 1199. This research is the work of Gary Lewis beginning with Thomas DeLowther and ending with Robert Lowther who immigrated to America from Ireland in about 1738.[21] The research of Lewis states that William Lowther, Jr., Robert's father, was born in Ireland and died in Bucks County Pennsylvania in 1750. These dates seem to indicate that they came to America together.

My first cousin, Phyllis Cutright McComas, sent the Lowther coat of arms to me. On it one can see that it has the name, Henry Lowther. None of our ancestors were named Henry according to Lewis' research, however, one of Robert's sons was named Henry.

As one reads the family tree, it is apparent that there are several names that are the same and seem to be family names. As seen in Lewis' research some of our ancestors were born at Lowther Castle, Lowther, Westmoreland, England. Apparently, there was a royal line of this family, which had a great bit of clout in England, which continues today according to Minnie Lowther.

She wrote in her book that from 1300 through the following five hundred years that no Parliament sat which did not include a Lowther or a Lowther's direct nominee.[22] The more interesting historical fact for me was that they had come to England "with William the Conqueror, from Normandy in France, during the autumn of 1066."[23] This was the year of the Norman invasion of England.

Minnie Lowther notes in her book that Lowthers did appear in America until 1681 in Pennsylvania but that our ancestor, Robert, had no connection with them. One of William Lowther, Jr.'s children, Ruth, died in Pennsylvania according to Lewis. Lowther disputes any relationship with the Pennsylvania family but this appears to be a connection for me.

Robert did settle in Albermarle County, Virginia but married Aquilla Reese in Philadelphia, Pennsylvania.[24] She was born in Plumstead Twp. Bucks Co., Pennsylvania. This is another connection, which indicates that our ancestors were in Pennsylvania before migrating to Virginia.

But we must move on to the contributions made by these Lowther ancestors in the formation of our great nation. It is William, Robert's son, who is the hero of this ancestral line. He came to Harrison County in June, 1773 with his wife, Sudna, and their three oldest children. Their fourth child, Jesse, and our ancestor is said to have been the first white male born in that county.[25]

Col. William Lowther Cabin

Minnie Lowther states in her book published in 1911 in a footnote on page 7 that the cabin was still standing. It was located one one-half miles below West Milford, on the Clarksburg road. This picture was taken in 1908 and at that time some of the descendants still lived in it.[26]

She was in possession of an old land grant that validates his early settlement at West Milford. It was made to him "on June 8, 1785 and signed by Patrick Henry, on November 14, 1786, while he was Governor of Virginia..."[27]

Lowther's book (which was sent to me by Jinny Collins, one of the 'cousins' I found during my research) and *Chronicles of Border Warfare*, (a gift from my nephew, Robert Edward Thompson) were my best resources for the Lowthers in America. In them were the stories and accomplishments of William in the areas of politics, military ventures and settlement,

William was the "first Justice of the Peace in the district of West Augusta; the first Sheriff of Harrison and Wood counties, and was at one time a member of the General Assembly at Richmond, Virginia."[28] His service in the political arena was continued through my father and sister.

William was an Indian fighter and helped in building Simpson's fort, West's fort and Nutter's fort.[29] Some of his encounters with Indians are documented in Wither's book.[30]

He joined the Revolutionary War effort in 1774. In a footnote of Wither's book he wrote, "His military merits carried him through the subordinate grades to the rank of Colonel."[31]

It was of great interest when it was learned that none other than General George Rogers Clarke commissioned him a Major in 1781.[32] His movement through the ranks was found in the *History of Harrison County:* commissioned Major, 1781, (204), Captain January 25, 1793 (129) and Lt. Colonel in March 1793 (219).

The following excerpt from Sue Tilzer's York Volunteer Listing, which I obtained online shows him with the rank of lst Lt. in 1776.

Capt. Hugh Campbell's Company
Sept. 17, 1776
Col. Robert McPherson's Second Battalion

Capt. Hugh Campbell	1st Lt. William Lowther
2nd Lt. Robert McIlhinney	Ensign Simon Vanarsdalen

Based on the information and documentation of Lowther's participation, Marjorie and Coleta Hardman, my two sisters, along with my Aunt Lora Hardman Cutright Queen became members of the Daughters of the American Revolution.

A copy of a document from the *Hacker' Creek Journal* supports his promotion to Major. It is dated 20 April 1785.

Publick claims – Major William Lowther appeared in court, proved to the satisfaction of the court same that he or is in the Volunteer Units under the command of General George Roger Clark in the year 1781 and obtained from the General a Major's commission and acted in that capacity from 21 day of June until the eleventh day of august and then obtained a discharge, also that he was seven days from the date of his discharge to his arrival home and that he obtained his discharge near (? Oastoned by tickney) and the discharge was lost and ordered to be copied.[33]

In Chapter one of Lowther's book, she gives a narrative of Col. William Lowther and the Hughes brother's expedition, which took them from Hacker's Creek to the Ohio River. On the way they named the streams and tributaries with one of special interest, the Hughes River. This river is named for Jesse Hughes, Col. William's brother-in-law.

I believe that it was Jinny Collins who told me in an e-mail that the town of Williamstown in Wood County was named for the Colonel. Lowther's book suggests that they may have been the first "paleface strangers" which had ever trod the present bounds of Ritchie County.[34] I know that as I travel down Rt.14 south towards Spencer it reminds me that our ancestors brought civilization to the area.

At his death the Colonel was buried near to the cabin where his life in West Virginia began. Sudna, his wife, moved to Berea and lived with her son, Elias. She is buried at Flanagan burying-ground near there which is off of Rt. 14.[35]

We know Jesse, his son, returned to the Parkersburg area and established a home on Neal's Island. It was here that Elias Jackson Lowther, his son and our ancestor, was born. Jesse returned to West Milford with his family later.[36] This is where Elias met our ancestor, Rebecca Celina McWhorter.

They were the parents of Granville Sharp Lowther, our great grandfather, who moved to Braxton County. Granville Sharp Lowther was the father of Bessie Maude Lowther, our grandmother. On her marriage to John William Hardman, our grandfather, Granville gave her a homestead on Fall Run, Braxton County, West Virginia. McComas' letter she tells a sad tale about this inheritance. After they were married John William convinced her to put the land in his name only. Unfortunately, he died at the age of fifty and Bessie Maude had to borrow $500.00 from her sister Carrie to pay the inheritance.

Judy Ramsey, our cousin, is in possession of the medical book Granville used in his practice of medicine. The book and his recipes for good health were very interesting. They used the naturally grown remedies to cure the flu, a cold and other common maladies. . . Phyllis Cutright McComas' letter states that Bessie Maude continued the practice of medicine on Fall Run as a midwife. She told Phyllis she had delivered sixty-five babies and never lost a mother or child.

33

In the distribution of Hazel Bowyer Hardman, our mother, I was given the homestead, which I have restored. McComas' letter says that Bessie Maude was a gifted artist and had, at one time, a picture she drew of a cat lying in front of the fireplace. The picture is long gone but the fireplace remains.

I restored it to the original walnut wood, which had no less than five coats of various kinds of paint on it. When our home place at Burnsville, pictured above, was torn down, Marjorie, my sister, gave me brick from its fireplace. James William Roe, my son, put them in the Hardman homestead fireplace. Something of the home in which our parent's lives began together joined with the home where we spent most of our childhood.

Below is a picture of Grandma Hardman in front of the cellar on the home place of which only a few stones remain. Phyllis suggested that she had a still in it and used the proceeds to take care of her six living children after being widowed. I know she had a recipe because at the age of nine on a visit to her home in Ryder, West Virginia she gave me my first taste of beer. She also taught me how to play solitaire that summer.

Below is a picture of my father, on the right, with a friend leaning on the fence along the creek.

As children, our parents took us to the farm where we spent many delightful hours. The most fun was playing in this creek. Just a short piece from the house was a pool of water deep enough to swim in. We would swing from grape vines in the trees and drop into the water. The things kids will do when the parents are not watching.

It was just a few miles down the road where our parents met. Hazel Bowyer was a teacher at Falls Mill School and George Dencil played ball every Sunday at the Falls. Just how they met I do not know but they were married and set up housekeeping at the homestead with Bessie Maude. I am in possession of the cherry dining room table and chairs they bought at that time. Their marriage brings all of our ancestors together as one family, Hardmans.

Life Sketch of the

Nicholas Hardman Family

Hardman

 We know nothing of Nicholas Hardman except that he was the father of the immigrant, Peterman Hardman who lived in Inglehiem-am-Rhine. My overview of our Hardman ancestors is taken from the *Hacker's Creek Journal.*[37] Peterman and Charlotte Lazier had paid for their passage in full, however, the ship was so overcrowded they got off in England. They did not have the money for the second ship and were "farmed out" on their arrival to work at hard labor for benefactors for seven months. After this debt was paid Peterman married Charlotte and proceeded to what is now Hardy County, WV.

He had received a grant of this land from Lord Fairfax in 1781. While I have no documentation of his fighting in the Revolutionary this was the custom of payment for having done so.

With the advent of the Revolutionary War and the great threat of Indian outrages, Peterman went to Cumberland, Maryland with his family.

He left the homestead in the care of Joseph Hanks and George Terry. On his return he found that Hanks had gone to faraway Kentucky and given a deed of trust to one Peterman. According to Paul Hardman he was, possibly, the father of Nancy Hanks, Lincoln's mother.

Peterman migrated farther to the west to the Hacker's Creek area of now Lewis Co., West Virginia. His children continued the settling of America process as they emigrated to Ohio, Iowa, Indiana, Kentucky—parts west and south.

Peterman Hardman and our ancestor's families stayed on Little Skin Creek. It is here that our Indian story takes place. One can place him there in May of 1792 by the account of the capture of Elizabeth Waggoner, his future daughter-in-law, by Tecumseh.[38]

The account of this attack is best described in the obituary written by Perry Worthington Hardman, her grandson, both of who are our ancestors.

> On the 6th day of May, 1792, a part of Shawanese Indians, with the since justly celebrated General Tecumseh at their head, approached the little mansion where Mr. Waggoner's family was quietly domiciled. Mr. Waggoner, who was at some distance from the house, was observed by Tecumseh, who immediately discharged at him the contents of his gun; but fortunately, the leaden messenger of death failed of its errand and left him (Waggoner) uninjured, and who, looking in the direction of his house, beheld it already surrounded by the residue of the Indians. Knowing that resistance would be in vain and only tend to excite the savage fiends to greater acts of cruelty, he made use of the only means left him whereby he might escape the

hard fate of his family, and fled from before his wily adversary, who, finding himself outstripped by the swift-footed hunter, soon gave up the pursuit and joined the party at the house, who, after killing and scalping a child that they found in the yard, had made prisoners of Mrs. Waggoner and her children, among whom was Mrs. Hardman, then about twelve years old. They not only departed with all possible dispatch, but finding that a portion of their captives were not able to travel with much speed, and wishing to be stripped of every impediment to a swift retreat, they fell upon them with their tomahawks and murdered them with every aggravation of savage cruelty, leaving their mangled bodies strewed promiscuously along the way, weltering in crimson gore.

Mrs. Hardman, who witnessed this horrid deed, by which she was robbed of an affectionate mother, a dear little brother, and a lovely sister, was now borned far away from her native land to the Indian towns on the Maumee River, where, agreeable to the custom of the Indians, she was exposed to sale, and purchased by a squaw, who exacted of her the hardest kind of servitude.

It may not be improper here to say something in relation to Tecumseh, who, though a savage, was yet a magnanimous chief. Although an inveterate enemy of the whites, he did much to alleviate the sufferings of the prisoners.

Observing one day, Mrs. Hardman's tyrannical mistress beating her in a most shocking and cruel manner, he immediately interposed, and with menacing gestures and commanding voice, bade her to abandon not only for the present, but in time to come, such detestable acts of barbarity. This was only one among the many instances in which he manifested a regard for the welfare of the prisoners…Mrs. Hardman soon became weary of living in the forest among the assassins of her countrymen. She

39

longed to return to the bosom of her broken-hearted father, and the associates of her childhood.

About this time (late in the fall of 1793) General Anthony Wayne began his campaign against the Indians, who were actively engaged in preparing to give him battle. For several days, company after company of the war-like
tribes thronged the Shawanese towns, brandishing above their heads the gleaming steel.

They made the woods resound with their war whoops and savage yells. At length, they all left the towns and repaired to the place whether they expected to meet General Wayne. Mrs. Hardman and another captive (then Miss Sallie Johnson) now determined on attempting their escape. Having succeeded in eluding the vigilance of the Indians, they set out late in the evening, and directed their steps toward Detroit. They had not traveled far before the sable current of night closed around them, but animated by the prospect of being restored to the society of their friends, the continued to travel the whole night through the dreary wilderness.

Some time during the next day they met a white man, an Indian trader, garnished them with some provisions, and gave them directions how to proceed in order to escape detection and to reach the Settlement.

They now traveled many miles without seeing a human being, but were at length overtaken by two white men who conducted them safely to a settlement at Detroit, where Mrs. Hardman made her home with a Mr. Sisney, until after the treaty was concluded with the Indians in 1795. Mr. Sisney, here kind benefactor, then conveyed her to the neighborhood of Wheeling, and left her with her uncle, Lewis Bonnett. Thence, she was conveyed to her father, whose joy at meeting with his long-lost child may be better imagined that described…

A note by Reuben Gold Thwaites, editor of the 1895 edition of Wither's book, gives an account of this incident on page 410. Above it was shared that Henry McWhorter, our ancestor, helped carry the bodies to West's fort. Jesse Hughes, brother of Sudna, our ancestor carried the news to the fort.

The Hardman mentioned in the note was Peterman Hardman, the immigrant and our ancestor, who was out hunting when the call from Elizabeth's father came. This is also confirmed in a deed made by Charlotte Hardman, his wife, on 15 June 1827, which reads,

"...corner to said Hardman and John Waggoner with sd Waggoners line...do hereby certify that Charlotte Hardman Widow of Peter Hardman party to a certain deed bearing the date on the fifteenth of June 1827..."

The incident was also noted at the bottom of the last will and testament of John D. Hardman, which was probated on Nov 13th 1865.[39] Thus ends our only, but very famous, Indian story in the lives of our ancestors.

The family made some notable contributions to religion on the frontier. John G. Hardman, Elizabeth's husband, became an itinerant preacher in the Methodist Episcopal Church late in life. He left the church and joined the Methodist Protestant Church when the church split over the slavery issue.[40]

"Early in the inception of reformed Methodism, a society was organized on Little Skin Creek, not far from where Georgetown is located, in Lewis County, West Virginia. There are many names now precious in our memory, which once belonged to this class at old Mount Gilead Church. The old church house is gone, and so are nearly all the old members—Rev. A. Spore and wife, Rev. John Hardman and wife,...This is the headquarters society of the Georgetown Circuit."[41] The formation of the church began in 1830; John would have been about 60 years old, late in life as stated above. In John D. Hardman's will he left his saddle bridle and saddle pockets and all his wearing apparel to his son, John G. Hardman and his Bible to a son, Samuel B. Hardman.[42]

41

Our religious heritage in the Methodist Church continues through Perry Worthington Hardman, John G. Hardman's son. He was a trustee in the planting of the Fall Run Methodist Church. As you can see in the following document the Hardmans and Lowthers were first united in an effort to build a church at Fall Run, Braxton County, West Virginia. A picture of the church taken in 1935, an overview of its history and the deed for the land are below.

Fall Run United Methodist Church

What was one time a laurel and white growth, graced by rhododendron, is now the setting of Fall Run United Methodist Church. The land for the church and cemetery was donated by Emery Berry and wife Caroline on June 14, 1890, and was cleared by G. S. Lowther and his son Harrison.

The church was built of white poplar, which was donated, and labor was free. It had the first ringing bell for miles around. The lectern was hand made by Jefferson Mick.

Dedication services were in 1892 and first pastor was John Cobb. In the flood of July 24, 1935, the church was washed from its foundation facing the hill to the present location facing Rt. 19, with very little damage.

The first members as of May 1893 were: Emery Berry (Leader), D.H. Prince, G.S. Lowther, C.B. Hardman, J.R. Casto, W.H. Hardman, M.E. Hardman, S.F. Hardman, Virginia Hardman, Cora Prince, P.W. Hardman, M.M. Hardman, Lidda Heaton, Cora White, Bessie Lowther, Sara Mick, Simeon Ware, Nannie Casto, Harriet Bull, Jennie Ware, Abraham Sponaugle, Cora Cummings, Lillie Barrickham, Otis Barrickham, W.L Prince, Mary Sponaugle, Mary Ware, Edwin Cummins, Maggie Cumins, William Cummins, E.M. Casto, George Brown, R.W. Casto, John White, Sara Ware, L.W. Ware and T.B. Hardman.

The church in the vale is still ringing out its welcome to its many friends near and far. 237 words
Submitted by Eva Bull, Sect./Tres.

This deed made this 14° day
of June 1890 between Emery A. Berry and Caroline Berry
his wife of the one part and, L. D. Leatto, Emery A. Berry
and P. H. Hardman trustees of the Methodist Protestant
Church of the second part all of Braxton County, West
Virginia Witnesseth That in consideration of the sum
of ten dollars in hand paid the receipt whereof is hereby
acknowledged they the said parties of the first part do
grant and convey to the said parties of the second part and
to their successors in office for the use and benefit of
the said Methodist Protestant Church all of the following described lot or parcel of land in the county and
State aforesaid and near the forks of fall run Bounded
as follows to-wit: Beginning at a stake near the forks
of said run in a line of C. E. Heaton thence S 47½ W
3 poles to a stake by the side of the road thence with the
road N 8¾ W 20 poles to a stake N 5 W 2 poles to a stake
at the run and with the run N 63½ E 20 poles to stake
S 50 E 8 poles to the Beginning containing one hundred and
thirty six poles surface measure. It is expressly agreed
and understood by and between the parties hereto that
in case the M. P. Church should fail to erect a house
for public religious worship on the lot hereby conveyed
and should said house of worship be erected and afterward
cease to be used as a house for religious worship that the
lot of land and its appurtenances shall revert to the parties of the first part or to their heirs or assigns. Witness
the following signatures and seals.
                              E. A. Berry [seal]
                              Caroline V. Berry [seal]

State of West Virginia
        County of Braxton to-wit:
I P. H. Hardman a Justice of the county aforesaid do certify
that Emery A. Berry whose name is signed to the writing
above bearing date on the 14 day of June 1890 has this day
acknowledged the same before me in my said county. And
I do further certify that Caroline Berry the wife of Emery A.
Berry whose names are signed to the writing above bearing

43

date on the 14th day of June 1890 personally appeared before me in the county aforesaid and being examined by me privately and apart from her husband and Reading the said writing fully explained to her, she the said Caroline Berry acknowledged the said writing to be her act and declared that she had willingly executed the same and does not wish to retract it. Given under my hand this 18th day of June 1890.

P. W. Hardman, Justice

State of West Virginia

Braxton County Court Clerks office July 1st 1890
The foregoing deed with the certificate of acknowledgment thereto annexed was this day presented in said office and admitted to record.

Teste   C. H. Newlon, clerk.

The words "church" in line 11, "worship" in line 25 and "shall" in line 26 of the foregoing deed and "she" in line 13 of the acknowledgment thereof, are interlineations.

Teste   C. H. Newlon, clerk.

This deed made and entered into this 12th day of March 1890 between H. D. Mitchell and Nancy his wife of the first part and J. H. Bibbee of the second part all of the county of Braxton and State of West Virginia Witnesseth that for and in consideration of two hundred dollars paid to J. S. Jenkins the receipt of which is hereby acknowledged doth grant bargain sell and convey to the aforesaid J. H. Bibbee the following described tract or parcel of land lying in the town of Burnsville county of Braxton and State of West Virginia known as lot No 34 and bounded as follows to wit: Beginning at a stake in Walnut street thence with Bailiff alley S 3 E 147 feet to a stake thence N 81 E 12 feet to a stake in Sweethen alley N 3 N 147 feet to Walnut street thence with same S 87 N 120 feet to the beginning containing one rood and thirty poles more or less to have and hold his heirs and assigns forever

The members named in the historical account, G. S. Lowther and P. W. Hardman, are our paternal great grandfathers. Bessie Lowther is our paternal grandmother

44

and Harrison Lowther is her brother. It was while attending this church that I received my call to preach. Like John G. Hardman, our ancestor, it was late in life at the age of fifty-eight. Ironically, both of us were born on October 7 one hundred and sixty-seven years apart.

It is no wonder that the Hardmans finally settled in West Virginia. Their homes were always in a mountainous terrain with a river or creek running through the valley. This is the same kind of setting Peterman Hardman immigrated from in 1764.

I had an opportunity to go to the homeland in 1998. I found myself boating down the Rhine river, near Inglehiem-am-Rhine. On either side of the river rose mountains reaching to the sky. The locations of Little Skin Creek and Fall Run were synonymous with our Hardman ancestor's homeland. This is the Rhine River in Germany near Kolb in the state of Hesse. Inglehiem-am-Rhine is near hear and the place of Hardman origin.

I was fascinated when I saw castles all along the way—one on every block if you will. The German hosts explained the history of them on the Rhine. They were tollbooths—whoever owned the castle had to be paid before one could pass through their section of the river.

Below is a picture of a castle, which sets in the Rhine River at Kolb, Germany.

Perry Worthington, John G. Hardman's son, migrated to what is now Braxton County, only about ten miles from his home place. As noted above, when Bessie Maude Lowther married John William, Perry's son, her father gave her the land where the home place stands that George Dencil I Hardman, our father, was raised.

As noted above there was no documentation that our Hardman ancestors served in the Revolutionary War. Jacob, Peterman's brother, served in that war under Col. William Lowther, our descendant. The same is true of the Civil War but William Hardman, the brother of Perry Worthington, died as a Union prisoner at Point Lookout. He served with Imboden's command and then under "Stonewall Jackson."[43]

Our ancestors or their family members contributed to the "fight for freedom" in the wars that plagued their day. This effort was continued by our immediate family in the same or different ways. During World War II our mother and father were members of the Civil Defense in Alexandria, Virginia.

Alexandria is a short distance from Washington, D. C. My heart still quivers when I am reminded by the historians how close the German submarines came to our shores at Chesapeake Bay. George, our father, had a rifle hanging beside the bed. The song, "Turns The Lights Down Low And Listen To The Radio," was an integral part of our lives. During air raids the green blinds were pulled, the lights turned off and we listened to the radio.

Our father was drafted in April of 1944 and passed the physical to become a member of the armed forces. However, he was not called to active duty until after his birthday in June and could not serve. That did not deter him from contributing in another way. He brought his family back to West Virginia and went to work in the Navy yards at Baltimore, Maryland.

In the next confrontation for freedom, the Korean War, Russell Beryl Thompson, Coleta's husband, and James Roe, Edith Sharon's husband, answered their country's call. Sadly, Robert Burke, Marjorie's brother-in-law, was killed in the last six hours of battle.

The heritage of political involvement has continued through our family. George, our father, and Hazel, our mother, carried on the interest and service in politics, which our ancestors had. They both had the privilege of being invited to the inauguration of President Franklin Delano Roosevelt when we lived in Alexandria. Their interest continued in West Virginia.

George Dencil Hardman I, our father, won the nomination of the Democratic ticket for a county commissioner on August 3, 1954. In the general election on November 2, 1954, he won that seat and served for six years. He was the president during the last two years of his term. During his years of service he was active in the planning of Interstate 77 as it passed through Braxton County.

My father's activities were rewarded with an appointment as the Maintenance Superintendent at the then Weston State Hospital in the early 1970's. His life's experience as a carpenter qualified him for this position. During his tenure he won an engineering award for redoing the antiquated heating system.

Unfortunately, political power changes and his position was challenged by the new governor. Since my father did not have a high school diploma he would lose the position. With the fortitude and 'gumption' of his ancestors, he proceeded to get his GED at the age of sixty. He passed it with flying colors, with a score of a sophomore in college; this man with only an formal eight grade education.

Marjorie Carol Hardman, our sister, and Billy Burke, her husband, became involved in politics on their retirement from pipelining. They served as representatives of the constituents of Gilmer, Braxton and part of Calhoun County in the West Virginia House of Delegates for several years. Marjorie had the honor of being the first woman to hold the position of Majority Whip , Speaker Pro Tem and to preside over the House during her tenure.

The following are letters, which are examples of our parents' interest in politics.

August 11, 1960

Mr. Hulett Smith, Chairman
State Democratic Executive Committee
Nelson Building
Charleston, West Virginia

Dear Sir,

On June 28, 1960, I wrote you a letter informing you that the Democratic Executive Committee of Braxton County meeting held on June 27, 1960 had resulted in a tie vote, so far I have not had any information from you in this matter.

I am very much interested in this matter, also, several other leading Democrats in the County are anxious to have this issue settled immediately so we can start organizing for the General Election campaign.

I hope the following information might help you in making the right decision.

In the Primary Election Campaign of 1956 when Robert H. Mollohan was the successful Democratic candidate for Governor, John L. Fox and William M. Kidd managed Mr. Mollohans' campaign in Braxton County, although Milton Ferguson carried Braxton County.

When the General Election Campaign was in progress Mr. Mollohan visited Sutton and contacted Mr. Doyle McLaughlin, County Chairman, they went to the office of Mr. Kidd and Mr. Fox. In discussing the campaign Mr. Kidd and Mr. Fox told Mr. Mollohan they could not be for him if Doyle McLaughlin and his followers were for him. (How's that for Good Democrats?) Mr. McLaughlin followers having lost their candidate in the State started working immediately for Mr. Mollohan. The above can be confirmed by Mr. Mollohan if you wish to contact him, but, since you were very close to him in his campaign you may have heard this from him.

Mr. Mollohan carried Braxton County in the General Election by

324 votes.

In the beginning of the recent Primary campaign, Cecil Facemire, Charles Duffield and William Kidd were supporting Pauley for Governor, Mr. Harry Brown and his family were supporting Skeen and Robert Carr was supporting you. These people belong to the same faction and must have had a particular reason for supporting three different candidates for Governor. The supposition is that they wanted to get as much money from State and National candidates as they could to pool it for support of their County slate.

In Burnsville (a Democratic stronghold) the following names were on their Slate: Paul S. Moyers, House of Delegates, William M. Kidd, Prosecuting Attorney, Woodrow Vankirk, Sheriff, Cecil Moyers, Assessor, Eugene Facemire, County Commissioner, Arden Dean and Susan Steele, Executive Committee and Hugh Brown, Board of Education.

Hugh Brown is the Son of Harry Brown who was campaign manager for Skeen and Susan Steele is a first cousin to Harry Brown.

Your name was not on their slate. Mr. O. B. McPherson of Burnsville has one of the slips of paper that those names were printed on. He will be glad to show it to you if you want to see it.

In view of the above facts, it is my opinion that you should appoint Doyle V. McLaughlin, Chairman of the Braxton County Democratic Executive Committee, forthwith and immediately.

With warmest political and kindest personal regards, I am

Very truly yours,

George D. Hardman
Secretary

cc: W. W. Barron

As for settling the United States Of America, no but we
have spread far and wide over our nation. Today some of us
live in Gilmer, Wood and Braxton County, West Virginia, the
states of Virginia, Ohio, Tennessee, and Kentucky all part of
the pioneering efforts of our ancestors. We have traversed
this nation just as our ancestors did when they paved the way
to Ohio, Kentucky, and points west, east, north and south.

There was an expression of their pioneering spirit by
some of the descendants. William Raymond Hardman I, our
brother, Robert Edward and Russell Beryl Thompson, Coleta's
son and husband, respectively, went to Alaska and helped

build the Alaskan Pipeline. Pictured below are Coleta's son and husband working on that pipeline. Billy Burke, Marjorie's

husband, was a pipeliner also. In their years as pipeliners they all traveled over the United States building the pipelines so that others could have a better life.

Edith Sharon Hardman was somewhat of a pioneer in the field of laboratory medicine. She entered it during its infant stage and taught Medical Technology at her Alma Mater, Alderson-Broaddus College in the early 1970's. She had the opportunity to assist in the development of a Medical Laboratory at the Osteopathic School of Medicine in Lewisburg, West Virginia. Thus, while not a doctor like our ancestor, Granville Sharp, or a nurse, like Bessie Maude Lowther, we continued to contribute to the medical profession.

Our generation still has the drive to venture and take risks just as our ancestors. Three of us were entrepreneurs in the business world just as Henry McWhorter built that first mill. George Dencil Hardman I owned several gas stations, when they still washed windshields and checked the oil, in the area of Alexandria and Fairfax County, Virginia. Marjorie Carol Hardman and Billy Burke returned to Gilmer County and purchased a hardware in Glenville, West Virginia. During Robert Edward's school years, Coleta Dare had a dry cleaners in Glenville, West Virginia.

CONCLUSION

In my research there is historical documentation of the contributions that our ancestors and their descendants have made to the growth of our nation. It is established that Col. William Lowther, Henry McWhorter and Caleb Stout, our ancestral grandfathers, all fought in the Revolutionary War. Peterman Hardman received a land grant from Lord Fairfax for his land in Maryland. As stated above this was customary payment for fighting. He was from the State of Hesse in Germany and may have been a Hessian soldier, which aided in turning that conflict in our favor.

Below are pictures of the land grants the Declaration of Independence, written in German, and a Hessian soldier, which was taken on my trip to Germany. This was at Hessen Park; a museum in Germany dedicated to those who migrated to America and fought in the War for Independence.

Our ancestors played an important role in the settling of the Hacker's Creek area and the establishment of towns, one of which is the county seat of Lewis County. They did not stop there and are purported to have left that area and paved the way for the settlement of counties to the west—Ritchie and Wood County.

Our ancestors fought for freedom from the human oppression of slavery in two ways. Some joined the Confederate army, fighting, being imprisoned and dying for this cause. Rev. John G. Hardman sought resolution in the area of the Church by withdrawing from one, which supported slavery.

Our ancestors suffered much but persevered in their confrontations with the Indians. One ancestor lived in the teepee of Chief Tecumseh because the squaw she served beat her. But our ancestors were forgiving, in her obituary there are kind words for the chief. Another chose to parley with them and bought their land; they did not just take it.

Our ancestors contributed to the political process and law enforcement in their day. They served as justice of the peace, sheriff and in the Virginia State Assembly. They tried to make a difference in the lives and living of others. Rather than make a profit one chose to feed his neighbors and friends.

Our heritage is one that challenged us to follow in their footsteps as noted in the life sketches above. Our family has done just that and one of us remains currently serves in the United Methodist Church as a pastor.

And so, the heritage continues as we pass on to our generations after us the spirit to dare and the will to achieve. We are many and we shall be more before this book is published a great grandchild will be added to my immediate family.

This is the story of our family but we must make note that many of the descendants of the immigrants share our story and the contributions of our common ancestors. My work would not be as complete without their research and knowledge of our ancestors. It is necessary, however, to leave the writing of their stories to them.

The Generations of the

John Stout Family

1. John STOUT (b.1570)
sp: Elizabeth BEE/GEE (a.1609 m.1609)
 +-2. Richard STOUT (b.1615 d.1705)
   sp: Penelope KENT/VAN PRINCIN (b.1622 d.1732)
   |-3. David STOUT (b.1667 d.1734)
   | sp: Rebecca ASHTON (b.1672 m.1688)
   | |-4. James STOUT (b.1694 d.1727)
   | | sp: Catharine SIMPSON (b.1692 m.1712 d.1749)
   | | |-5. James STOUT (b.1715 d.1754)
   | | | sp: Jemima Reeder REEDER (m.1740)
   | | | |-6. Caleb STOUT (b.1742 d.1838)
   | | | | sp: Elizabeth LA BAW (b.1740 m.1764 d.1832)
   | | | | |-7. James STOUT (b.1780 d.1863)
   | | | | | sp: Phoebe JACKSON (b.1793 m.1811)
   | | | | | |-8. Edward Jackson STOUT (b.1819)
   | | | | | | sp: Amanda BLAKE (b.1827 m.1839)
   | | | | | | |-9. George Washington STOUT (b.1847
                   d.1924)
   | | | | | | | sp: Mary Matilda BOWYER (b.1853 m.1871)
   | | | | | | | |-10. W. Elhue STOUT (b.1872 d.1895)
   | | | | | | | |-10. Della M. C. STOUT (b.1874)
   | | | | | | | | sp: John H. DILLEY (m.1898)
   | | | | | | | |-10. Icie Elizabeth STOUT (b.1876)
   | | | | | | | | sp: Joseph STRALEY (m.1902)
   | | | | | | | |-10. Mary Catora STOUT (b.1878 d.1954)
   | | | | | | | | sp: Hugh Raymond BOWYER (b.1877
                   d.1966)
   | | | | | | | | |-11. Hazel BOWYER
   | | | | | | | | |-11. Franklin BOWYER
   | | | | | | | | |-11. Mary Edith BOWYER
   | | | | | | | | +-11. Worthy Lee BOWYER, SR.
   | | | | | | | |-10. Leonard Oscar STOUT (b.1881 d.1881)
   | | | | | | | |-10. Effie Marie STOUT (b.1884)
   | | | | | | | | sp: Rev. William W. STEELE (m.1916)
   | | | | | | | |-10. Anthony Ernest STOUT (b.1887 d.1961)
   | | | | | | | | sp: Anna Elizabeth HOLDEN (m.1912)
   | | | | | | | | |-11. Clarence Paul STOUT (b.1913)
   | | | | | | | | +-11. Kenneth Earl STOUT (b.1925 d.1987)

```
| | | | | | | |-10. Colista STOUT (b.1889 d.1973)
| | | | | | | | sp: James MORRELL (m.1915)
| | | | | | | | | |-11. Wanneta MORRELL (b. ~1920
                        d. ~1998)
| | | | | | | | | sp: George HENDERSON (d.1957)
| | | | | | | | | | |-12. Phyllis HENDERSON
| | | | | | | | | | +-12. Georgeanna HENDERSON
| | | | | | | | | +-11. Mondalea MORRELL (b.1916 d.1990)
| | | | | | | | |   sp: William C. DENNISON
| | | | | | | |     |-12. Darryl MORRELL
| | | | | | | |     |  sp: UNKNOWN
| | | | | | | |     |  +-13. James MORRELL (d.1995)
| | | | | | | |     |-12. Dennis MORRELL
| | | | | | | |     |  sp: UNKNOWN
| | | | | | | |     |  |-13. Traci MORRELL
| | | | | | | |     |  +-13. Lori MORRELL
| | | | | | | |     |-12. Linda DENNISON
| | | | | | | |     +-12. Wilma DENNISON
| | | | | | | +-10. Warder Martin STOUT (b.1893 d.1970)
| | | | | | |   sp: Virgie MCCOY (b.1895 m.1921 d.1974)
| | | | | | |   |-11. Lloyd George STOUT (b.1919 d.1973)
| | | | | | |   | sp: Opal STARCHER (a.1949)
| | | | | | |   | sp: Josephine MARTIN
| | | | | | |   |-11. Auldra McCoy STOUT (b.1922)
| | | | | | |   | sp: Bernice ROBERTS (m.1948)
| | | | | | |   | +-12. Charlotte Ann STOUT (b.1949)
| | | | | | |   |   sp: John CHIDESTER (b.1948 m.1973)
| | | | | | |   |   +-13. Ann Marie CHIDESTER (b.1976)
| | | | | | |   |     sp: Jason Eric HYRE (m.2000)
| | | | | | |   |-11. Vernon Bernell STOUT (b.1924)
| | | | | | |   | sp: Vivian Ruth CUTLIP (b.1926 d.1988)
| | | | | | |   | |-12. Larry STOUT (b.1947)
| | | | | | |   | | sp: Cheryl CARLISLE (m.1968)
| | | | | | |   | | |-13. Aaron P. STOUT (b.1972)
| | | | | | |   | | +-13. Seth STOUT (b.1979)
| | | | | | |   | |-12. Judith Carol STOUT (b.1949)
| | | | | | |   | | sp: James HANNA
| | | | | | |   | | |-13. Paul D. HANNA (b.1968)
| | | | | | |   | | |-13. Paula D. HANNA (b.1971)
```

```
| | | | | | |   | | sp: Fred ORUM JR. (m.1990)
| | | | | | |   | +-12. Susan STOUT (b.1954)
| | | | | | |   |   sp: Kerry SCARLETT (m.1970)
| | | | | | |   |   |-13. Bryan SCARLETT (b.1970)
| | | | | | |   |   | sp: Sue NOLL
| | | | | | |   |   +-13. Jeremy SCARLETT (b.1975)
| | | | | | |   |-11. Eunice Lorraine STOUT (b.1926)
| | | | | | |   | sp: Howard TEMPLETON (b.1927 m.1951)
| | | | | | |   | |-12. Linda Sue TEMPLETON (b.1953
| | | | | | |   |       d.1953)
| | | | | | |   | +-12. Charles Edward TEMPLETON
| | | | | | |   |       (b.1955)
| | | | | | |   |   sp: Pamela MARTIN (m.1978(div))
| | | | | | |   |-11. Roy Glendon STOUT (b.1928)
| | | | | | |   | sp: Kay HAMRIC (b.1933 m.1954)
| | | | | | |   | |-12. Betsy Jane STOUT (b.1958)
| | | | | | |   | | sp: Dwight JONES, JR.
| | | | | | |   | |-12. Taffey Ann STOUT (b.1962)
| | | | | | |   | | sp: Greg GORCZYNSKI (m.1992)
| | | | | | |   | +-12. Renee' Michelle STOUT (b.1964)
| | | | | | |   |   sp: Richard FAIRCLOTH (m.1987)
| | | | | | |   |   |-13. Austin FAIRCLOTH (b.1987)
| | | | | | |   |   |-13. Parker David FAIRCLOTH (b.1991)
| | | | | | |   |   |-13. Aaron Alexander FAIRCLOTH
| | | | | | |   |       (b.1996)
| | | | | | |   |   |-13. Stephen FAIRCLOTH (b.1998)
| | | | | | |   |   +-13. Sierra Joy FAIRCLOTH
| | | | | | |   |-11. Mavis Jean STOUT (b.1930)
| | | | | | |   |-11. George Leonard STOUT (b.1933)
| | | | | | |   | sp: Betty WILLIAMS (b.1938 m.1957)
| | | | | | |   | |-12. Debra K. STOUT (b.1958)
| | | | | | |   | | sp: Joel MANN (m.1976(div))
| | | | | | |   | | |-13. Christopher MANN (b.1976)
| | | | | | |   | | |-13. Benjamin MANN (b.1978)
| | | | | | |   | | | sp: Jo Carrol TRUETT (m.2001)
| | | | | | |   | | |-13. Joshua MANN (b.1979)
| | | | | | |   | | |-13. Joel MANN (b.1982)
| | | | | | |   | | sp: Mark VOGAN
| | | | | | |   | | +-13. Elijah VOGAN
```

```
| | | | | | |   | +-12. Michael A. STOUT (b.1960)
| | | | | | |   |   sp: Cynthia HARTZELL (m.1989)
| | | | | | |   |    +-13. Kylie STOUT (b.1990)
| | | | | | |   |-11. Donald Wayne STOUT (b.1936)
| | | | | | |   | sp: Mary DYER (b.1936 m.1962)
| | | | | | |   |  |-12. David STOUT (b.1971)
| | | | | | |   |  +-12. Christie STOUT (b.1977)
| | | | | | |   +-11. Rendal Lee STOUT (b.1939)
| | | | | | |     sp: Judy WALDECK (b.1943 m.1961)
| | | | | | |      +-12. Randal L. STOUT (b.1963)
| | | | | | |        sp: Kimberly ODE (m.1989)
| | | | | | |         |-13. Emily Marie STOUT (b.1992)
| | | | | | |         |-13. Erin Lee STOUT (b.1994)
| | | | | | |         |-13. Ryan John STOUT (b.1998)
| | | | | | |         +-13. Andrew Joseph STOUT (b. 2001)
```

First Generation

1. **John STOUT**[1,2] was born ~1570/1580.

    John married[3] **Elizabeth BEE/GEE** on 13 Nov 1609 in Nottinghamshire, England. Elizabeth published notice of marriage 13 Nov 1609 .

    They had the following child:

    +   2   M   i.   **Richard STOUT** was born 1615 and died ~1705.

Second Generation

2. **Richard STOUT**[1,4] (John) was born 1615. He died ~1705.

    Richard married **Penelope KENT/VAN PRINCIN** on 1644. Penelope was born 1622. She died 1732.

    They had the following children:

       3   M   i.   **John STOUT** was born 1645. He died 1724.

       4   M   ii.   **Richard STOUT** was born 1646. He died 1717.

       5   M   iii.   **James STOUT** was born 1648.

       6   F   iv.   **Mary STOUT** was born 1650.

       7   F   v.   **Alice Deliverance STOUT** was born 1652.

       8   M   vi.   **Peter STOUT** was born 1654. He died 1703.

       9   F   vii.   **Sarah STOUT** was born 1656.

      10   M   viii.   **Jonathan STOUT** was born 1660. He died 1722.

    + 11   M   ix.   **David STOUT** was born 1667 and died 1734.

      12   M   x.   **Benjamin STOUT** was born 1669. He died 1734.

Third Generation

11. **David STOUT**[5,6] (Richard, John) was born 1667. He died 1734 and was buried in Hunterdon Co., N. J.--Stout Plot.

David married **Rebecca ASHTON** on 1688 in Freehold, N.J. Rebecca was born 1672.

They had the following children:

13	F	i.	**Sarah STOUT** was born 1689.
14	F	ii.	**Rebecca STOUT** was born 1691. She died 1772.
+ 15	M	iii.	**James STOUT** was born 1694 and died 1727.
16	M	iv.	**Freegift STOUT** was born 1695. He died 1709.
17	M	v.	**David STOUT** was born 1695. He died 1781.
18	M	vi.	**Joseph STOUT** was born 1698. He died 1770.
19	F	vii.	**Deliverance STOUT** was born 1701.
20	M	viii.	**Benjamin STOUT** was born 1707. He died 1789.

Fourth Generation

15. **James STOUT**[5,7] (David, Richard, John) was born 1694 in Middleton, N. J. He died 1727.

James married **Catharine SIMPSON** on 1712. Catharine was born 1692. She died 1749.

They had the following children:

21	M	i.	**John STOUT** was born 1713. He died 1790.
+ 22	M	ii.	**James STOUT** was born 1715 and died 1754.

| 23 | M | iii. | **Joseph STOUT** was born 1717. He died 1760. |

23 M iii. **Joseph STOUT** was born 1717. He died 1760.

24 M iv. **David STOUT** was born 1719. He died 1781.

25 M v. **Jacob STOUT** was born 1721. He died 1785.

26 M vi. **Jonathan STOUT** was born 1723. He died 1811.

27 F vii. **Rebecca STOUT** was born 1727. She died 1788.

Fifth Generation

22. **James STOUT**[7,8] (James, David, Richard, John) was born 1715. He died 1754.

James married **Jemima Reeder REEDER** on 1740.

They had the following children:

28 M i. **Abel STOUT** was born 1740. He died 1797.

+ 29 M ii. **Caleb STOUT** was born 1742 and died 1838.

30 F iii. **Amy STOUT**.

31 F iv. **Mary STOUT**.

32 F v. **Elinor STOUT** was born 1749. She died 1828.

33 M vi. **James STOUT** died 1807.

Sixth Generation

29. **Caleb STOUT**[2,9] (James, James, David, Richard, John) was born 1742. He died 1838.

Caleb married **Elizabeth LA BAW** on 1764. Elizabeth was born 1740. She died 1832.

They had the following children:

| 34 | M | i. | **Abel STOUT** was born 1764. He died 1837. |

34 M i. **Abel STOUT** was born 1764. He died 1837.

35 F ii. **Susannah STOUT** was born 1769. She died[10] 1814/1837.

36 F iii. **Jemima STOUT** was born 1780. She died 3 Mar 1854.

37 M iv. **Samuel STOUT** was born 1792. He died 1874.

+ 38 M v. **James STOUT** was born 1780 and died 1863.

39 F vi. **Deliverance STOUT**.

40 M vii. **David STOUT** died 1825.

41 F viii. **Eleanor STOUT**.

42 M ix. **Gideon STOUT**.

43 M x. **Jeremiah STOUT**.

44 M xi. **Titus STOUT**.

Seventh Generation

38. **James STOUT**[2,5] (Caleb, James, James, David, Richard, John) was born 1780. He died 1863.

James married[13] **Phoebe JACKSON**, daughter of Edward JACKSON and Martha MILLER, on 24 Dec 1811 in Harrison Co., WV. Phoebe was born 19 Jul 1793.

They had the following children:

45 M i. **Nathaniel D. STOUT** was born[14] 22 Oct 1814. He died 13 Jan 1892.

+ 46 M ii. **Edward Jackson STOUT** was born 1819.

47 M iii. **Daniel STOUT** was born 1822. He died 1901.

48 F iv. **Irene STOUT** was born 1826.

49 F v. **Martha STOUT**.

Eighth Generation

46. **Edward Jackson STOUT**[2] (James, Caleb, James, James, David, Richard, John) was born 1819. He died in Missouri.

Edward married **Amanda BLAKE** on 1839. Amanda was born 1827.

They had the following children:

    50 F   i. **Elizabeth STOUT**.

    51 F   ii. **Belinda STOUT** was born 1844.

    52 F   iii. **Amaretta STOUT**.

+   53 M iv. **George Washington STOUT** was born 24 Oct 1847 and died 31 Oct 1924.

    54 F   v. **Louvenia STOUT** was born 1848.

    55 F   vi. **Melissa STOUT** was born 1851.

               Melissa married **George BOWYER**.

    56 F vii. **Mary Melinda STOUT** was born 1852.

    57 M viii. **Thomas J. STOUT** was born 1859.

    58 M ix. **Jonathan STOUT**.

    59 M x. **Mortimer STOUT**.

    60 M xi. **William STOUT**.

Ninth Generation

53. **George Washington STOUT**[2,15,16] (Edward Jackson, James, Caleb, James, James, David, Richard, John) was born 24 Oct 1847 in Middle Island, Doddridge Co., WV. He died 31 Oct 1924.

George married **Mary Matilda BOWYER** on 24 Nov 1871 in Gilmer Co., WV. Mary was born 1853.

They had the following children:

    61 M   i. **W. Elhue STOUT**[17] was born 24 Sep 1872 in Doddridge Co., WV. He died 28 Feb 1895.

62 F   ii.   **Della M. C. STOUT**[17] was born 14 Oct 1874 in Braxton Co., WV. She died 11 Mar.

63 F iii. **Icie Elizabeth STOUT**[17] was born 24 Jul 1876 in Braxton Co., WV. She died in Weston, WV.

+   64 F iv. **Mary Catora STOUT** was born 23 May 1878 and died 23 Oct 1954.

65 M v. **Leonard Oscar STOUT**[17] was born 3 Aug 1881 in Braxton Co., WV. He died 15 Nov 1883.

66 F vi. **Effie Marie STOUT**[17] was born 15 May 1884 in Braxton Co., WV.

+   67 M vii. **Anthony Ernest STOUT** was born 16 Feb 1887 and died 23 Jun 1961.

+   68 F viii. **Colista STOUT** was born 22 Oct 1889 and died 13 May 1973.

+   69 M ix. **Warder Martin STOUT** was born 5 Dec 1893 and died 23 May 1970.

Tenth Generation

Mary Catora Stout Bowyer

64. **Mary Catora STOUT** "Tory"[18] (George Washington, Edward Jackson, James, Caleb, James, James, David, Richard, John) was born 23 May 1878 in Gilmer Co., WV. She died 23 Oct 1954 in Weston, WV and was buried in K & P, Burnsville, WV.

Tory married **Hugh Raymond BOWYER** on 24 May 1906 in Burnsville, WV. Hugh was born 2 Oct 1877 in Horn Creek, Gilmer Co., WV. He died 22 Jan 1966 in Weston, WV and was buried in K & P, Burnsville, WV.

They had the following children:

   70 F   i. **Hazel BOWYER**.

   71 M   ii. **Franklin BOWYER**.

   72 F   iii. **Mary Edith BOWYER**.

   73 M iv. **Worthy Lee BOWYER, SR.**.

67. **Anthony Ernest STOUT** "Ernie"[17] (George Washington, Edward Jackson, James, Caleb, James, James, David, Richard, John) was born 16 Feb 1887 in Copen, WV. He died 23 Jun 1961 in Maxwells Run, WV.

Ernie married **Anna Elizabeth HOLDEN** on 20 Sep 1912 in Braxton Co., WV.

They had the following children:

   74 M   i. **Clarence Paul STOUT** was born 31 Aug 1913.

   75 M   ii. **Kenneth Earl STOUT** was born 17 Mar 1925. He died 25 Feb 1987.

68. **Colista STOUT**[19] (George Washington, Edward Jackson, James, Caleb, James, James, David, Richard, John) was born 22 Oct 1889 in Braxton Co., WV. She died 13 May 1973 in Burnsville, WV and was buried in K & P, Burnsville, WV.

Colista married **James MORRELL** "Jim" on 22 Dec 1915 in Burnsville, WV.

They had the following children:

+   76 F   i. **Wannetta MORRELL** was born 30 June about 1920 and died about 1998.

+   77 F   ii. **Mondalea MORRELL** was born 25 Sep 1916 and died 3 Apr 1990.

69. **Warder Martin STOUT**[16] (George Washington, Edward Jackson, James, Caleb, James, James, David, Richard, John) was born 5 Dec 1893. He died 23 May 1970 in Copen, WV and was buried in King Cemetery, Copen, WV.

Warder married **Virgie MCCOY** on 6 Mar 1921. Virgie was born 12 Sep 1895. She died 4 Mar 1974 in Copen, WV and was buried in King Cemetery, Copen, WV.

They had the following children:

   78 F   i. **Lloyd George STOUT** [16,20] was born 13 Mar 1919 in Boggs, Webster Co., WV. He died 18 May 1973 in Clarksburg, WV and was buried in King Cemetery, Copen, WV.

                Lloyd married (1) **Opal STARCHER**. Opal was divorced May 1949 .

                Lloyd also married (2) **Josephine MARTIN**.

+   79 M   ii. **Auldra McCoy STOUT** "Bull" was born 26 Apr 1922.

+   80 M   iii. **Vernon Bernell STOUT** was born 12 Jun 1924.

+   81 F   iv. **Eunice Lorraine STOUT** was born 14 Jul 1926.

+   82 M   v. **Roy Glendon STOUT** was born 4 Aug 1928.

   83 F   vi. **Mavis Jean STOUT**[20] was born 8 Oct 1930 in Copen, WV.

+   84 M   vii. **George Leonard STOUT** was born 28 Aug 1933.

+   85   M   viii.   **Donald Wayne STOUT** was born 20 Apr 1936.

+   86   M   ix.   **Rendal Lee STOUT** was born 18 Feb 1939.

Eleventh Generation

76. **Wannetta MORRELL**[19] (Colista STOUT, George Washington, Edward Jackson, James, Caleb, James, James, David, Richard, John).

Wannetta married **George HENDERSON**. He died 6 May 1957.

They had the following children:

   87   F   i.   **Phyllis HENDERSON** was born 9 May 1941. She married **Donald SHUVOICH** about 1962.

   88   F   ii.   **Georgeanna HENDERSON** was born in 1944 and died July 1958.

77. **Mondalea MORRELL** "Mondy"[19] (Colista STOUT, George Washington, Edward Jackson, James, Caleb, James, James, David, Richard, John) was born 25 Sep 1916 in Burnsville, WV. She died 3 Apr 1990 in Jefferson, Ohio.

She had the following children:

+   89   M   i.   **Darryl MORRELL** was born 3 Jul 1938.

+   90   M   ii.   **Dennis MORRELL** was born 3 May 1941.

Mondy married **William C. DENNISON** "Bud" about 1947. He had the following children:

   91   F   iii.   **Linda DENNISON**[19] was born 3 Mar 1948. She married/divorced **Harold MELLIN**. They had the following children: **Shannon MELLIN**. **Joshua MELLIN**.

   92   F   iv.   **Wilma DENNISON**[19] was born 1 Jan 1950. She married **Michael SEELEY**. They had the following children:

Kevin SEELEY.
Matthew SEELEY.

79. **Auldra McCoy STOUT** "Bull"[16,20] (Warder Martin, George Washington, Edward Jackson, James, Caleb, James, James, David, Richard, John) was born 26 Apr 1922 in Copen, WV.

Bull married **Bernice ROBERTS** on 13 Jul 1948.

They had the following child:

+   93 F   i.   **Charlotte Ann STOUT** was born 27 May 1949.

80. **Vernon Bernell STOUT** "Benny"[16,20] (Warder Martin, George Washington, Edward Jackson, James, Caleb, James, James, David, Richard, John) was born 12 Jun 1924 in Copen, WV.

Benny married **Vivian Ruth CUTLIP** on 19 Oct 1945. Vivian was born 29 Jul 1926. She died 7 Sep 1988 and was buried in Ravenna, Ohio.

They had the following children:

+   94 M   i.   **Larry STOUT** was born 16 Jun 1947.

+   95 F   ii.   **Judith Carol STOUT** was born 6 Jun 1949.

+   96 F   iii.   **Susan STOUT** was born 2 Apr 1954.

81. **Eunice Lorraine STOUT**[16,20] (Warder Martin, George Washington, Edward Jackson, James, Caleb, James, James, David, Richard, John) was born 14 Jul 1926 in Copen, WV.

Eunice married **Howard TEMPLETON** on 1 Nov 1951. Howard was born 10 Aug 1927. He was buried in Alamogordo, NM.

They had the following children:

   97 F   i.   **Linda Sue TEMPLETON** was born 15 Dec 1953. She died 15 Dec 1953.

98 M ii. **Charles Edward TEMPLETON** was born 25 Aug 1955.

Charles married **Pamela MARTIN** on ~3 June 1978. The marriage ended in divorce.

82. **Roy Glendon STOUT** "Bill Jake"[16,20] (Warder Martin, George Washington, Edward Jackson, James, Caleb, James, James, David, Richard, John) was born 4 Aug 1928 in Copen, WV.

Bill Jake married **Kay HAMRIC** on 12 Jul 1954. Kay was born 12 Jul 1933.

They had the following children:

99 F i. **Betsy Jane STOUT**[16,20] was born 9 Aug 1958.

Betsy married **Dwight JONES, JR.**

100 F ii. **Taffey Ann STOUT** was born 8 Apr 1962.

Taffey married **Greg GORCZYNSKI** on Nov 1992.

+ 101 F iii. **Renee' Michelle STOUT** was born 13 May 1964.

84. **George Leonard STOUT** "Peck"[16,20] (Warder Martin, George Washington, Edward Jackson, James, Caleb, James, James, David, Richard, John) was born 28 Aug 1933 in Copen, WV.

Peck married **Betty WILLIAMS** on 3 Jul 1957. Betty was born 5 Jan 1938.

They had the following children:

+ 102 F i. **Debra K. STOUT** was born 18 Mar 1958.

+ 103 M ii. **Michael A. STOUT** was born 7 Mar 1960.

85. **Donald Wayne STOUT**[16] (Warder Martin, George Washington, Edward Jackson, James, Caleb, James, James, David, Richard, John) was born 20 Apr 1936 in Copen, WV.

Donald married **Mary DYER**, daughter of **Stephen and Nellie WILLIAMS DYER**, on 25 Aug 1962 in Heaters, WV. Mary was born 21 Mar 1936.

They had the following children:

    104 M   i. **David STOUT** was born 11 Sep 1971. David married **Allison STRICKLAND** 17 Jul 2004.

    105 F   ii. **Christie STOUT** was born 25 Jun 1977.

86. **Rendal Lee STOUT** "Ren"[16,20] (Warder Martin, George Washington, Edward Jackson, James, Caleb, James, James, David, Richard, John) was born 18 Feb 1939 in Copen, WV.

Ren married **Judy WALDECK** on 11 Jun 1961. She was born 12 Aug 1943. Her parents were **John and Polly WALDECK.**

They had the following children:

+   106 M   i. **Randal L. STOUT** was born 25 Feb 1963.

Twelfth Generation

89. **Darryl MORRELL**[19] (Mondalea MORRELL, Colista STOUT, George Washington, Edward Jackson, James, Caleb, James, James, David, Richard, John).

He had the following child:

    107 M   i. **James MORRELL** died 1995.

90. **Dennis MORRELL**[19] (Mondalea MORRELL, Colista STOUT, George Washington, Edward Jackson, James, Caleb, James, James, David, Richard, John).

He had the following children:

    108 F   i. **Traci MORRELL** was born 17 Jul 1965.

    109 F   ii. **Lori MORRELL** was born 1 Feb 1968.

Dennis also married **Dorothy COGSWELL.**

93. **Charlotte Ann STOUT**[16,20] (Auldra McCoy, Warder Martin, George Washington, Edward Jackson, James, Caleb, James, James, David, Richard, John) was born 27 May 1949.

Charlotte married **John CHIDESTER** on 30 Aug 1973. John was born 29 Dec 1948.

They had the following children:

    110 F   i. **Ann Marie CHIDESTER** was born 15 Nov 1976.

                    Ann married **Jason Eric HYRE** on 15 May 2000.

94. **Larry STOUT**[16,20] (Vernon Bernell, Warder Martin, George Washington, Edward Jackson, James, Caleb, James, James, David, Richard, John) was born 16 Jun 1947.

Larry married **Cheryl CARLISLE** on 30 Nov 1968. Her parents were **Kenneth and Lila CARLISLE.**

They had the following children:

    111 M   i. **Aaron P. STOUT** was born 5 Sep 1972.

    112 M   ii. **Seth STOUT** was born 12 Dec 1979.

95. **Judith Carol STOUT**[16,20] (Vernon Bernell, Warder Martin, George Washington, Edward Jackson, James, Caleb, James, James, David, Richard, John) was born 6 Jun 1949.

Judith married (1) **James HANNA**.

They had the following children:

    113 M   i. **Paul D. HANNA** was born 13 Aug 1968.

    114 F   ii. **Paula D. HANNA** was born 7 Sep 1971.

Judith also married (2) **Fred ORUM JR.** on ~22 Sept 1990.

96. **Susan STOUT**[16,20] (Vernon Bernell, Warder Martin, George Washington, Edward Jackson, James, Caleb, James, James, David, Richard, John) was born 2 Apr 1954.

Susan married **Kerry SCARLETT** on 23 Jun 1970.

They had the following children:

117 M   i.   **Bryan SCARLETT** was born 18 Dec 1970.

               Bryan married **Sue NOLL**.

116 M   ii. **Jeremy SCARLETT** was born 24 Jun 1975.

101.**Renee' Michelle STOUT** (Roy Glendon, Warder Martin, George Washington, Edward Jackson, James, Caleb, James, James, David, Richard, John) was born 13 May 1964.

Renee' married **Richard FAIRCLOTH** on 20 Apr 1987.

They had the following children:

117 M   i.   **Austin FAIRCLOTH** was born 15 Jun 1987.

118 M   ii. **Parker FAIRCLOTH** was born 16 Feb 1991.

119 M iii. **Aaron FAIRCLOTH** was born 19 Feb 1996.

120 M iv. **Stephen FAIRCLOTH** was born 10 Feb 1998.

121 F   v. **Sierra Joy FAIRCLOTH**.

102.**Debra K. STOUT**[16,20] (George Leonard, Warder Martin, George Washington, Edward Jackson, James, Caleb, James, James, David, Richard, John) was born 18 Mar 1958.

Debra married (1) **Joel MANN** on 12 Jun 1976. The marriage ended in divorce.

They had the following children:

122 M   i.   **Christopher MANN** was born 25 Dec 1976.

123 M   ii. **Benjamin MANN** was born 24 May 1978.

               Benjamin married **Jo Carrol TRUETT** on 15 Sep 2001.

124 M iii. **Joshua MANN** was born 8 Dec 1979.

125　M　iv.　**Joel MANN** was born 23 Jan 1982.

Debra also married (2) **Mark VOGAN**.

They had the following child:

126　M　v.　**Elijah VOGAN** was born 4 Aug 1992.

103.**Michael A. STOUT** "Mike"[16,20] (George Leonard, Warder Martin, George Washington, Edward Jackson, James, Caleb, James, James, David, Richard, John) was born 7 Mar 1960.

Mike married **Cynthia HARTZELL** on 15 Jul 1989.

She had the following children:

> **Chad HARTZELL** was born 17 Mar 1979. He married **Angela STULTZ**.
>
> **Chad and Angela HARTZELL** had the following children:
>
>> **Alexis Nicole HARTZELL** was born 7 Dec 1996.
>>
>> **Cassandria Kaye HARTZELL** was born 21 Jun 2001.
>> **Jeremy HARTZELL** was born 19 Apr 1980. He married **Shannon SMITH** 8 Nov 2003.
>> **Sarah HARTZELL** was born 7 Jan 1984.

They had the following child:

127　M　i.　**Kylie STOUT** was born 28 Apr 1990.

106.**Randal L. STOUT**[16,20] (Rendal Lee, Warder Martin, George Washington, Edward Jackson, James, Caleb, James, James, David, Richard, John) was born 25 Feb 1963.

Randal married **Kimberly ODE** on 3 Jun 1989.

They had the following children:

128　F　i.　**Emily Marie STOUT** was born 17 Dec 1992.

129　F　ii.　**Erin Lee STOUT** was born 25 Sep 1994.

130 M   iii. **Ryan John STOUT** was born 27 Sep 1998.

131 M   iv. **Andrew Joseph STOUT** was born
17 Oct 2001.

108 **Traci MORRELL** (Dennis, Mondalea MORRELL, Colista
STOUT, George Washington, Edward Jackson, James,
Caleb, James, James, David, Richard, John)

She had the following children:

132 F   i.   Errin

133 M   ii.   Neal

134 M   iii. Ryan

135 F   iv. Ilish

The Generations of the

Felix Grimes Family

1. Felix GRIMES (GRAHAM) (b.1749)
sp: Catharine HULL (b.1752 d.1826)
 |-2. Arthur GRIMES , SR. (b.1774 d.1850)
 | sp: Mary SHARP (b.1774 d.1806)
 | |-3. Sally GRIMES (b.1797)
 | |-3. Rachel GRIMES (b.1798 d.1850)
 | |-3. Rebecca GRIMES (b.1804)
 | |-3. Sarah Elizabeth GRIMES (b.1805 d.1880)
 | **sp: Peggy WAUGH (m.1806)**
 | |-3. Arthur GRIMES, JR. (b.1808)
 | |-3. Sally GRIMES (b.1808)
 | **|-3. Nancy Jane GRIMES (b.1810 d.1849)**
 | **| sp: Leonard BOWYER (BOYER) II**
 | |-3. Rebecca J. GRIMES (b.1818 d.1880)
 | +-3. John GRIMES (b.1819 d.1861)
 |-2. Margaret GRIMES (GRAHAM)
 |-2. Mary GRIMES (GRAHAM)
 |-2. Sally GRIMES (GRAHAM)
 |-2. Nancy GRIMES (GRAHAM)
 |-2. John GRIMES (GRAHAM)
 |-2. Charles GRIMES (GRAHAM)
 |-2. Henry GRIMES (GRAHAM)
 |-2. James GRIMES (b.1796 d.1873)
 | **sp: Mary Magdaline BURNER (b.1796 m.1822 d.1890)**
 | **|-3. Catharine GRIMES (b.1822 d.1859)**
 | **| sp: Leonard BOWYER (BOYER) II (m.1850)**
 | |-3. Abraham GRIMES (b.1823 d.1893)
 | |-3. Mary GRIMES (b.1828)
 | |-3. Allen D. GRIMES (b.1829 d.1888)
 | |-3. Margaret Elizabeth GRIMES (b.1832)
 | |-3. George S. (C.) GRIMES (b.1834)
 | |-3. James H. GRIMES (b.1836)
 | |-3. Charles Bryson GRIMES (b.1840 d.1859)
 | +-3. Clarissa R. GRIMES (b.1844)

First Generation

1. **Felix GRIMES (GRAHAM)**[1,2] was born 1749 in Ireland. He died Aft Dec 13 1813 and Bef Feb 1814.

   Felix married **Catharine HULL**. Catharine was born 1752 in Ireland. She died 1826 in Bath Co., Va.

   They had the following children:

   +   2   M   i.   **Arthur GRIMES (GRAHAM) Sr.** was born 1774 and died 1850.

         3   F   ii.   **Margaret GRIMES (GRAHAM)**.

         4   F   iii.   **Mary GRIMES (GRAHAM)**.

         5   F   iv.   **Sally GRIMES (GRAHAM)**.

         6   F   v.   **Nancy GRIMES (GRAHAM)**.

         7   M   vi.   **John GRIMES (GRAHAM)** was born in 1819.

         8   M   vii.   **Charles GRIMES (GRAHAM)**.

         9   M   viii.   **Henry GRIMES (GRAHAM)**.

   +   10   M   ix.   **James GRIMES (GRAHAM)** was born about 1796 and died 16 Jul 1873.

Second Generation

2. **Arthur GRIMES (GRAHAM)**[2] (Felix) was born 1774 in Augusta Co., Va. He died 1850 in Pocahontas Co., (W)V.

   Arthur married (1) **Mary SHARP**, daughter of William SHARP and Mary MEEKS, on 21 Jan 1797 in Pocahontas Co., (W)V. Mary was born about 1774 in Huntersville, Pocahontas Co., (W)V. She died before 1 May 1806 in Bath Co., Va.

   They had the following children:

       11   F   i.   **Sally GRIMES** was born after 1797 in Bath Co., Va.

12 F ii. **Rachel GRIMES** was born 1798/1800 in Pocahontas Co., (W)V. She died 1850 in (W)V.

13 F iii. **Rebecca GRIMES** was born about 1804 in Bath Co., Va.

14 F iv. **Sarah Elizabeth GRIMES** was born 1805 in Bath Co., Va. She died after 1880 in Pocahontas Co., (W)V.

Arthur Sr. also married (2) **Peggy WAUGH** on 1 May 1806 in Bath Co., Va.

They had the following children:

15 M v. **Arthur GRIMES, Jr.** was born 1808 in Pocahontas Co., (W)V.

Arthur Jr. married Elizabeth Comston on 27 Feb 1830.

16 F vi. **Sally GRIMES** was born about 1808 in Pocahontas Co., (W)V.

17 F vii. **Nancy Jane GRIMES**[2,4] was born 1810/1820 in Bath Co., Va. She died 1 Aug 1849 in Highland Co., Va.

Nancy married **Leonard BOWYER II**.

18 F viii. **Rebecca J. GRIMES** was born 1818 in Bath Co., Va. She died after 1880.

19 M ix. **John GRIMES** was born 1819 in Bath Co., Va.. He died 1861/1864 in Buckhannon, Upshur Co., WV.

10. **James GRIMES (GRAHAM)** (Felix) was born about 1796 in Va. He died 16 Jul 1873 in Hillsboro, Pocahontas Co.

He had the following children:

20 F i. **Catharine GRIMES**[3,5,6] was born 1822 in Pocahontas Co., (W)V. She died 1 Aug 1859 in Highland Co., Va. Catharine married **Leonard BOWYER II** on 14 Feb

1850.

21 M   ii.   **Abraham GRIMES** was born 1823 in Pocahontas Co., (W)V. He died 1893.

22 F   iii.   **Mary GRIMES** was born 1828 in Pocahontas Co., (W)V.

23 M   iv.   **Allen D. GRIMES** was born 28 Oct 1829 in Mill Point, Pocahontas Co. He died 5 Feb 1888 in Mill Point, Pocahontas Co. and was buried in McNeel Cemetery, Hillsboro, WV.

24 F   v.   **Margaret Elizabeth GRIMES** was born about 1832 in Pocahontas Co., (W)V.

25 M   vi.   **George S. (C.) GRIMES** were born about 1834 in Pocahontas Co., (W)V.

26 M   vii.   **James H. GRIMES** was born about 1836 in Pocahontas Co., (W)V.

27 M   viii.   **Charles Bryson GRIMES** was born about 1840.

The Generations of the

Leonard Bowyer (Boyer) I Family

1. Leonard BOWYER (BOYER) I (d.1815)
 sp: UNKNOWN
|-2. **Leonard (Leonidas) BOWYER (BOYER) II (b.1808 d.1900)**
| **sp: Nancy Jane GRIMES (b.1810 m.1833 d.1849)**
| |-3. Ellen V. BOWYER (b.1841 d.1898)
| | sp: Enoch G. WATSON
| | |-4. David O. W. WATSON (b.1859)
| | |-4. Leonard L. WATSON (b.1861)
| | |-4. Clarissa R. H. WATSON (b.1864)
| | |-4. George W. WATSON (b.1866)
| | |-4. James S. H. WATSON (b.1868)
| | |-4. Warder W. W. WATSON (b.1871)
| | |-4. Marion WATSON (b.1873)
| | |-4. Lidn WATSON (b.1876)
| | +-4. Dora C. B. WATSON (b.1879)
| |-3. **Charles Osbourne BOWYER (b.1849 d.1915)**
| | **sp: Mary (Merry) Catherine RICHARDS (b.1853 d.1932)**
| | |-4. Henry BOWYER (b.1871)
| | |-4. Olive Jane BOWYER (b.1875 d.1953)
| | | sp: James SPAUR (b.1867 m.1895 d.1927)
| | | |-5. Ora Myrtle SPAUR (b.1896 d.1974)
| | | | sp: George Henry RIFFLE (b.1885 m.1915 d.1968)
| | | | |-6. Noah Lester RIFFLE (b.1915)
| | | | | sp: Irene MCHENRY (b.1921)
| | | | | |-7. Virginia Ann RIFFLE (b.1943)
| | | | | |-7. Theodore Lester RIFFLE (b.1945)
| | | | | +-7. Raymond Eugene RIFFLE (b.1948)
| | | | |-6. Alta Mae RIFFLE (b.1917)
| | | | | sp: Arnold COOPER (b.1914 m.1946)
| | | | | +-7. Sandra Diania COOPER (b.1947)
| | | | |-6. Charles Burley RIFFLE (b.1921)
| | | | | sp: Lois Ann BROWN (b.1934 m.1951)
| | | | | |-7. Sheldon Bruce RIFFLE (b.1952)
| | | | | |-7. Shannon Michael RIFFLE (b.1958 d.1981)
| | | | | |-7. Louwann Violene RIFFLE (b.1955)
| | | | | +-7. Tammy Dawn RIFFLE (b.1960)
| | | | |-6. Clarence Cecil RIFFLE (b.1924 d.1986)
| | | | | sp: Joyce SMITH

```
| | | | | sp: Patricia Ann SHERRER (m.1954)
| | | | |-6. Emma Virnie RIFFLE (b.1926)
| | | | | sp: Overt SNIDER (b.1926 m.1947)
| | | | | +-7. Betty Jo SNIDER (b.1954)
| | | | |   sp: Charles Franklin HEATER (b.1953 m.1980)
| | | | |-6. George Clendon RIFFLE (b.1930 d.1951)
| | | | |-6. Mary Catherine RIFFLE (b.1932 d.1933)
| | | | +-6. Monna Regina RIFFLE (b.1939)
| | | |   sp: Lloyd ALLMAN (m.1959)
| | | |   |-7. George Allan ALLMAN (b.1961)
| | | |   |-7. Barbara Kathern ALLMAN (b.1962)
| | | |   |-7. Phyllis Renee ALLMAN (b.1963)
| | | |   |-7. Anita Lynn ALLMAN (b.1966)
| | | |   |-7. Lisa Sue ALLMAN (b.1967)
| | | |   |-7. Sharon Lea ALLMAN (b.1970)
| | | |   sp: Wilbur WILLISTON
| | | |-5. Charles Dewey SPAUR (b.1899)
| | | |-5. Minnie Byrd SPAUR (b.1900)
| | | |-5. James Anthony SPAUR (b.1902)
| | | |-5. Vena Valena SPAUR (b.1907)
| | | |-5. Queen Ester SPAUR (b.1910)
| | | |-5. Melba Belle SPAUR (b.1919)
| | | +-5. Woodrow SPAUR
| | |-4. Hugh Raymond BOWYER  (b.1877 d.1966)
| | | sp: Mary Catora STOUT (b.1878 m.1871 d.1954)
| | | |-5. Hazel BOWYER (b.1908 d.1992)
| | | | sp: George Dencil HARDMAN I (m.1928)
| | | | |-6. George Dencil HARDMAN II
| | | | |-6. Mary Alice HARDMAN
| | | | |-6. Marjorie HARDMAN
| | | | |-6. Coleta Dare HARDMAN
| | | | |-6. Edith Sharon HARDMAN
| | | | +-6. William Raymond HARDMAN I
| | | |-5. Frankie BOWYER  (b.1910 d.1911)
| | | |-5. Mary Edith BOWYER  (b.1912 d.2001)
| | | | sp: Paul Dean MAYSE (m.1937)
| | | | |-6. Sandra Sue MAYSE
| | | | +-6. Anna Raye MAYSE (b.1946 d.2001)
| | | +-5. Worthy Lee BOWYER  (b.1915 d.1989)
```

```
| | |   sp: Ruth JACKSON (m.1937)
| | |   |-6. Worthy Lee BOWYER, JR. (b.1938)
| | |   | sp: Dolores BUBON (b.1936)
| | |   |-6. Raymond BOWYER  (b.1941)
| | |   +-6. Rodney BOWYER  (b.1945)
| | |     sp: Susan NESPECA (b.1950 m.1975)
| | |     |-7. Rodney BOWYER, JR. (b.1969)
| | |     +-7. Julie BOWYER  (b.1983)
| | |-4. Nancy Elizabeth BOWYER  (b.1886 d.1975)
| | | sp: John SHOLES (b.1877 d.1951)
| | | |-5. Minnie SHOLES (b.1905 d.1968)
| | | |-5. Okie Frank SHOLES (b.1908 d.1974)
| | | |-5. Roy C. SHOLES (b.1912)
| | | | sp: Barbara Lee BERRY (b.1910 m.1937 d.1999)
| | | +-5. Juanita SHOLES (b.1924 d.1994)
|-2. Nancy BOWYER (BOYER) (b.1811)
+-2. Anthony BOWYER (BOYER) (b.1812)
```

First Generation

Leonard BOWYER (BOYER) I[1] died 11 Feb-4 Apr 1815 in Pendleton Co., (W)V.

He had the following children:

+   2   M   i.   **Leonard (Leonidas) BOWYER (BOYER) II** was born 1808 and died ~1900.

      3   F   ii.   **Nancy BOWYER (BOYER)** was born 1811 in Pendleton Co., (W)V.

      4   M   iii.   **Anthony BOWYER (BOYER)** was born about 1812.

Leonidas (Leonard) Boyer (Bowyer)

Second Generation

2.   **Leonard (Leonidas) BOWYER (BOYER) II**[2,3,4,5] (Leonard) was born 1808. He died ~1900 in Braxton Co., WV and was buried in Nutter's Farm, Near Cox Mills, Gilmer Co. WV.

Leonard married[6] (1) **Nancy Jane GRIMES**[6], daughter of Arthur GRIMES and Mary SHARP, on 6 Aug 1833 in Highland Co., VA. Nancy was born 1810/1815 in Bath Co., Va.. She died[7] 1849 in Highland Co., VA.

They had the following children:

+   5   M   i.   **Washington Cicero BOWYER** was born 1835.

+   6   M   ii.   **James Leonard BOWYER** was born 1836.

+   7   F   iii.   **Rebecca BOWYER** was born 1839.

+   8   F   iv.   **Ellen V. BOWYER** was born 13 Jul 1841 and died 16 Oct 1898.

+   9   F   v.   **Margaret Elizabeth BOWYER** was born 1846.

+   10   M   vi.   **Charles Osbourne BOWYER** was born 17 Sep 1849 and died 2 Mar 1915.

Leonard also married[2,6] (2) **Catherine GRIMES**[6,8,9,10], daughter of James GRIMES and Mary BURNER, on 14 Feb 1850 in Bath Co., Va. Catherine was born 1822 in Bath Co., Va. She died 1 Aug 1859 in Highland Co., Va.

They had the following children:

+   11   M   vii.   **George Allen BOWYER** was born 1851 and died 6 Feb 1932.

    12   F   viii.   **Mary Matilda BOWYER** [9] was born 1853.

                  Mary married **George Washington STOUT**[11] on 24 Nov 1871 in Gilmer Co., WV.

Third Generation

5. **Washington Cicero BOWYER** [4] (Leonard (Leonidas) BOWYER (BOYER) II, Leonard) was born 1835.

Washington married **Eliza QUEEN**.

They had the following children:

    13   M   i.   **James B. BOWYER** was born 1864.

    14   F   ii.   **Rebecca BOWYER** was born 1864.

    15   M   iii.   **Charles L. BOWYER** was born 1870.

    16   F   iv.   **Virginia N. BOWYER** was born 1874.

    17   F   v.   **Cora J. BOWYER** was born 1876.

    18   M   vi.   **Docia E. BOWYER** was born 1878.

6. **James Leonard BOWYER** [12] (Leonard (Leonidas) BOWYER (BOYER) II, Leonard) was born 1836.

James married **Mary E. UNKNOWN**.

They had the following children:

   19 M   i.   **Leonard BOWYER** was born 1869.

   20 M   ii.   **Frank BOWYER** was born 1870.

7. **Rebecca BOWYER** [13] (Leonard (Leonidas) BOWYER (BOYER) II, Leonard) was born 1839 in Pocahontas Co., (W)V.

Rebecca married **George Marion WOOFTER** on Feb 1867 in Leading Creek, Gilmer Co., WV.

They had the following children:

   21 F   i.   **Rebecca WOOFTER** was born 10 Oct 1863She died 12 Dec 1895.

   22 F   ii.   **Nancy WOOFTER** was born 3 Jan 1868. She died 4 Nov 1869.

   23 M   iii.   **Albert WOOFTER** was born 10 Jun 1869.

   24 M   iv.   **Lloyd Granville WOOFTER** was born 1871.

   25 M   v.   **William E. WOOFTER** was born 1873.

   26 F   vi.   **Amelia Mary WOOFTER** was born 1874. She died 13 Aug 1926.

   27 M vii.   **Emory WOOFTER** was born 13 Oct 1876.

   28 M viii. **Homer WOOFTER** was born 1877.

   29 M   ix.   **Roy WOOFTER** was born 1878.

   30 M   x.   **Esta WOOFTER** was born 1878. He died 21 Apr 1882.

8. **Ellen V. BOWYER** [14,15] (Leonard (Leonidas) BOWYER (BOYER) II, Leonard) was born 13 Jul 1841 in Pocahontas Co., (W)V. She died 16 Oct 1898 and was buried Ross in Upshur Co., Selbyville, WV.

Ellen married **Enoch G. WATSON**.

They had the following children:

31 M   i.   **David O. W. WATSON** was born 1859.

32 M   ii. **Leonard L. WATSON** was born 1861.

33 F   iii. **Clarissa R. H. WATSON** was born 1864.

34 M   iv. **George W. WATSON** was born 1866.

35 M   v.   **James S. H. WATSON** was born 1868.

36 M   vi. **Warder W. W. WATSON** was born 1871.

37 M   vii. **Marion WATSON** was born 1873.

38 M   viii. **Lidn WATSON** was born 1876.

39 F   ix. **Dora C. B. WATSON** was born 1879.

9. **Margaret Elizabeth BOWYER** [16] (Leonard (Leonidas) BOWYER (BOYER) II, Leonard) was born 1846. She was buried in Nutter's Farm, Near Cox Mills, Gilmer Co. WV.

Margaret married (1) **Albert MONEYPENNY**.

They had the following children:

+   40 M   i.   **Ace Elihue Lee MONEYPENNY** was born 31 Jan 1867 and died 31 May 1957.

Margaret also married (2) **Jonathan MARSH** in 1870 in Gilmer Co., WV.

He had the following child:

41 M   ii. **Jonathan MARSH II** was born[17] 1867.

They had the following child:

42 F   iii. **Hester MARSH** was born 1874.

Charles Osbourne and Merry Richards Bowyer

10. **Charles Osbourne BOWYER**[7,18] (Leonard (Leonidas) BOWYER (BOYER) II, Leonard) was born 17 Sep 1849 in Highland Co., VA. He died 2 Mar 1915 in Burnsville, Braxton Co., WV and was buried K & P in Burnsville, Braxton Co., WV.

Charles married **Mary (Merry) Catherine RICHARDS**[19], daughter of John Richards RICHARDS and Jane MCQUAIN, on 7 Jan 1870 in Gilmer Co., WV. Mary was born 1 Aug 1853. She died 16 Jun 1932 in Braxton Co., WV and was buried K & P in Burnsville, Braxton Co., WV.

They had the following children:

+   43 M   i. **Henry BOWYER** was born 26 Nov 1871.

+   44 M   ii. **Emory Jackson BOWYER** was born 2 Feb 1873 and died 2 Feb 1957.

+   45 F   iii. **Olive Jane BOWYER** was born 1875 and died 28 Nov 1953.

+   46 M   iv. **Hugh Raymond BOWYER** was born 2 Oct 1877 and died 22 Jan 1966.

     47 M   v. **George Allan BOWYER** was born 2 Jul 1881 in Horn Creek, Gilmer Co., WV.

+   48 M   vi. **Washington Cicero BOWYER** was born 7 Jun 1844 and died before 1915.

+   **49 F vii.** **Nancy Elizabeth BOWYER** was born 13 Mar 1886 and died 1975.

+   **50 M viii.** **James S. BOWYER** was born 1889.

Ezra Minter Bowyer

+   **51 M ix.** **Ezra Minter BOWYER** was born 1894.

11. **George Allen BOWYER** [16,20] (Leonard (Leonidas) BOWYER (BOYER) II, Leonard) was born 1851 in Highland Co., VA. He died 6 Feb 1932 in Cox Mills, Gilmer Co., WV.

George married (1) **Melissa STOUT**. Melissa was born 1849.

They had the following children:

    52 M i. **Arlington E. BOWYER** was born 1874.

    53 M ii. **Claudies BOWYER** was born 1876.

    54 F iii. **Capitola Laura BOWYER** was born 25 Jul 1879.

    55 M iv. **Donald BOWYER** .

George also married (2) **Mary BURROWS** on 1883. Mary died 11 Jan 1942.

They had the following children:

    56 M v. **Jesse Lewis BOWYER** was born 1884.

    57 M vi. **Leonard O. BOWYER** was born 1886. He

died 1887.

58   F   vii.   **Leota Mae BOWYER** was born 7 May 1888.

59   F   viii.   **Ella C. BOWYER** was born 1889.

60   M   ix.   **Brison Leon BOWYER** was born 1891.

Fourth Generation

40. **Ace Elihue Lee MONEYPENNY**[21] (Margaret Elizabeth BOWYER , Leonard (Leonidas) BOWYER (BOYER) II, Leonard) was born 31 Jan 1867. He died 31 May 1957 in Ritchie Co., WV and was buried IOOF Cemetery in Harrisville, WV.

Ace married (1) **Eliza Ellen LAW** on 18 Apr 1889 in Gilmer Co., WV. Eliza died 12 Aug 1897 in Conings, Gilmer Co., WV.

They had the following children:

61   F   i.   **Clella Jane MONEYPENNY** was born 3 Mar 1890 in Gilmer Co., WV. She died 7 Dec 1967 in Warren, Ohio.

62   F   ii.   **Edith Edna MONEYPENNY** was born 15 Apr 1892.

63   F   iii.   **"Daughter" MONEYPENNY** was born 14 May 1897. She died 1897.

Ace also married (2) **Melvina Elizabeth FLESHER** on 23 Nov 1897. Melvina was born 11 Feb 1879.

They had the following children:

64   M   iv.   **William Rodney MONEYPENNY** was born 16 Nov 1898 in Conings, Gilmer Co., WV.

65   M   v.   **Albert MONEYPENNY** was born 30 Aug 1900.

66   F   vi.   **Roxie MONEYPENNY** was born 29 Jan 1902 in Conings, Gilmer Co., WV.

67 M vii. **Roy Lee MONEYPENNY** was born 3 Mar 1904 in Conings, Gilmer Co., WV.

68 M viii. **Randall MONEYPENNY** was born 6 Apr 1905.

69 M ix. **Ruhl MONEYPENNY** was born 17 Mar 1906.

70 M x. **Rinza MONEYPENNY** was born 1 Jan 1908 in Conings, Gilmer Co., WV.

71 M xi. **Rillis MONEYPENNY** was born 16 May 1911 in Alum Bridge, Lewis Co., WV.

72 F xii. **Regina Lea MONEYPENNY** was born 11 Jun 1916 in Doddridge Co., WV.

73 M xiii. **Paul Revere MONEYPENNY** was born 29 Aug 1919 in Cairo, Ritchie Co., WV.

74 M xiv. **Russell Gearl MONEYPENNY** was born 10 Jun 1922 in Cairo, Ritchie Co., WV.

43. **Henry BOWYER** [22] (Charles Osbourne BOWYER, Leonard (Leonidas) BOWYER (BOYER) II, Leonard) was born 26 Nov 1871 in Horn Creek, Gilmer Co., WV. Henry married **Hester MARSH**.

They had the following children:

75 F i. **Cora Ethel BOWYER** was born 1897.

76 F ii. **Mary Gay BOWYER** .

44. **Emory Jackson BOWYER** [23] (Charles Osbourne BOWYER, Leonard (Leonidas) BOWYER (BOYER) II, Leonard) was born 2 Feb 1873 in Horn Creek, Gilmer Co., WV. He died 2 Feb 1957 in Falls Mills, Braxton Co., WV.

Emory married (1) **Cornelia STUMP**, daughter of Hezekiah STUMP. Cornelia was born 1875.

They had the following children:

77 F i. **Cornelia Elma BOWYER** .

78 F ii. **Cornelia Lynn BOWYER** .

Emory also married (2) **Alberta SPAUR** on 25 Jun 1899.

They had the following children:

   79   F   iii.   **Dochie Eva BOWYER** was born 25 Jun 1900.

   80   F   iv.   **Mae BOWYER** was born 2 Jul 1902. She died 1993.

   81   M   v.   **Everette G. BOWYER** was born 2 Nov 1904. He died 1988.

   82   F   vi.   **Retha Leone BOWYER** was born 29 Oct 1906.

   83   F   vii.   **Winnie Letalia BOWYER** was born 8 Sep 1908.

   84   M   viii.   **Delbert C. BOWYER** was born 3 Oct 1910. He died 1972.

   85   F   ix.   **Ella Loma BOWYER** was born 23 Oct 1912. She died 1992.

   86   F   x.   **Wilma Gertrude BOWYER** was born 6 Feb 1915. She died 1984.

   87   F   xi.   **Grace BOWYER** was born 8 Sep 1918.

   88   F   xii.   **Ella Virginia BOWYER** was born 4 Jul 1921.

45. **Olive Jane BOWYER** [24] (Charles Osbourne BOWYER, Leonard (Leonidas) BOWYER (BOYER) II, Leonard) was born 1875 in Horn Creek, Gilmer Co., WV. She died 28 Nov 1953 in Sutton, WV and was buried K & P in Burnsville, Braxton Co., WV.

Olive married **James SPAUR**, son of John W. SPAUR and Jemina AMOS, on 6 Nov 1895 in Gilmer Co., WV. James was born 18 Aug 1867 in Skin Creek, Lewis Co., WV. He died Sep 1927 in Burnsville, Braxton Co., WV.

They had the following children:

+   89   F   i.   **Ora Myrtle SPAUR** was born 23 Aug 1896

and died 26 Jan 1974.

90 M ii. **Charles Dewey SPAUR** was born 22 Feb 1899 in Moore's Run, Gilmer Co., WV.

91 F iii. **Minnie Byrd SPAUR** was born 26 Jun 1900 in Moore's Run, Gilmer Co., WV.

92 M iv. **James Anthony SPAUR** was born 15 Sep 1902 in Beach Fork, Braxton Co., WV.

93 F v. **Vena Valena SPAUR** was born 7 Jan 1907 in Beach Fork, Braxton Co., WV.

94 F vi. **Queen Ester SPAUR** was born 8 Aug 1910 in Beach Fork, Braxton Co., WV.

95 F vii. **Melba Belle SPAUR** was born 19 Dec 1919 in Beach Fork, Braxton Co., WV.

96 M viii. **Woodrow SPAUR**.

Hugh Raymond Bowyer

46. **Hugh Raymond BOWYER** [25] (Charles Osbourne BOWYER, Leonard (Leonidas) BOWYER (BOYER) II, Leonard) was born 2 Oct 1877 in Horn Creek, Gilmer Co., WV. He died 22 Jan 1966 in Burnsville, Braxton Co., WV and was buried K & P in Burnsville, Braxton Co., WV.

Hugh married **Mary Catora STOUT** on 24 Nov 1871 in Gilmer Co., WV. Mary was born 23 May 1878. She died 23 Oct 1954 in Weston, WV and was buried in K & P, Burnsville, WV.

Hazel, Mary Edith, Worthy Lee Bowyer

They had the following children:

+   97   F   i.   **Hazel BOWYER** was born 13 Feb 1908 and died 8 Jan 1992.

     98   M   ii.   **Frankie BOWYER** was born 21 Nov 1910. He died 30 Jul 1911.

+   99   F   iii.   **Mary Edith BOWYER** was born 18 Oct 1912 and died 7 Jun 2001.

+   100   M   iv.   **Worthy Lee BOWYER** was born 26 Feb 1915 and died 1 Nov 1989.

48. **Washington Cicero BOWYER** [26,27] (Charles Osbourne BOWYER, Leonard (Leonidas) BOWYER (BOYER) II, Leonard) was born 7 Jun 1844 in Horn Creek, Gilmer Co., WV. He died before 1915.

Washington married **Zona TAYLOR**.

They had the following children:

  101   M   i.   **Charles Cicero BOWYER** .

  102   F   ii.   **Madge BOWYER** .

49. **Nancy Elizabeth BOWYER** [28] (Charles Osbourne BOWYER, Leonard (Leonidas) BOWYER (BOYER) II, Leonard) was born 13 Mar 1886 in Horn Creek, Gilmer Co., WV. She died 1975 in Burnsville, Braxton Co., WV.

Nancy married **John SHOLES**. John was born 1877. He died 1951.

They had the following children:

103　F　　i.　**Minnie SHOLES** was born 22 Aug 1905.
　　　　　　　She died 1979.

104　M　　ii.　**Okie Frank SHOLES** was born 1 May 1908.
　　　　　　　He died 1974.

105　M　　iii.　**Roy C. SHOLES** was born 6 Oct 1912.

　　　　　　　Roy married **Barbara Lee BERRY** on 9
　　　　　　　Jan 1937 in Burnsville, Braxton Co., WV.
　　　　　　　Barbara was born 14 May 1910 in
　　　　　　　Richwood, Nicholas Co., WV. She died 16
　　　　　　　Sep 1999 in Maryland.

106　F　　iv.　**Juanita SHOLES** was born 10 Feb 1924.
　　　　　　　She died 1994.

50. **James S. BOWYER** [29] (Charles Osbourne BOWYER,
Leonard (Leonidas) BOWYER (BOYER) II, Leonard) was
born 1889 in Horn Creek, Gilmer Co., WV.

James married **Eva EXLINE**.

They had the following children:

107　F　　i.　**Opal BOWYER** .

108　F　　ii.　**Mildred BOWYER** .

109　F　　iii.　**Georgie BOWYER**.

110　F　　iv.　**Mary BOWYER** .

111　M　　v.　**Arden BOWYER** .

112　F　　vi.　**Lola BOWYER** .

113　F　　vii.　**Gladys BOWYER** .

51. **Ezra Minter BOWYER** [29] (Charles Osbourne BOWYER,
Leonard (Leonidas) BOWYER (BOYER) II, Leonard) was
born 1894 in Horn Creek, Gilmer Co., WV.

Ezra married **Mary Mildred FISHER**.

They had the following children:

114 F   i.   **Marjorie BOWYER** .

115 M   ii. **William BOWYER** .

116 M   iii. **John BOWYER** .

117 M   iv. **Robert BOWYER** .

Fifth Generation

89. **Ora Myrtle SPAUR**[30] (Olive Jane BOWYER , Charles Osbourne BOWYER, Leonard (Leonidas) BOWYER (BOYER) II, Leonard) was born 23 Aug 1896 in Moore's Run, Gilmer Co., WV. She died 26 Jan 1974 in Roanoke, Lewis Co., WV and was buried in Mitchell Cemetery, Roanoke, WV.

Ora married **George Henry RIFFLE**[30], son of John Jackson RIFFLE and Nancy Susan BLAKE, on 1 Jan 1915 in Gilmer Co., WV. George was born 13 Aug 1885 in Bennett Siding, Lewis Co., WV. He died 24 Oct 1968 in Roanoke, Lewis Co., WV and was buried in Mitchell Cemetery, Roanoke, WV.
They had the following children:

+   118 M   i.   **Noah Lester RIFFLE** was born 15 Nov 1915.

+   119 F   ii. **Alta Mae RIFFLE** was born 14 Sep 1917.

+   120 M   iii. **Charles Burley RIFFLE** was born 16 Jul 1921.

    121 M   iv. **Clarence Cecil RIFFLE**[30] was born 6 Aug 1924 in Bennett Siding, Lewis Co., WV. He died 23 Jan 1986 in Lorain, Ohio.

             Clarence married (1) **Joyce SMITH**.

             He also married (2) **Patricia Ann SHERRER** .

+   122 F   v.   **Emma Virnie RIFFLE** was born 15 Dec 1926.

    123 M   vi. **George Clendon RIFFLE**[30] was born 9 Jun 1930 in Lewis Co., WV. He died 10 Oct

1951 was buried in Mitchell Cemetery, Roanoke, WV.

124 F vii. **Mary Catherine RIFFLE**[31] was born 1 Oct 1932 in Lewis Co., WV. She died 15 Mar 1933 and was buried in Posey Run Cemetery, Orlando, WV.

+ 125 F viii. **Monna Regina RIFFLE** was born 16 Jul 1939.

Hazel Bowyer

97.**Hazel BOWYER**[32] (Hugh Raymond BOWYER , Charles Osbourne BOWYER, Leonard (Leonidas) BOWYER (BOYER) II, Leonard) was born 13 Feb 1908 in Burnsville, WV. She died 8 Jan 1992 in Weston, WV and was buried in K & P, Burnsville, WV.

Hazel married **George Dencil HARDMAN I** on 23 Dec 1928 in Falls Mills, Braxton Co., WV.

They had the following children:

126 M i. **George Dencil HARDMAN II** .

127 F ii. **Mary Alice HARDMAN** .

128 F iii. **Marjorie HARDMAN** .

129 F iv. **Coleta Dare HARDMAN** .

130 F   v.   **Edith Sharon HARDMAN** .

131 M   vi.   **William Raymond HARDMAN I.**

Mary Edith Bowyer

99. **Mary Edith BOWYER** [33] (Hugh Raymond BOWYER ,
Charles Osbourne BOWYER, Leonard (Leonidas)
BOWYER (BOYER) II, Leonard) was born 18 Oct 1912 in
Burnsville, WV. She died 7 Jun 2001 and was buried in K &
P, Burnsville, WV.

Edith married **Paul Dean MAYSE** on 29 Oct 1937.

They had the following children:

132 F   i.   **Sandra Sue MAYSE** was born 1 May 1943.

Sandra married **Darwin PLUMLEE** on 6
June 1964.

133 F   ii.   **Anna Raye MAYSE** was born 4 Oct 1946.
She died 5 Apr 2001 in Weston, WV.

Worthy Lee Bowyer, Sr.

100.**Worthy Lee BOWYER , Sr.**[34] (Hugh Raymond BOWYER , Charles Osbourne BOWYER, Leonard (Leonidas) BOWYER (BOYER) II, Leonard) was born 26 Feb 1915 in Burnsville, WV. He died 1 Nov 1989 in Youngstown, Ohio and was buried in K & P, Burnsville, WV.

Worthy married **Ruth JACKSON** in 1937.

They had the following children:

   134 M   i. **Worthy Lee BOWYER, JR.** "Butch" was born[35] 29 Mar 1938.

                Butch married **Dolores BUBON**. Dolores was born 4 Feb 1936.

   135 M   ii. **Raymond BOWYER** was born[35] 2 Mar 1941.

+   136 M   iii. **Rodney BOWYER** was born 11 Dec 1945.

Sixth Generation

118.**Noah Lester RIFFLE**[30] (Ora Myrtle SPAUR, Olive Jane BOWYER , Charles Osbourne BOWYER, Leonard (Leonidas) BOWYER (BOYER) II, Leonard) was born 15 Nov 1915 in Bennett Siding, Lewis Co., WV.

Noah married **Irene MCHENRY**. Irene was born 20 Feb 1921.

They had the following children:

137 F i. **Virginia Ann RIFFLE**[31] was born 29 Apr 1943.

138 M ii. **Theodore Lester RIFFLE**[31] was born 15 Nov 1945..

139 M iii. **Raymond Eugene RIFFLE**[31] was born 9 Oct 1948.

119.**Alta Mae RIFFLE**[30] (Ora Myrtle SPAUR, Olive Jane BOWYER , Charles Osbourne BOWYER, Leonard (Leonidas) BOWYER (BOYER) II, Leonard) was born 14 Sep 1917 in Bennett Siding, Lewis Co., WV.

Alta married **Arnold COOPER** on 12 May 1946.

They had the following children:

140 F i. **Sandra Diania COOPER** was born 25 Mar 1947.

120.**Charles Burley RIFFLE**[30] (Ora Myrtle SPAUR, Olive Jane BOWYER , Charles Osbourne BOWYER, Leonard (Leonidas) BOWYER (BOYER) II, Leonard) was born 16 Jul 1921 in Bennett Siding, Lewis Co., WV.

Charles married **Lois Ann BROWN** on 6 Oct 1951. Lois was born 20 Jul 1934. They had the following children:

141 M i. **Sheldon Bruce RIFFLE**[31] was born 20 Aug 1952.

142 M ii. **Shannon Michael RIFFLE**[31] was born 2 Mar 1958. He died 3 Jul 1981.

143 F iii. **Louwann Violene RIFFLE**[30] was born 25 May 1955.

144 F iv. **Tammy Dawn RIFFLE**[31] was born 29 Mar 1960.

122.**Emma Virnie RIFFLE**[30] (Ora Myrtle SPAUR, Olive Jane BOWYER , Charles Osbourne BOWYER, Leonard (Leonidas) BOWYER (BOYER) II, Leonard) was born 15 Dec 1926 in Bennett Siding, Lewis Co., WV.

Emma married **Overt SNIDER**, son of Everett SNIDER and Sudie ISENHEART, on 21 Jun 1947. Overt was born 17 May 1926 in Gilmer Co., WV.

They had the following child:

145 F   i.   **Betty Jo SNIDER** was born 21 Feb 1954 in Lewis Co., WV.

                 Betty married **Charles Franklin HEATER** on 21 Jun 1980. Charles was born 29 Mar 1953 in Lewis Co., WV.

125. **Monna Regina RIFFLE** "Jean"[31] (Ora Myrtle SPAUR, Olive Jane BOWYER , Charles Osbourne BOWYER, Leonard (Leonidas) BOWYER (BOYER) II, Leonard) was born 16 Jul 1939 in Roanoke, Lewis Co., WV.

Jean married (1) **Lloyd ALLMAN** on 3 Jan 1959.

They had the following children:

146 M   i.   **George Allan ALLMAN** was born 26 May 1961 in Lewis Co., WV.

147 F   ii.   **Barbara Kathern ALLMAN** was born 12 Apr 1962 in Lewis Co., WV.

148 F   iii.   **Phyllis Renee ALLMAN** was born 23 Jul 1963 in Lewis Co., WV.

149 F   iv.   **Anita Lynn ALLMAN** was born 2 Oct 1966 in Lewis Co., WV.

150 F   v.   **Lisa Sue ALLMAN** was born 26 Oct 1967 in Lewis Co., WV.

151 F   vi.   **Sharon Lea ALLMAN** was born 1 Apr 1970 in Lewis Co., WV.

Jean also married (2) **Wilbur WILLISTON**.

The Generations of the

Henry McWhorter Family

1. Henry MCWHORTER (b.1760 d.1848)
sp: Mary FIELDS (b.1761 m.1783 d.1834)
 |-2. Thomas MCWHORTER (b.1785 d.1816)
 | sp: Delila STALNAKER (b.1789 m.1807 d.1872)
 | |-3. Talitha MCWHORTER (b.1808 d.1890)
 | |-3. Henry MCWHORTER (b.1809 d.1863)
 | |-3. Rebecca Celina MCWHORTER (b.1811 d.1882)
 | | sp: Elias Jackson LOWTHER (b.1801 m.1828 d.1887)
 | | |-4. Jesse LOWTHER (b.1829)
 | | |-4. Henry Marcellus LOWTHER (b.1830)
 | | |-4. John McWhorter LOWTHER (b.1832 d.1863)
 | | |-4. Calhoun LOWTHER (b.1834 d.1835)
 | | |-4. McDuffy LOWTHER (b.1834 d.1873)
 | | |-4. Granville Sharp LOWTHER (b.1836 d.1920)
 | | | sp: Elizabeth PRIBBLE (m.1862 d.1865)
 | | | |-5. Henry LOWTHER (b.1863 d.1866)
 | | | sp: Mary Jane LOWTHER (m.1865)
 | | | |-5. John D. LOWTHER (b.1867 d.1869)
 | | | |-5. Carrie Orvilla LOWTHER (b.1868 d.1927)
 | | | |-5. Lura May LOWTHER (b.1872 d.1872)
 | | | |-5. Lora Virginia LOWTHER (b.1872)
 | | | |-5. Bessie Maude LOWTHER (b.1872 d.1964)
 | | | | sp: John William HARDMAN (m.1899)
 | | | | |-6. Leatha Carrie HARDMAN
 | | | | |-6. Lora Arvilla HARDMAN
 | | | | |-6. Walter W. Hardman
 | | | | |-6. George Dencil Hardman I HARDMAN
 | | | | |-6. Delmas Emmett HARDMAN
 | | | | |-6. Retta Dale HARDMAN
 | | | | +-6. Lester HARDMAN
 | | | +-5. Harrison LOWTHER (b.1875)
 | | |-4. Camillus LOWTHER (b.1839 d.1902)
 | | |-4. Thomas Newton LOWTHER (b.1841 d.1934)
 | | |-4. Columbia Virginia LOWTHER (b.1844 d.1906)
 | | |-4. Mary M. LOWTHER (b.1846 d.1908)
 | | |-4. Elias Hughes LOWTHER (b.1848 d.1888)
 | | |-4. Celina (Celinda) Jane LOWTHER (b.1851 d.1923)
 | | +-4. William Alex LOWTHER (b.1854)
 | |-3. Rulina MCWHORTER (b.1813)

```
|  |-3. Mary MCWHORTER (b.1815 d.1905)
|  |-3. Margaret MCWHORTER (b.1816 d.1900)
|  +-3. Susanna MCWHORTER (b.1817)
```

First Generation

1. **Henry MCWHORTER**[1] was born 13 Nov 1760 in New Jersey. He died 4 Feb 1848 in (W)V and was buried in McWhorter Church Cemetery, McWhorter, (W)V.

   Henry married **Mary FIELDS**, daughter of M. Walter FIELDS, on 1 Aug 1783 in Bucks Co., Pa. Mary was born 28 Oct 1761 in Bucks Co., Pa. She died 28 Aug 1834 in McWhorter, (W)V and was buried in McWhorter Church Cemetery, McWhorter, (W)V.

   They had the following children:

       2 M   i. **John MCWHORTER** was born 28 Apr 1784. He died 14 Apr 1880.

   +   3 M   ii. **Thomas MCWHORTER** was born 15 Jul 1785 and died 28 Dec 1816.

       4 M   iii. **Walter Fields MCWHORTER** was born 31 Oct 1787. He died 12 Aug 1860.

Second Generation

3. **Thomas MCWHORTER**[2] (Henry) was born 15 Jul 1785. He died 28 Dec 1816.

   Thomas married **Delila STALNAKER** on Mar 1807. Delila was born 13 Feb 1789. She died 26 Feb 1872.

   They had the following children:

       5 F   i. **Talitha MCWHORTER** was born 13 Apr 1808. She died 13 Apr 1890.

                    Talitha married **David SMITH** on 27 Feb 1827.

       6 M   ii. **Henry MCWHORTER** was born 8 Oct 1809. He died 22 Jan 1863.

                    Henry married **Hannah JONES**, daughter of Lt. Samuel Z. JONES, on 1832. Hannah was born 9 Jul 1809. She died 5

105

Sep 1888.

+   7   F   iii.   **Rebecca Celina MCWHORTER** was born 22 Oct 1811 and died 10 Sep 1882.

     8   F   iv.   **Rulina MCWHORTER** was born 21 Nov 1813.

Rulina married (1) **Washington SLEETH**.

Rulina also married (2) **Lewis PATTON**.

Rulina also married (3) **Angus RADER**.

Rulina also married (4) **Levi MCWHORTER**.

Rulina also married (5) **James LYNCH**.

     9   F   v.   **Mary MCWHORTER** was born 17 Feb 1815. She died 1905.

Mary married **Hamilton G. NUTTER** on 1837.

   10   F   vi.   **Margaret MCWHORTER** was born 18 Apr 1816. She died 27 Nov 1900.

Margaret married **Leonard Shobe WARD** on 19 Oct 1837.

   11   F   vii.   **Susanna MCWHORTER** was born 17 Sep 1817.

Susanna married **William CRUMINE**.

Third Generation

7. **Rebecca Celina MCWHORTER**[3] (Thomas, Henry) was born 22 Oct 1811. She died 10 Sep 1882.

Rebecca married **Elias Jackson LOWTHER**[3], son of Jesse LOWTHER and Mary RAGAN, on 17 Jul 1828. Elias was born[4] 1 Jan 1801 in Neal's Island, Parkersburg, WV. He died 27 Feb 1887.

They had the following children:

   12   M   i.   **Jesse LOWTHER** was born 9 Apr 1829.

13 M ii. **Henry Marcellus LOWTHER** was born 22 Oct 1830.

14 M iii. **John McWhorter LOWTHER** was born 5 Sep 1832. He died 17 Mar 1863.

John married **Eliza BOOTH** on 1855.

15 M iv. **Calhoun LOWTHER** was born 16 Apr 1834. He died Feb 1835.

16 M v. **McDuffy LOWTHER** was born 16 Apr 1834. He died 3 Jul 1873.

+ 17 M vi. **Granville Sharp LOWTHER** was born 6 Nov 1836 and died 20 Mar 1920.

18 M vii. **Camillus LOWTHER** was born 9 Jul 1839. He died 26 Mar 1902.

19 M viii. **Thomas Newton LOWTHER** was born 24 Dec 1841. He died 10 Feb 1934.

20 F ix. **Columbia Virginia LOWTHER** was born 24 Jul 1844. She died 27 Oct 1906.

21 F x. **Mary M. LOWTHER** was born 17 Sep 1846. She died 1908.

22 M xi. **Elias Hughes LOWTHER** was born 5 Nov 1848. He died 8 Jan 1888.

23 F xii. **Celina (Celinda) Jane LOWTHER** was born 18 May 1851. She died 30 Oct 1923.

24 M xiii. **William Alex LOWTHER** was born 20 Dec 1854.

Fourth Generation

17. **Granville Sharp LOWTHER**[5] (Rebecca Celina MCWHORTER, Thomas, Henry) was born 6 Nov 1836 in Harrison Co., WV. He died 20 Mar 1920 in Fall Run, Braxton Co., WV and was buried in Green Hill Cemetery, Green Hill, WV.

Granville married (1) **Elizabeth PRIBBLE** on 10 Nov 1862

in Braxton Co., WV. Elizabeth died 16 Feb 1865 in Braxton Co., WV and was buried in Green Hill Cemetery, Green Hill, WV.

They had the following children:

    25 M   i.   **Henry LOWTHER** was born 26 Nov 1863 in Fall Run, Braxton Co., WV. He died 9 Mar 1866 in Fall Run, Braxton Co., WV.

Granville also married (2) **Mary Jane LOWTHER** on 20 Dec 1865 in Fall Run, Braxton Co., WV.

They had the following children:

    26 M   ii.   **John D. LOWTHER** was born 13 Jan 1867. He died 13 Oct 1869.

    27 F   iii.   **Carrie Orvilla LOWTHER** was born 18 Oct 1868. She died 1927.

    28 F   iv.   **Lura May LOWTHER** was born 23 Feb 1872 in Fall Run, Braxton Co., WV. She died 23 Feb 1872 in Fall Run, Braxton Co., WV.

    29 F   v.   **Lora Virginia LOWTHER** was born 23 Feb 1872 in Fall Run, Braxton Co., WV.

+   30 F   vi.   **Bessie Maude LOWTHER** was born 26 Jun 1872(73) and died 1964.

    31 M vii.   **Harrison LOWTHER** was born 21 Sep 1875 in Fall Run, Braxton Co., WV.

The Generations of the

Thomas De Lowther Family

1. Thomas DE LOWTHER (b.1199)
sp: MOULTON
  +-2. Gervase DE LOWTHER (b.1212)
    sp: Miss ROSS
    +-3. Hugh DE LOWTHER (b.1260)
      sp: Margaret L'Inglishe DE LUCY
      +-4. Hugh DE LOWTHER (b.1280)
        sp: Margaret (Moriceby) WHALE (b.1284)
        |-5. Hugh LOWTHER (b.1313)
        | sp: Matilda DE TILLIOL (b.1318 m.1338)
        | |-6. Hugh LOWTHER (b.1340 d.1373)
        | | sp: Margaret QUALE (b.1345 m.1365)
        | | |-7. Robert LOWTHER (b.1368 d.1430)
        | | | sp: Margaret STRICKLAND (b.1370 m.1397
d.1440)
        | | | |-8. Hugh LOWTHER (b.1395)
        | | | | sp: Mary Anne DE DERWENTWATER (b.1395
        | | | | |-9. Hugh LOWTHER (b.1415 d.1475)
        | | | | | sp: Miss STAPLETON (b.1417 m.1434)
        | | | | | +-10. Hugh LOWTHER (b.1435 d.1475)
        | | | | | sp: Mabel LANCASTER (b.1437 m.1455
d.1475)
        | | | | | |-11. Hugh LOWTHER (b.1451 d.1510)
        | | | | | | sp: Ann THRELKELD (b.1480 m.1480)
        | | | | | | +-12. John LOWTHER (b.1488 d.1551)
        | | | | | | sp: Lucy CURWEN (b.1490 m.1501)
        | | | | | | |-13. Hugh LOWTHER (b.1508 d.1546)
        | | | | | | | sp: Dorothy DE CLIFFORD (b.1512
d.1562)
        | | | | | | | |-14. Richard LOWTHER (b.1529
d.1606)
        | | | | | | | | sp: Frances MIDDLETON (b.1533
        | | | | | | | | |-15. William LOWTHER (b.1573
d.1642)
        | | | | | | | | | sp: Eleanor WELBURY (b.1578
d.1641)
        | | | | | | | | | +-16. George LOWTHER (b.1618
                                      d.1683)

-17. William LOWTHER, SR. (b.1642 d.1727)
  sp: Isabel LANCASTER (b.1644 m.1679)
    -18. William LOWTHER, JR. (b.1693 d.1750)
      sp: Martha UNKNOWN (b.1691 m.1710 d.1748)
        -19. Robert LOWTHER (b.1714 d.1780)
          sp: Aquilla REESE (b.1717 d.1750)
            -20. Col. William LOWTHER (b.1742
              sp: Sudna HUGHES (b.1745 d.1829)
                -21. Jesse LOWTHER (b.1773 d.1854)
                  sp: Mary RAGAN (b.1770 d.1857)
                  +-22. Elias Jackson LOWTHER
                        (b.1801)
                      sp: Rebecca Celina
                          MCWHORTER (b.1811)
-23. Granville Sharp LOWTHER (b.1836
  sp: Mary Jane LOWTHER
  -24. Bessie Maude LOWTHER
        sp. John William HARDMAN
          -25. Leatha Carrie HARDMAN
          -25. Lora Arvilla HARDMAN
          -25. Walter W. Hardman
          -25. George Dencil Hardman I HARDMAN
          -25. Delmas Emmett HARDMAN
          -25. Retta Dale HARDMAN
          +-25. Lester HARDMAN

First Generation

1. **Thomas DE LOWTHER**[7] was born 1199.

   Thomas married **MOULTON**.

   They had the following child:

   + 2 M i. **Gervase DE LOWTHER** was born about 1212.

Second Generation

2. **Gervase DE LOWTHER** (Thomas) was born about 1212.

   Gervase married **Miss ROSS**.

   They had the following child:

   + 3 M i. **Hugh DE LOWTHER** was born about 1260.

Third Generation

3. **Hugh DE LOWTHER** (Gervase, Thomas) was born about 1260 in Rydal, Westmoreland, England.

   Hugh married **Margaret L'Inglishe DE LUCY**.

   They had the following child:

   + 4 M i. **Hugh DE LOWTHER** was born 1280.

Fourth Generation

4. **Hugh DE LOWTHER** (Hugh, Gervase, Thomas) was born 1280 in Lowther, Westmoreland, England.

   Hugh married **Margaret (Moriceby) WHALE**. Margaret was born 1284 in Lowther, Westmoreland, England.

   They had the following children:

   + 5 M   i.   **Hugh LOWTHER** was born about 1313.
      6 F   ii. **Alice DE LOWTHER** was born 1330 in England.
      7 M   iii. **Thomas DE LOWTHER**.

Fifth Generation

5. **Hugh LOWTHER** (Hugh, Hugh, Gervase, Thomas) was born about 1313 in Lowther, Westmoreland, England.

Hugh married **Matilda DE TILLIOL** about 1338 in Scaleby Castle, Cumberland, England. Matilda was born about 1318 in Scaleby Castle, Cumberland, England.

They had the following children:

    8 M   i. **Thomas LOWTHER** was born about 1339 in Lowther, Westmoreland, England.

+   9 M   ii. **Hugh LOWTHER** was born about 1340 and died after 1373.

   10 F   iii. **Joan LOWTHER** was born[1] about 1341 in Lowther, Westmoreland, England.

Sixth Generation

9. **Hugh LOWTHER** (Hugh LOWTHER, Hugh, Hugh, Gervase, Thomas) was born about 1340 in Lowther, Westmoreland, England. He died after 1373.

Hugh married (1) **Margaret LUCY**. Margaret was born about 1327.

Hugh also married (2) **Margaret QUALE** about 1365 in Lowther, Westmoreland, England. Margaret was born about 1345 in Lowther, Westmoreland, England.

They had the following children:

   11 M   i. **John LOWTHER** was born[2] about 1347 in Lowther, Westmoreland, England.

+   12 M   ii. **Robert LOWTHER** was born about 1368 and died 9 Apr 1430.

   13 M   iii. **William LOWTHER** was born about 1369 in Lowther, Westmoreland, England.

Seventh Generation

12. **Robert LOWTHER** (Hugh LOWTHER, Hugh LOWTHER,

Hugh, Hugh, Gervase, Thomas) was born about 1368 in Lowther, Westmoreland, England. He died 9 Apr 1430.

Robert married **Margaret STRICKLAND** about 1397. Margaret was born about 1370 in Lizbergh, Westmoreland, England. She died 1440.

They had the following children:

+   14   M   i.   **Hugh LOWTHER** was born about 1395.

      15   M   ii.   **William LOWTHER** was born about 1400 in Lowther, Westmoreland, England.

Eighth Generation

14. **Hugh LOWTHER** (Robert LOWTHER, Hugh LOWTHER, Hugh LOWTHER, Hugh, Hugh, Gervase, Thomas) was born about 1395 in Lowther, Westmoreland, England.

Hugh married **Mary Anne DE DERWENTWATER** about 1415 in Lowther, Westmoreland, England. Mary was born about 1395 in Edenhall, Cumberland, England.

They had the following children:

+   16   M   i.   **Hugh LOWTHER** was born about 1415 and died 4 Aug 1475.

      17   M   ii.   **William LOWTHER** was born about 1417 in Lowther, Westmoreland, England.

      18   F   iii.   **Isabel LOWTHER** was born about 1419 in Lowther, Westmoreland, England.

      19   M   iv.   **Robert LOWTHER** was born about 1421 in Lowther, Westmoreland, England.

Ninth Generation

16. **Hugh LOWTHER** (Hugh LOWTHER, Robert LOWTHER, Hugh LOWTHER, Hugh LOWTHER, Hugh, Hugh, Gervase, Thomas) was born about 1415 in Lowther, Westmoreland, England. He died 4 Aug 1475.

Hugh married **Miss STAPLETON** about 1434 in Edenhall,

Cumberland, England. Miss was born about 1417 in Edenhall, Cumberland, England.

They had the following child:

+ 20 M i. **Hugh LOWTHER** was born about 1435 and died 17 Sep 1475.

Tenth Generation

20. **Hugh LOWTHER** (Hugh LOWTHER, Hugh LOWTHER, Robert LOWTHER, Hugh LOWTHER, Hugh LOWTHER, Hugh, Hugh, Gervase, Thomas) was born about 1435 in Lowther, Westmoreland, England. He died 17 Sep 1475.

Hugh married **Mabel LANCASTER** on 18 Aug 1455 in Lowther, Westmoreland, England. Mabel was born about 1437 in Hartsop, Westmoreland, England. She died 4 Aug 1475.

They had the following children:

+ 21 M i. **Hugh LOWTHER** was born 1451 and died Bet 1510-1511.

22 M ii. **James LOWTHER** was born about 1463 in Lowther, Westmoreland, England. He died Bet 1510-1511.

23 F iii. **Joan LOWTHER** was born about 1465 in Lowther, Westmoreland, England.

Eleventh Generation

21. **Hugh LOWTHER**[3] (Hugh LOWTHER, Hugh LOWTHER, Hugh LOWTHER, Robert LOWTHER, Hugh LOWTHER, Hugh LOWTHER, Hugh, Hugh, Gervase, Thomas) was born 1451 in Lowther, Westmoreland, England. He died Bet 1510-1511.

Hugh married **Ann THRELKELD** on 1480 in Lowther, Westmoreland, England. Ann was born 1480 in Yanwath Hall, Cumberland, England.

They had the following children:

24 F   i. **Jane LOWTHER** was born 1477 in Lowther, Westmoreland, England.

25 F   ii. **Mabel LOWTHER** was born 1479 in Lowther, Westmoreland, England.

26 M   iii. **Lancelot LOWTHER** was born 1481 in Lowther, Westmoreland, England.

27 M   iv. **Robert LOWTHER** was born 1483 in Lowther, Westmoreland, England.

28 F   v. **Elizabeth LOWTHER** was born 1484 in Lowther, Westmoreland, England.

+   29 M   vi. **John LOWTHER** was born 1488 and died 3 Feb 1551/1552.

Twelfth Generation

29. **John LOWTHER** (Hugh LOWTHER, Hugh LOWTHER, Hugh LOWTHER, Hugh LOWTHER, Robert LOWTHER, Hugh LOWTHER, Hugh LOWTHER, Hugh, Hugh, Gervase, Thomas) was born 1488 in Lowther Castle, Westmoreland, England. He died 3 Feb 1551/1552.

John married **Lucy CURWEN** on 27 Jan 1501/1502 in Workington, Cumberland, England. Lucy was born 1490 in Workington, Cumberland, England.

They had the following children:

+   30 M   i. **Hugh LOWTHER** was born 1508 and died 1546.

31 F   ii. **Elizabeth LOWTHER** was born 1511 in Lowther, Westmoreland, England.

32 F   iii. **Joan LOWTHER** was born 1513 in Lowther, Westmoreland, England.

33 F   iv. **Mabel LOWTHER** was born 1515 in Lowther, Westmoreland, England.

Thirteenth Generation

30. **Hugh LOWTHER** (John LOWTHER, Hugh LOWTHER, Hugh LOWTHER, Hugh LOWTHER, Hugh LOWTHER, Robert LOWTHER, Hugh LOWTHER, Hugh LOWTHER, Hugh, Hugh, Gervase, Thomas) was born 1508 in Lowther Hall, Lowther, Westmoreland, England. He died 1546.

Hugh married **Dorothy DE CLIFFORD** on 1529 in Skipton, Yorkshire, England. Dorothy was born 1512 in Lowther Hall, Lowther, Westmoreland, England. She died 13 Sep 1562 in Lowther, Cumberland, England and was buried 13 Sep 1562 in Lowther, Cumberland, England.

They had the following children:

+   34   M   i.   **Richard LOWTHER** was born 14 Jan 1529/1530 and died 27 Jan 1606/1607.

      35   F   ii.   **Margaret LOWTHER** was born 1534 in Lowther, Westmoreland, England.

      36   M   iii.   **Gerald LOWTHER** was born 1534 in Lowther, Westmoreland, England. He died Dec 1596 in Ireland.

      37   F   iv.   **Anne LOWTHER** was born 1538 in Lowther, Westmoreland, England.

      38   F   v.   **Barbara LOWTHER** was born 1541 in Lowther, Westmoreland, England.

      39   F   vi.   **Frances LOWTHER** was born 1542 in Lowther, Westmoreland, England.

Fourteenth Generation

Richard LOWTHER[3] (Hugh LOWTHER, John LOWTHER, Hugh LOWTHER, Hugh LOWTHER, Hugh LOWTHER, Hugh LOWTHER, Robert LOWTHER, Hugh LOWTHER, Hugh LOWTHER, Hugh, Hugh, Gervase, Thomas) was born 14 Jan 1529/1530 in Lowther Hall, Lowther, Westmoreland, England. He died 27 Jan 1606/1607 in England.

Richard married (1) **Margaret EDEN** before 1853/1854.

They had the following child:

    40 F   i. **Anne LOWTHER** was born 15 Jan 1553/1554 in Lowther, Westmoreland, England.

Richard also married (2) **Frances MIDDLETON** on 1554 in Lowther, Westmoreland, England. Frances was born about 1533 in Middleton, Westmoreland, England.

They had the following children:

    41 M ii. **John LOWTHER** was born 18 Feb 1554/1555 in Lowther, Westmoreland, England. He died about 1558.

    42 M iii. **William LOWTHER** was born 1556 in Ireland.

    43 M iv. **Christopher LOWTHER** was born 8 Sep 1557 in Lowther, Westmoreland, England. He died 29 Jul 1617 in Lowther Castle, Westmoreland, England.

    44 M v. **George LOWTHER** was born 23 Oct 1558 in Lowther, Westmoreland, England and died 28 Jul 1562 in Lowther, Westmoreland, England.

    45 F vi. **Florence LOWTHER** was born 7 Sep 1559 in Lowther, Westmoreland, England.

    46 F vii. **Frances LOWTHER** was born 26 Jan 1560/1561 in Lowther, Westmoreland, England.

    47 M viii. **Gerald LOWTHER** was born 21 Dec 1561 in Lowther, Westmoreland, England. He died 14 Oct 1624.

    48 F ix. **Agnes LOWTHER** was born 1562 in Lowther, Westmoreland, England.

    49 M x. **Hugh LOWTHER** was born 1563 in Lowther,

Westmoreland, England. He died 1654.

50 F xi. **Margaret LOWTHER** was born 1565 in Lowther, Westmoreland, England.

51 F xii. **Dorothy LOWTHER** was born 9 Apr 1566 in Lowther, Westmoreland, England. She died 21 Jun 1567 in Lowther, Westmoreland, England.

52 F xiii. **Mabel LOWTHER** was born 12 Sep 1567 in Lowther, Westmoreland, England. She died 10 Nov 1568 in Lowther, England.

53 M xiv. **Richard LOWTHER** was born 4 Jan 1568/1569 in Lowther, Westmoreland, England. He died 8 Aug 1575.

54 M xv. **Lancelot LOWTHER** was born 1 Oct 1571 in Lowther, Westmoreland, England. He died 10 Jan 1636/1637.

55 F xvi. **Agnes LOWTHER** was born 1572 in Meath, Ireland.

+ 56 M xvii. **William LOWTHER** was born 30 Jan 1573/1574 and died 21 Jul 1642.

57 F xviii. **Frances LOWTHER** was born 10 Aug 1578 in Lowther, Westmoreland, England.

Fifteenth Generation

56. **William LOWTHER**[3] (Richard LOWTHER, Hugh LOWTHER, John LOWTHER, Hugh LOWTHER, Hugh LOWTHER, Hugh LOWTHER, Hugh LOWTHER, Robert LOWTHER, Hugh LOWTHER, Hugh LOWTHER, Hugh, Hugh, Gervase, Thomas) was born 30 Jan 1573/1574 in Lowther, Westmoreland, England. He died 21 Jul 1642.

William married **Eleanor WELBURY** on 1599 in Castle Eden, Durham, England. Eleanor was born 1578 in Castle Eden, Durham, England. She died Aug 1641. They had the following children:

58 F   i.   **Anne LOWTHER** was born 21 Nov 1600 in Lowther, Westmoreland, England.

59 M   ii.   **Richard LOWTHER** was born 30 Apr 1602 in Lowther, Westmoreland, England. He died 1645.

60 M   iii.   **Gerald LOWTHER** was born 21 Apr 1603 in Lowther, Westmoreland, England. He died 25 May 1604 in Lowther, Westmoreland, England.

61 M   iv.   **Hugh LOWTHER** was born 5 Jun 1604 in Lowther, Westmoreland, England. He died 24 Oct 1604 in Lowther, Westmoreland, England.

62 M   v.   **Lancelot LOWTHER** was born 1 Sep 1605 in Lowther, Westmoreland, England. He died 7 Apr 1661 in Lowther Castle, Lowther, Westmoreland, England.

63 M   vi.   **John LOWTHER** was born 10 May 1607 in Lowther Castle, Lowther, Westmoreland, England. He died 10 May 1607 in Lowther Castle, Lowther, Westmoreland, England.

64 M   vii.   **Robert LOWTHER** was born 29 Jan 1609/1610 in Ingleton, West Riding, Yorkshire, England.

65 F   viii.   **Frances LOWTHER** was born 1 May 1612 in Ingleton, West Riding, Yorkshire, England.

66 F   ix.   **Eleanor LOWTHER** was born 11 Jun 1613 in Ingleton, West Riding, Yorkshire, England.

67 F   x.   **Florence LOWTHER** was born 22 Oct 1614 in Ingleton, West Riding, Yorkshire, England.

+   68 M   xi.   **George LOWTHER** was born 12 Jul 1618

and died 1683.

Sixteenth Generation

68. **George LOWTHER** (William LOWTHER, Richard LOWTHER, Hugh LOWTHER, John LOWTHER, Hugh LOWTHER, Hugh LOWTHER, Hugh LOWTHER, Hugh LOWTHER, Robert LOWTHER, Hugh LOWTHER, Hugh LOWTHER, Hugh, Hugh, Gervase, Thomas) was born 12 Jul 1618 in Ingleton, West Riding, Yorkshire, England. He died 1683 in Longhill, Armagh, Northern Ireland.

George married (1) **Francis PIERS**.

They had the following children:

   69 M   i. **Edward LOWTHER**.

   70 M ii. **Lancelot LOWTHER**.

George also married (2) **Jana JONES**.

They had the following children:

   71 F iii. **Jana LOWTHER**.

   72 F iv. **Elleanor LOWTHER**.

   73 F v. **Anne LOWTHER**.

George also married (3) **Elizabeth FITZGERALD** on 1638 in Ingleton, West Riding, Yorkshire, England. Elizabeth was born 1620 in Ingleton, West Riding, Yorkshire, England. She died 1683.

They had the following children:

+   74 M vi. **William LOWTHER, SR.** was born 13 Nov 1642 and died 1727.

   75 F vii. **Daughter LOWTHER** was born 1648 in Ingleton, West Riding, Yorkshire, England.

   76 F viii. **Daughter LOWTHER** was born 1650 in Ingleton, West Riding, Yorkshire, England.

77 F ix. Daughter LOWTHER was born 1652 in Ingleton, West Riding, Yorkshire, England.

78 F x. Daughter LOWTHER was born 1654 in Ingleton, West Riding, Yorkshire, England.

Seventeenth Generation

74. **William LOWTHER, SR.**[3] (George LOWTHER, William LOWTHER, Richard LOWTHER, Hugh LOWTHER, John LOWTHER, Hugh LOWTHER, Hugh LOWTHER, Hugh LOWTHER, Hugh LOWTHER, Robert LOWTHER, Hugh LOWTHER, Hugh LOWTHER, Hugh, Hugh, Gervase, Thomas) was born 13 Nov 1642 in Ingleton, West Riding, Yorkshire, England. He died 1727 in Ireland.

William married (1) **Jane KELSO** on 1671 in Lurgen, Armagh, Ireland. Jane died 1677.

They had the following children:

79 M i. Henry LOWTHER was born 1672 in Armagh, Ireland.

80 F ii. Elizabeth LOWTHER was born 1677 in Armagh, Ireland.

William also married (2) **Isabel LANCASTER** on 24 Jul 1679 in Lurgen, Armagh, Ireland. Isabel was born about 1644 in Inniskillen, Northern Ireland.

They had the following children:

81 M iii. Samuel LOWTHER was born Nov 1681 in Lurgen Armagh, Ireland.

82 F iv. Mary LOWTHER was born May 1684 in Lurgen Armagh, Armagh, Northern Ireland.

83 F v. Catherine LOWTHER was born Mar 1686/1687 in Lurgen, Armagh, Ireland.

84 F vi. Hannah LOWTHER was born Apr 1691 in

Lurgen, Armagh, Northern Ireland.

+ 85 M vii. **William LOWTHER, JR.** was born Jan 1693/1694 and died 3 Oct 1750.

86 M viii. **John LOWTHER** was born Jan 1696/1697 in Tober, Kings Co. now Derry Co., Ireland.

Eighteenth Generation

85. **William LOWTHER, JR.** (William LOWTHER, SR., George LOWTHER, William LOWTHER, Richard LOWTHER, Hugh LOWTHER, John LOWTHER, Hugh LOWTHER, Hugh LOWTHER, Hugh LOWTHER, Hugh LOWTHER, Robert LOWTHER, Hugh LOWTHER, Hugh LOWTHER, Hugh, Hugh, Gervase, Thomas) was born Jan 1693/1694 in Tober, Kings County (now Derry) Or Offaly County Ireland. He died 3 Oct 1750 in Buckingham Twp., Bucks Co., VA.

William married **Martha UNKNOWN** on 1710/1712 in Westmeath, Ireland. Martha was born 1691 in Tober, Kings Co. Now Derry Co., Ireland. She died 1748 in Pennsylvania.

They had the following children:

87 F i. **Sarah LOWTHER** was born about 1713 in Westmeath, Ireland. She died 1775 in Maryland.

+ 88 M ii. **Robert LOWTHER** was born ~1714 and died ~1780.

89 M iii. **Joel LOWTHER** was born about 1715 in Westmeath, Ireland.

90 F iv. **Ruth LOWTHER** was born about 1720 in Westmeath, Ireland. She died 10 Feb 1800.

91 F v. **Martha LOWTHER** was born about 1723 in Westmeath, Ireland. She died 7 Nov

1774.

92 F   vi. **Mary LOWTHER** was born about 1725 in Ireland.

93 M   vii. **William LOWTHER** was born in Ireland.

Nineteenth Generation

88. **Robert LOWTHER**[4,5,6] (William LOWTHER, JR., William LOWTHER, SR., George LOWTHER, William LOWTHER, Richard LOWTHER, Hugh LOWTHER, John LOWTHER, Hugh LOWTHER,Hugh LOWTHER, Hugh LOWTHER,Hugh LOWTHER, Robert LOWTHER, Hugh LOWTHER, Hugh LOWTHER, Hugh, Hugh, Gervase, Thomas) was born ~1714 in Westmeath, Ireland and immigrated ~1738 to Albermarle County, Va. He died ~1780 in Hacker's Creek, WV and was buried in Hacker's Creek, WV.

Robert married **Aquilla REESE** on ~1738. Aquilla was born ~1717 in Plumstead Twp, Bucks Co., Pa. She died ~1750 in Hacker's Creek, WV and was buried in Hacker's Creek, WV.

They had the following children:

94 M   i. **Thomas LOWTHER** died was probably killed by Indians.

95 M   ii. **Henry LOWTHER** died was probably Albermarle County, Va.

96 M   iii. **Jonathan LOWTHER** died was probably killed by Indians.

97 M   iv. **Joel LOWTHER** probably died in Harrison County, (W)V.

+   98 M   v. **Col. William LOWTHER** was born 22 Dec 1742 and died 28 Oct 1814.

99 M   vi. **Joseph LOWTHER** died 1800.

Twentieth Generation

98. **Col. William LOWTHER**[4,6,7] (Robert LOWTHER, William LOWTHER, JR., William LOWTHER, SR., George

LOWTHER, William LOWTHER, Richard LOWTHER, Hugh LOWTHER, John LOWTHER, Hugh LOWTHER, Hugh LOWTHER, Hugh LOWTHER, Hugh LOWTHER, Robert LOWTHER, Hugh LOWTHER, Hugh LOWTHER, Hugh, Hugh, Gervase, Thomas) was born 22 Dec 1742 in Albermarle Co., Va.. He died 28 Oct 1814 in Hacker's Creek, WV and was buried in Hacker's Creek, WV.

Col. married **Sudna HUGHES** on 1 Jun 1763 in Hardy Co., (W)V. Sudna was born 1745 in Hardy Co., (W)V. She died 1829 in Berea, Wirt Co., WV and was buried in Flanagan Burial Ground near Berea, WV.

They had the following children:

100 M i. **Robert LOWTHER** was born 1 Oct 1765. He died 16 Nov 1832 in Hacker's Creek, (W)V.

101 M ii. **Thomas LOWTHER** was born 7 Mar 1767. He died 1816.

102 M iii. **William B. LOWTHER** was born 27 Jan 1769 in South Branch Of Potomac River. He died 26 Nov 1857 in West Milford, (W)V and was buried in Lowther Burying Grounds.

+ 103 M iv. **Jesse LOWTHER** was born 21 Jul 1773 and died 15 Oct 1854.

104 F v. **Sudna LOWTHER**.

105 M vi. **Major Elias E. LOWTHER** was born 16 Sep 1776 in Hacker's Creek, (W)V. He died 1845 in Staunton, Va.

Major married **Rebecca COBURN**. Rebecca was born 11 Dec 1779 in Harrison Co., (W)V. She died 1850 in Berea, Wirt Co., WV and was buried in Flanagan Burial Ground near Berea, WV.

106 F vii. **Mary LOWTHER**.

107 F viii. **Hannah LOWTHER**.

108 F ix. **Nancy LOWTHER**.

Twenty-First Generation

103. **Jesse LOWTHER**[5,8] (Col. William LOWTHER, Robert LOWTHER, William LOWTHER, JR., William LOWTHER, SR., George LOWTHER, William LOWTHER, Richard LOWTHER, Hugh LOWTHER, John LOWTHER, Hugh LOWTHER, Hugh LOWTHER, Hugh LOWTHER, Hugh LOWTHER, Robert LOWTHER, Hugh LOWTHER, Hugh LOWTHER, Hugh, Hugh, Gervase, Thomas) was born 21 Jul 1773. He died 15 Oct 1854 in West Milford, (W)V and was buried in Lowther Burying Grounds.

Jesse married **Mary RAGAN** on 8 Aug 1791 in Harrison Co., WV. Mary was born 25 Dec 1770. She died Apr 1857 and was buried in Pullman Churchyard, Ritchie Co., (W)V.

They had the following children:

109 M i. **William J. LOWTHER** was born 1791.

110 M ii. **Dr. Jesse LOWTHER** died in Little Rock, Arkansas.

111 F iii. **Sarah Sallie LOWTHER** was born 1795. She died 1870.

112 F iv. **Margaret LOWTHER** died in West Milford, (W)V.

113 F v. **Mary Ann LOWTHER** died 1876.

114 F vi. **Millie M. LOWTHER** died in Woodsfield, Ohio.

115 M vii. **Dr. Robert LOWTHER**.

116 F viii. **Sudna LOWTHER** was born in West Milford, (W)V. She died in West Milford, (W)V.

117 M ix. **Uriah LOWTHER** was born 1793. He died in

youth.

118 F x. **Drusilla LOWTHER** died in Zanesville, Ohio.

119 F xi. **Elizabeth LOWTHER**.

+ 120 M xii. **Elias Jackson LOWTHER** was born 1 Jan 1801 and died 27 Feb 1887.

Twenty-Second Generation

120. **Elias Jackson LOWTHER**[5,9,10] (Jesse LOWTHER, Col. William LOWTHER, Robert LOWTHER, William LOWTHER, JR., William LOWTHER, SR., George LOWTHER, William LOWTHER, Richard LOWTHER, Hugh LOWTHER, John LOWTHER, Hugh LOWTHER, Hugh LOWTHER, Hugh LOWTHER, Hugh LOWTHER, Robert LOWTHER, Hugh LOWTHER, Hugh LOWTHER, Hugh, Hugh, Gervase, Thomas) was born[8] 1 Jan 1801 in Neal's Island, Parkersburg, WV. He died 27 Feb 1887.

Elias married **Rebecca Celina MCWHORTER**[9], daughter of Thomas MCWHORTER and Delila STALNAKER, on 17 Jul 1828. Rebecca was born 22 Oct 1811. She died 10 Sep 1882.

They had the following children:

121 M i. **Jesse LOWTHER** was born 9 Apr 1829.

122 M ii. **Henry Marcellus LOWTHER** was born 22 Oct 1830.

123 M iii. **John McWhorter LOWTHER** was born 5 Sep 1832. He died 17 Mar 1863.

124 M iv. **Calhoun LOWTHER** was born 16 Apr 1834. He died Feb 1835.

125 M v. **McDuffy LOWTHER** was born 16 Apr 1834. He died 3 Jul 1873.

+ 126 M vi. **Granville Sharp LOWTHER** was born 6 Nov 1836 and died 20 Mar 1920.

127 M vii. **Camillus LOWTHER** was born 9 Jul 1839.

He died 26 Mar 1902.

128 M viii. **Thomas Newton LOWTHER** was born 24 Dec 1841. He died 10 Feb 1934.

129 F ix. **Columbia Virginia LOWTHER** was born 24 Jul 1844. She died 27 Oct 1906.

130 F x. **Mary M. LOWTHER** was born 17 Sep 1846. She died 1908.

131 M xi. **Elias Hughes LOWTHER** was born 5 Nov 1848. He died 8 Jan 1888.

132 F xii. **Celina (Celinda) Jane LOWTHER** was born 18 May 1851. She died 30 Oct 1923.

133 M xiii. **William Alex LOWTHER** was born 20 Dec 1854.

Twenty Third Generation

Granville Sharp Lowther

126.**Granville Sharp LOWTHER**[11,12] (Elias Jackson LOWTHER, Jesse LOWTHER, Col. William LOWTHER, Robert LOWTHER, William LOWTHER, JR., William LOWTHER, SR., George LOWTHER, William LOWTHER, Richard LOWTHER, Hugh LOWTHER, John LOWTHER, Hugh LOWTHER, Hugh LOWTHER, Hugh LOWTHER, Hugh LOWTHER, Robert LOWTHER, Hugh LOWTHER, Hugh LOWTHER, Hugh, Hugh, Gervase, Thomas) was born 6 Nov 1836 in Harrison Co., WV. He died 20 Mar

1920 in Fall Run, Braxton Co., WV and was buried in Green Hill Cemetery, Green Hill, WV.

Granville married (1) **Elizabeth PRIBBLE** on 10 Nov 1862 in Braxton Co., WV. Elizabeth died 16 Feb 1865 in Braxton Co., WV and was buried in Green Hill Cemetery, Green Hill, WV. They had the following children:

134　M　i.　**Henry LOWTHER** was born 26 Nov 1863 in Fall Run, Braxton Co., WV. He died 9 Mar 1866 in Fall Run, Braxton Co., WV.

Granville also married (2) **Mary Jane LOWTHER** on 20 Dec 1865 in Fall Run, Braxton Co., WV.

They had the following children:

135　M　ii.　**John D. LOWTHER** was born 13 Jan 1867. He died 13 Oct 1869.

136　F　iii.　**Carrie Orvilla LOWTHER** was born 18 Oct 1868. She died 1927.

137　F　iv.　**Lura May LOWTHER** was born 23 Feb 1872. She died 23 Feb 1872.

138　F　v.　**Lora Virginia LOWTHER** was born 23 Feb 1872.

+　139　F　vi.　**Bessie Maude LOWTHER** was born 26 Jun 1872(73) and died 1964.

140　M　vii.　**Harrison LOWTHER** was born 21 Sep 1875.

Twenty Fourth Generation

Bessie Maude Lowther

139.   **Bessie Maude LOWTHER**[13,14,15,16] (Granville Sharp
LOWTHER, Elias Jackson LOWTHER, Jesse LOWTHER,
Col. William LOWTHER, Robert LOWTHER, William
LOWTHER, JR., William LOWTHER, SR., George
LOWTHER, William LOWTHER, Richard LOWTHER,
Hugh LOWTHER, John LOWTHER, Hugh LOWTHER,
Hugh LOWTHER, Hugh LOWTHER, Hugh LOWTHER,
Robert LOWTHER, Hugh LOWTHER, Hugh LOWTHER,
Hugh, Hugh, Gervase, Thomas) was born[17] 26 Jun
1872(73) in Fall Run, Braxton Co., WV. She died 1964 in
Lost Creek, WV and was buried in Green Hill Cemetery,
Green Hill, WV.

Bessie married **John William HARDMAN** on 12 Jul 1899.
They had the following children:

141   F   i.   **Leatha Carrie HARDMAN.**

142   F   ii.   **Lora Arvilla HARDMAN.**

143   M   iii.   **Walter Worthington Hardman.**

144   M   iv.   **George Dencil Hardman I HARDMAN.**

145   M   v.   **Delmas Emmett HARDMAN.**

146   F   vi.   **Retta Dale HARDMAN.**

147   M   vii.   **Lester HARDMAN.**

The Generations of the

Nicholas Hardman Family

1. Nicholas HARDMAN (b.1720)
sp: Margaret NMN (b.1720)
+-2. Peterman HARDMAN (b.1745 d.1827)
  sp: Charlotte LAZIER/LEZIER (b.1748 m.1765 d.1835)
 |-3. John D. HARDMAN (b.1770 d.1864)
 | sp: Elizabeth WAGGONER (b.1779 m.1798 d.1854)
 | |-4. John G. HARDMAN (b.1817 d.1897)
 | | sp: Malinda FORINASH (b.1822 m.1838 d.1884)
 | | |-5. Perry Worthington HARDMAN (b.1850)
 | | | sp: Mary Melissa BERRY (b.1853 m.1870)
 | | | |-6. John William HARDMAN (b.1876 d.1897)
 | | | | sp: Bessie Maude LOWTHER (b.1873 m.1899
           d.1966)
 | | | | |-7. Leatha Carrie HARDMAN (b.1901 d.1950)
 | | | | |-7. Lora Arvilla HARDMAN (b.1902 d.1992)
 | | | | | sp: Orla CUTRIGHT, SR.
 | | | | |-7. George Dencil HARDMAN I (b.1906 d.1972)
 | | | | | sp: Hazel BOWYER (b.1908 m.1928 d.1992)
 | | | | | |-8. George Dencil HARDMAN II (b.1929
d.1982)
 | | | | | | sp: Jane Grey GREGORY (b.1933 m.1950)
 | | | | | | +-9. Georgia Grey HARDMAN (b.1951)
 | | | | | | sp: John Allen COFFEY (b.1948 m.1973)
 | | | | | | +-10. Brian Michael COFFEY (b.1976)
 | | | | | |-8. Mary Alice HARDMAN (b.1931 d.1931)
 | | | | | |-8. Marjorie Carol HARDMAN (b.1932)
 | | | | | | sp: Billy Brown BURKE (m.1950)
 | | | | | | |-9. Roberta Diane BURKE (b.1956)
 | | | | | | | sp: Michael HATTON (m.1987)
 | | | | | | +-9. Carolyn Sue BURKE (b.1958)
 | | | | | | sp: William HOLVEY (m.(div))
 | | | | | | |-10. Burke Ashley HOLVEY (b.1984)
 | | | | | | +-10. Samantha Sue HOLVEY (b.1986)
 | | | | | |-8. Coleta Dare HARDMAN (b.1934 d.1991)
 | | | | | | sp: Russell Beryl THOMPSON (b.1929
m.1951)
 | | | | | | | +-9. Robert Edward THOMPSON (b.1954)
 | | | | | | | sp: Sandra Kay ANDERSON (b.1953
m.1994)

```
| | | | | |-8. Edith Sharon HARDMAN  (b.1937)
| | | | | | sp: James ROE (m.(div) d.1991)
| | | | | | |-9. James William ROE (b.1962)
| | | | | | | sp: Sonya HARPER (m.(div))
| | | | | | | +-10. James Bradley ROE (b.1994)
| | | | | | |-9. John Neil ROE (b.1963)
| | | | | | | sp: Mary MILLER (m.(nm))
| | | | | | | +-10. Taylor Marie RUSSELL (b.1995)
| | | | | | |-9. Sherrie Anne ROE (b.1963)
| | | | | | | sp: Timothy MCDANIEL (m.(div))
| | | | | | | |-10. Kimberly Anne MCDANIEL (b.1980)
| | | | | | | | sp: Chad GARDNER (m.(nm))
| | | | | | | | +-11. Kyler GARDNER (b.2000)
| | | | | | | |-10. Kara Alyce MCDANIEL (b.1984)
| | | | | | | | sp: Charles KEENER (m.(nm))
| | | | | | | |-10. Robert Charles MCDANIEL (b.1987)
| | | | | | | | sp: Robert HART (m.(div))
| | | | | | |-9. Barbara Ruth ROE (b.1965)
| | | | | | | sp: David VICE (m.1994)
| | | | | | | |-10. Courtney Sharon Elizabeth VICE
                     (b.1998)
| | | | | | | | |-10. Christopher David VICE (b.1998)
| | | | | | | | sp: Jeffrey KERSEY (m.(div))
| | | | | | | sp: Norman Leo WEST (b.1931 m.1986)
| | | | | | +-8. William Raymond HARDMAN  (b.1947
                     d.1996)
| | | | | |  sp: Emma Jean WILLIAMS (m.1969)
| | | | | |  |-9. William Oran HARDMAN  (b.1970)
| | | | | |  |-9. George Dencil HARDMAN III (b.1973)
| | | | | |  | sp: Virginia WEBB (m.1995)
| | | | | |  | |-10. Tray WEBB
| | | | | |  | |-10. William Raymond HARDMAN II
(b.1997)
| | | | | |  | |-10. George Dencil HARDMAN IV (b.1998)
| | | | | |  | +-10. Dalton Lee HARDMAN  (b.2001)
| | | | | |  +-9. Katheryn Mischelle HARDMAN  (b.1976)
| | | | | |  sp: William Sean BURCHETT (m.(nm))
| | | | | |  +-10. Raymond Michael HARDMAN (b.1999)
| | | | |-7. Retta Dale HARDMAN (b.1910 d.1977)
```

```
| | | | |sp: Edward BILDSTIEN (m.1955)
| | | | | |-8. Oleta HARDMAN (b.1928)
| | | | | | sp: George Edward CARTER (m.1955 d.1992)
| | | | | +-8. Irwin HARDMAN (b.1930)
| | | | |    sp: UNKNOWN
| | | | |    |-9. Dale HARDMAN
| | | | |    |-9. Deborah HARDMAN
| | | | |    +-9. Brett HARDMAN
```

First Generation

1. **Nicholas HARDMAN**[1] was born 1720 in Inglehiem-am-Rhine, Germany.

   Nicholas married **Margaret NMN**. Margaret was born ~1720 in Inglehiem-am-Rhine, Germany.

   They had the following children:

   +   2   M   i.   **Peterman HARDMAN** was born 10 Mar 1745 and died 13 May 1827.

Second Generation

2. **Peterman HARDMAN**[2] (Nicholas) was born 10 Mar 1745 in Inglehiem-am-Rhine, Germany. He died 13 May 1827 in Jane Lew, Lewis Co., (W)V and was buried in Harmony Cemetery, Jane Lew, Lewis Co., WV.

   Peterman married **Charlotte LAZIER/LEZIER** on ~1765 in New Jersey/New York. Charlotte was born ~1748 in Germany. She died Nov 1835 in Lewis Co., WV and was buried in Harmony Cemetery, Jane Lew, Lewis Co., WV.

   They had the following children:

   +   3   M   i.   **John D. HARDMAN** was born 7 Oct 1770 and died 9 May 1864.

        4   F   ii.   **Elizabeth HARDMAN** was born 8 Oct 1774. She died 6 Jan 1861.

             Elizabeth married **Caleb SMITH** on 7 Apr 1792.

        5   M   iii.   **Peter HARDMAN** was born 23 Jul 1776 in Harrison Co., (W)V. He died 30 Jul 1859 in Greene Co., Ohio and was buried in Witman Cemetery, Greene Co., Ohio.

             Peter married (1) **Margaret HACKER** on 5 Dec 1798 in Harrison Co., (W)V. Margaret was born 27 Dec 1776 in Bush's Fort, Now Buckhannon, WV. She died 20

Jul 1815 in Greene Co., Ohio and was buried in Witman Cemetery, Greene Co., Ohio.

Peter also married (2) **Sarah ADAMS** on 26 Oct 1815 in Greene Co., Ohio. Sarah was born 18 Aug 1786 in near Greeneville, TN. She died 25 Aug 1875 in Greene Co., Ohio and was buried in Witman Cemetery, Greene Co., Ohio.

6 M iv. **Henry HARDMAN** was born 1 May 1781. He died 2 Oct 1870 in Lewis Co., WV.

Henry married (1) **Elizabeth HACKER** on 19 Sep 1808. Elizabeth was born 1784 in Bush's Fort, Now Buckhannon, WV. She died 1811 in Greene Co., Ohio and was buried in Witman Cemetery, Greene Co., Ohio.

Henry also married (2) **Juliana R(H)INEHART** on 14 Apr 1815 in Harrison Co., (W)V. Juliana was born 1794 in Monongalia (Preston Co.) (W)V. She died 3 Jul 1880 in Lewis Co., WV.

7 F v. **Catherine HARDMAN** was born 26 Feb 1784 and published notice of marriage 4 Nov 1814. She died 2 Apr 1867 in Lewis Co., WV and was buried in Harmony Cemetery.

Catherine married (1) **James HYDE** on 20 Mar 1801.

Catherine also married (2) **Peter WAGGONER** on 4 Nov 1814.

8 M vi. **Daniel HARDMAN** was born 17 Nov. He died Jan 1826 in Marion Co., Ohio.

Daniel married **Nancy FOWLER** on 9 Jun 1806.

136

Third Generation

3. **John D. HARDMAN**[3] (Peterman, Nicholas) was born 7 Oct 1770 in Big Youghigany, PA. He died 9 May 1864 in Lewis Co., WV and was buried in Mt. Gilead Church, Georgetown, WV.

John married (1) **Elizabeth WAGGONER** "Betty", daughter of John WAGGONER and Margaret BONNETT, on 10 Nov 1798 in Harrison Co., (W)V. Betty was born 5 Nov 1779. She died 1 Feb 1854.

They had the following children:

9   i.   **Unnamed HARDMAN** was born ~1798.

10 M   ii.   **Jacob Wolf HARDMAN** was born 1801 in Little Skin Creek, Lewis Co., (W)V. He died 1874 in Louisville, Ky.

Jacob married **Marion RODMAN** on 4 Feb 1829 in Washington Co., Ind.

11 M   iii.   **Henry D. HARDMAN** was born 19 Feb 1803 in Lewis Co., WV. He died 24 Dec 1886 in Lewis Co., WV and was buried in Vandalia Cemetery, Vandalia, WV.

Henry married **Mary WEST** on 30 Mar 1826 in Lewis Co., WV.

12   iv.   **Unnamed HARDMAN** was born 1804. Unnamed died 1804 in died in infancy.

13 M   v.   **Samuel Baxter HARDMAN** was born 1805. He died 27 Jan 1891 in Groveland, ILL.

Samuel married (1) **Margaret BONNETT** 27 Jan 1845.

Samuel also married (2) **Mary Francis BERRY** on 27 Jan 1845 in Tazewell Co., ILL. Mary was born 7 Dec 1814 in New Hampshire. She died 19 Oct 1894.

14 M   vi.   **Thomas HARDMAN** was born 10 Feb 1807

in Lewis Co., WV. He died 13 Jun 1883.

Thomas married (1) **Rebecca CLARK** on 30 Sep 1831.

Thomas also married (2) **Tamzen PATTEN** on 16 Oct 1854.

15 M vii. **William HARDMAN** was born 1809. He died 1840.

16 M viii. **Joshua HARDMAN** was born 5 Jul 1811. He died 16 Apr 1893 in Lewis Co., WV and was buried in Vandalia Cemetery, Vandalia, WV.

Joshua married **Susan FULTZ** on ~1837.

17 F ix. **Elizabeth HARDMAN** was born 24 Jun 1813. She died 4 Sep 1855 in Lewis Co., WV and was buried in Mt. Gilead Church, Georgetown, WV.

Elizabeth married **Jacob W. HUDSON** on 10 Oct 1833.

+ 18 M x. **John G. HARDMAN** was born 2 May 1817 and died 10 Nov 1897.

19 M xi. **Peter Jamison HARDMAN** was born 1819. He died 1891 in Warsaw, Ind.

Peter married **Hannah FINLEY**.

20 M xii. **Daniel HARDMAN** was born 1822 in Little Skin Creek, Lewis Co., (W)V. He died ~1826 and was buried in Mt. Gilead Church, Georgetown, WV.

21 M xiii. **David HARDMAN** was born 1826. He died ~1826 and was buried in Mt. Gilead Church, Georgetown, WV.

John also married (2) **Elizabeth Jane LOCKHART** on 25 Nov 1791.

Fourth Generation

18. **John G. HARDMAN**[3] (John D., Peterman, Nicholas) was born 2 May 1817 in Lewis Co., WV and 23 Dec 1838 in Braxton Co., WV. He died 10 Nov 1897 in Braxton Co., WV and was buried in Green Hill Cemetery, Green Hill, WV.

John married **Malinda FORINASH**, daughter of Jacob FORINASH and Katherine CRITES, on 23 Dec 1838 in Lewis Co., WV. Malinda was born 5 Mar 1822. She died 8 Apr 1884 in Braxton Co., WV and was buried in Green Hill Cemetery, Green Hill, WV.

They had the following children:

22 M i. **Jacob Miflin HARDMAN** was born 12 Jul 1840.

Jacob married **Virginia SIMMONS** on 2 Aug 1862.

23 M ii. **William H. HARDMAN** was born 1842. He died ~1861-65 in Point Lookout, Md.

24 F iii. **Martha A. HARDMAN** was born 1844. She died 5 Feb 1881 in Lewis Co., WV.

Martha married **James E. MORRIS** on 24 Dec 1863 in Lewis Co., WV.

25 F iv. **Mary E. HARDMAN** was born 1846.

26 F v. **Cintha J. HARDMAN** was born 1847.

+ 27 M vi. **Perry Worthington HARDMAN** was born 27 Jun 1850.

28 F vii. **Margaret HARDMAN** was born 26 May 1855 in Little Skin Creek, Lewis Co., (W)V.

Margaret married **R. MORRISON** on 6 Mar 1873 in Lewis Co., WV.

F viii. **Hannah M. HARDMAN** was born 1858.

F ix. **Virginia C. HARDMAN** was born 1861.

139

F x.   **Sarah Ellen HARDMAN** was born 1863.

29 M xi.   **Perry Andrew HARDMAN** was born[4] 28 Jul 1866.

30 M ix.   **Samuel M. HARDMAN** was born[5] ~1866.

Samuel married (1) **Mary CUMMINS** on 14 Sep 1871 in Lewis Co., WV. The marriage ended in divorce.

Samuel also married (2) **Alice PROPST**.

Fifth Generation

27. **Perry Worthington HARDMAN**[6] (John G., John D., Peterman, Nicholas) was born 27 Jun 1850. He died in Braxton Co., WV.

Mary Melissa Berry

Perry married **Mary Melissa BERRY**, daughter of William D. BERRY and Hannah Laverna MCCRAY, on 16 Mar 1870 in Kanawha District., WV. Mary was born 16 Nov 1853 in Upshur Co., (W)V. She died 14 Jul 1898 in Braxton Co., WV.

They had the following children:

31 F i.   **Anna HARDMAN** was born 28 Feb 1871. She died 5 Nov 1877.

32 F ii.   **Laverna A. HARDMAN** was born 25 Apr

1872. She died 25 Oct 1877.

33 F iii. **Georgia E. HARDMAN** was born 8 Jul 1874. She died 19 Oct 1877.

John William Hardman

+ 34 M iv. **John William HARDMAN** was born 5 Jan 1876 and died 10 Nov 1925.

35 M v. **Donlas HARDMAN** was born 23 Sep 1878.

36 F vi. **Stella B. HARDMAN** was born 13 Mar 1882. She died Sep 1899.

F vii. **Maggie HARDMAN** was born 1886. She died 6 Jul 1890.

37 M viii. **Earl HARDMAN** was born 26 Jul 1896. He died 25 Oct 1951.

F ix. **Mary Matilda HARDMAN** was born and died 14 Jul 1898.

He also married (2) **Cora A. PRINCE** in 1898. She was born 12 Jan 1853. She died 2 May 1924.

Sixth Generation

34. **John William HARDMAN**[7,8,9] (Perry Worthington, John G., John D., Peterman, Nicholas) was born 5 Jan 1876. He died 10 Nov 1925 in Fall Run, Braxton Co., WV and was buried in Green Hill Cemetery, Green Hill, WV.

John married[7] **Bessie Maude LOWTHER** on 12 Jul 1899 in Fall Run, Braxton Co., WV. Bessie was born 26 Jun

1873 in Braxton Co., WV. She died 1966 in Harrison Co., WV.

The John William and Bessie Maude Lowther Hardman Family

They had the following children:

38 F i. **Leatha Carrie HARDMAN**[10] was born 12 Jun 1901. She died[11] Dec 1950 in Wheeling, WV.

39 F ii. **Lora Arvilla HARDMAN**[12] was born 23 Feb 1902. She died 1 Apr 1992 in Clarksburg, WV.

+ 40 M iii. **Walter W. HARDMAN** was born 15 May 1904 and died 20 Apr 1970.

+ 41 M iv. **George Dencil HARDMAN I** was born 15 Jun 1906 and died 20 Sep 1972.

42 M v. **Delmas Emmett HARDMAN** was born 3 Oct 1908 in Fall Run, Braxton Co., WV. He died 9 May 1976.

+ 43 F vi. **Retta Dale HARDMAN** was born 10 Nov 1910 and died 5 Oct 1977.

142

44 M vii. **Lester HARDMAN** was born 25 Nov 1912.
He died 17 Jan 1918.

Seventh Generation

40. **Walter W. HARDMAN**[10,13,14] (John William, Perry
Worthington, John G., John D., Peterman, Nicholas) was
born 15 May 1904. He died 1970.

Walter married **Gertrude HAMILTON**. They had the
following children:

45 F i. **Naomi HARDMAN**.

46 F ii. **Nina HARDMAN**.

47 M iii. **Noel HARDMAN**.

48 M iv. **Norman HARDMAN**.

49 M v. **Nelson HARDMAN**.

George Dencil I and Hazel Bowyer Hardman

41. **George Dencil HARDMAN I**[15] (John William, Perry
Worthington, John G., John D., Peterman, Nicholas) was
born 15 Jun 1906. He died 20 Sep 1972 in Weston, WV
and was buried in K & P, Burnsville, WV.

George married **Hazel BOWYER** "Juanita", daughter of

Hugh Raymond BOWYER and Mary Catora STOUT, on 23 Dec 1928 in Braxton Co., WV. Juanita was born 13 Feb 1908. She died 8 Jan 1992 in Weston, WV and was buried in K & P, Burnsville,WV.

Bessie   *Marge*   *Boots*

Toots   *Biggy Bill*

They had the following children:

+   50 M   i.   **George Dencil HARDMAN II** was born 5 Sep 1929 and died 22 Jun 1982.

     51 F   ii. **Mary Alice HARDMAN** was born 24 Jul 1931 in Burnsville, WV. She died 27 Oct 1931was buried in K & P, Burnsville, WV.

+   52 F   iii. **Marjorie Carol HARDMAN** was born 14 Nov 1932.

+   53 F   iv. **Coleta Dare HARDMAN** was born 6 Oct 1934 and died 11 Jan 1991.

.+   54 F   v.   **Edith Sharon HARDMAN** was born 7 Oct 1937.

+   55 M   vi. **William Raymond HARDMAN** was born

1 May 1947 and died 7 Mar 1996.

43. **Retta Dale HARDMAN** (John William, Perry Worthington, John G., John D., Peterman, Nicholas) was born 10 Nov 1910 in Fall Run, Braxton Co., WV. She died 5 Oct 1977 in Glen Burnie, Md.

Retta married **Edward BILDSTIEN** on ~1955.

They had the following children:

   56 F   i. **Oleta HARDMAN** was born 31 May 1928 in Fall Run, Braxton Co., WV.

               Oleta married **George Edward CARTER** on 1 Dec 1955. George died 13 May 1992.

+   57 M   ii. **Irwin HARDMAN** was born 28 Feb 1930.

               He had the following children:

69	F	i.	**Dale HARDMAN**.
70	F	ii.	**Deborah HARDMAN**.
71	M	iii.	**Brett HARDMAN**.

Eighth Generation

George Dencil II and Jane Grey Gregory Hardman Family

50. **George Dencil HARDMAN II**[15,16] (George Dencil HARDMAN I, John William, Perry Worthington, John G., John D., Peterman, Nicholas) was born 5 Sep 1929. He died 22 Jun 1982 in Interlachen, Fl. and was buried 26 Jun 1982 in K & P, Burnsville, WV.

George married **Jane Grey GREGORY**, daughter of James Vincent GREGORY and Dora BROWN, on 9 Sep 1950 in Burnsville, WV. Jane was born 27 Aug 1933 in Gregory, Braxton Co., WV.

Georgia Grey Hardman

They had the following child:

+   58 F   i.   **Georgia Grey HARDMAN** was born 9 Jul 1951.

52. **Marjorie Carol HARDMAN** [17] (George Dencil HARDMAN I, John William, Perry Worthington, John G., John D., Peterman, Nicholas) was born 14 Nov 1932.

Marjorie married **Billy Brown BURKE** on 20 Dec 1952 in Burnsville, WV.

Roberta Diane and Carolyn Sue Burke

They had the following children:

59 F   i. **Roberta Diane BURKE**[18] was born 27 Mar 1956 in Weston, WV.

Roberta married **Michael HATTON** on 28 Nov 1987 in Sand Fork, WV.

+ 60 F   ii. **Carolyn Sue BURKE** was born 24 Jan 1958.

The Russell Beryl and Coleta Dare Hardman Thompson Family

53. **Coleta Dare HARDMAN** [19] (George Dencil HARDMAN I, John William, Perry Worthington, John G., John D., Peterman, Nicholas) was born 6 Oct 1934. She died 11 Jan 1991 in Sand Fork, WV.

Coleta married **Russell Beryl THOMPSON**[20], son of Charles J. THOMPSON and Arnetta Bell CONRAD, on 15 Mar 1951 in Sutton, Braxton Co., WV. Russell was born 15 Mar 1929 in Gilmer Co., WV.

They had the following child:

Robert Edward and Sandra Kaye Anderson Thompson

61 M i. **Robert Edward THOMPSON**[21] was born 30 May 1954 in Sutton, Braxton Co., WV.

Robert married **Sandra Kay ANDERSON**[22], daughter of **Russell RICE** and **Florence STRAIGHT**, on 14 Feb 1994 in Gilmer Co., WV. Sandra was born 16 Nov 1953 in Muddy Creek, Tyler Co., WV.

54. **Edith Sharon HARDMAN** [23] (George Dencil HARDMAN I, John William, Perry Worthington, John G., John D., Peterman, Nicholas) was born 7 Oct 1937 in Fall Run, Braxton Co., WV.

Sharon married (1) **James ROE**, son of Lafayette ROE and Nellie SCOTT. The marriage ended in divorce. James was born in Grahn, KY. He died 10 Jan 1991 in St. Petersburg, Fl. and was buried in Florida National Cemetery.

They had the following children:

The James and Edith Sharon Hardman Roe Children

+ 62 M i. **James William ROE** was born 20 Jun 1962.

+ 63 M ii. **John Neil ROE** was born 26 Jun 1963.

+ 64 F iii. **Sherrie Anne ROE** was born 14 Jun 1963.

+ 65 F iv. **Barbara Ruth ROE** was born 15 Jul 1965.

Sharon also married (2) **Norman Leo WEST** on 24 May 1986 in St. Mary's, WV. Norman was born 21 Feb 1931.

55. **William Raymond HARDMAN**[24] (George Dencil HARDMAN I, John William, Perry Worthington, John G., John D., Peterman, Nicholas) was born 1 May 1947 in Burnsville, WV. He died 7 Mar 1996 in Columbus, Ohio and was buried in Mt Hebron, WV.

William married **Emma Jean WILLIAMS** on 23 Aug 1969 in St. Mary's, WV.

The William Raymond and Emma Jean Williams Hardman Children

They had the following children:

  66 M   i. **William Oran HARDMAN** [24] was born 17 Nov 1970 in Parkersburg, WV.

+   67 M   ii. **George Dencil HARDMAN III** was born 9 Jun 1973.

+   68 F   iii. **Katheryn Mischelle HARDMAN** was born 31 Oct 1976.

Ninth Generation

The John Allen and Georgia Grey Hardman Coffey Family

58. **Georgia Grey HARDMAN** (George Dencil HARDMAN II, George Dencil HARDMAN I, John William, Perry Worthington, John G., John D., Peterman, Nicholas) was born 9 Jul 1951 in Sutton, Braxton Co., WV.

Georgia married **John Allen COFFEY**, son of **James Francis COFFEY** and **Mary KEOGH**, on 27 Oct 1973 in Alexandria, VA. John was born 11 Feb 1948 in Brocton, Mass.

They had the following child:

Brian Michael Coffey

72 M i. **Brian Michael COFFEY** was born 15 Apr 1976 in Fairfax, VA.

60. **Carolyn Sue BURKE**[18] (Marjorie Carol HARDMAN , George Dencil HARDMAN I, John William, Perry Worthington, John G., John D., Peterman, Nicholas) was born 24 Jan 1958 in Weston, WV.

Carolyn married **William HOLVEY**. The marriage ended in divorce.

Burke Ashley and Samantha Carol Holvey

They had the following children:

73 F i. **Burke Ashley HOLVEY** was born 2 Sep 1984 in Houston, TX.

74 F ii. **Samantha Carol HOLVEY** "Sam" was born 1 Mar 1986 in Houston, TX.

James William Roe

62. **James William ROE**[25] (Edith Sharon HARDMAN , George Dencil HARDMAN I, John William, Perry Worthington, John G., John D., Peterman, Nicholas) was born 20 Jun 1962 in Columbus, Ohio.

James married **Sonya HARPER**. The marriage ended in divorce. They had the following child:

James Bradley Roe

   75 M   i. **James Bradley ROE**[25] was born 30 Sep 1994 in Parkersburg, WV.

John Neil Roe

63. **John Neil ROE**[25] (Edith Sharon HARDMAN , George Dencil HARDMAN I, John William, Perry Worthington, John G., John D., Peterman, Nicholas) was born 26 Jun 1963 in Columbus, Ohio. John was not married to **Mary MILLER**.

They had the following child:

76　F　i.　**Taylor Marie RUSSELL**[25] was born 3 Aug 1995.

Taylor Marie Russell

Gene and Sherrie Anne Roe Streight

64. **Sherrie Anne ROE**[25] (Edith Sharon HARDMAN , George Dencil HARDMAN I, John William, Perry Worthington, John G., John D., Peterman, Nicholas) was born 14 Jun 1963 in Columbus, Ohio.

Sherrie married **Timothy MCDANIEL**. The marriage ended in divorce.

She had the following children:

Kara Alyce, Kimberly Anne, Robert Charles McDaniel

+   77   F   i.   **Kimberly Anne MCDANIEL** was born 9 Jan 1980.

    78   F   ii.   **Kara Alyce MCDANIEL** was born 31 Jan 1984.

Sherrie was also not married to **Charles KEENER**.

They had the following child:

   79   M   iii.   **Robert Charles MCDANIEL** was born 18
                   Mar 1987 in Philippi, WV.

Sherrie also married **Robert HART**. The marriage ended in divorce.

Sherrie also married **Gene STREIGHT** on 19 August 2005.

David Bruce and Barbara Ruth Roe Vice

65. **Barbara Ruth ROE**[25] (Edith Sharon HARDMAN ,
    George Dencil HARDMAN I, John William, Perry
    Worthington, John G., John D., Peterman, Nicholas)
    was born 15 Jul 1965 in Alexandria,VA.

Barbara married (1) **Jeffrey KERSEY.** The marriage ended
in divorce.

Barbara married (2) **David VICE** on 26 May 1994 in Mt.
Sterling, Ky. David was born 1 Jul 1955.

They had the following children:

Christopher   *Courtney*

80 F i. **Courtney Sharon Elizabeth VICE**[25] was born 9 Jun 1998 in Mt. Sterling, Ky.

81 M ii. **Christopher David VICE**[25] was born 2 Mar 1998 in Weston, WV and was adopted 10 May 1999 in Sutton, Braxton Co., WV.

George and Virginia Webb Hardman III Family

67. **George Dencil HARDMAN III**[24] (William Raymond HARDMAN , George Dencil HARDMAN I, John William, Perry Worthington, John G., John D., Peterman, Nicholas) was born 9 Jun 1973 in Parkersburg, WV.

George married **Virginia WEBB** on 6 Oct 1995 in Sand Fork, WV. They had the following children:

82 M i. **Tray WEBB**.

83 M ii. **William Raymond HARDMAN II** was born May 1997.

84 M iii. **George Dencil HARDMAN IV** was born 27 Nov 1998

85 M iv. **Dalton Lee HARDMAN** was born 25 Jan 2001.

86 M v. **James Wyatt HARDMAN** was born 14 Oct 2004.

68. **Katheryn Mischelle HARDMAN** [26] (William Raymond HARDMAN George Dencil HARDMAN I, John William,

Perry Worthington, John G., John D., Peterman, Nicholas) was born 31 Oct 1976 in Parkersburg, WV.

Katheryn was not married to **William Sean BURCHETT**.

They had the following children:

   86   M   i. **Raymond Michael HARDMAN** was born 29 Dec 1999.

Tenth Generation

77. **Kimberly Anne MCDANIEL**[25] (Sherrie Anne ROE, Edith Sharon HARDMAN , George Dencil HARDMAN I, John William, Perry Worthington, John G., John D., Peterman, Nicholas) was born 9 Jan 1980 in Elkins, WV.

Kimberly was not married to **Chad GARDNER**.

They had the following children:

Kyler and Shane Gardner

   87   M   i. **Kyler GARDNER** was born 13 Jun 2000 in Marietta, Ohio.

   88   M   ii. **Shane GARDNER** was born 4 Jan 2003 in Marietta, Ohio.

And so are the ancestors and generations of the George Dencil Hardman I Family. We end with the beginning of a new generation. This is the continuing story of those who have gone before us as an example in the making of a nation. This generation continues to carry the mantle, which has been passed to us. The children of George I and Hazel Bowyer Hardman are in the winter of their years with only two surviving, Marjorie and Edith Sharon Hardman. We are now passing on that mantle to the generations, which follow us.

The Generations of the

Orla and Lora Arvilla Hardman Cutright Family

First Generation

Orla and Lora Arvilla Hardman Cutright

1. **Orla CUTRIGHT, SR.** "Cutty" died 21 Oct 1969 in Harrison
    Co., WV.

    Cutty married **Lora Arvilla HARDMAN**[1] on 19 Aug 1919 in
    Oakland, Md. Lora was born 23 Feb 1902 in Fall Run,
    Braxton Co., WV. She died 1 Apr 1992 in Clarksburg, WV.

    They had the following children:

    +   2   F   i.   **Bessie Irene CUTRIGHT** was born 11 Apr
    1921.

          3   F   ii.   **Vivian Grey CUTRIGHT** was born 20 Sep
    1922.

    +   4   M   iii.   **Orla E. CUTRIGHT, JR.** was born 27 Sep
    1924.

    +   5   F   iv.   **Lora Phyllis CUTRIGHT** was born 7 Dec
    1926.

    +   6   M   v.   **Rex CUTRIGHT** was born 26 Jun 1934.

Second Generation

2. **Bessie Irene CUTRIGHT** (Orla) was born 11 Apr 1921 in
    Harrison Co., WV.

Irene married (1) **Ferrell C. ROMINE** on 20 Apr 1939 in Elkton, Md. Ferrell died 3 Nov 1986.

They had the following children:

> 7 M i. **Gary Lee ROMINE** was born 8 Sep 1940.
>
> Gary married **Karen HEDBLOM.**

+ 8 M ii. **Richard ROMINE** was born 7 Apr 1943.

+ 9 F iii. **Renee Lora ROMINE** was born 1952.

> 10 M iv. **Thomas Jay ROMINE** was born 1956.

Irene also married (2) **Howard PAUGH** on 1992.

4. **Orla E. CUTRIGHT, JR.** (Orla) was born 27 Sep 1924 in Lost Creek, WV.

Orla married (1) **Iris Irene FINDLEY** on 14 Dec 1947.

They had the following children:

> 11 M i. **Stanford Delmas CUTRIGHT.**
>
> 12 M ii. **Edward Emmitt CUTRIGHT.**
>
> 13 F iii. **Loretta Christine CUTRIGHT.**

Orla also married (2) **Helen PORTARO** in 1967.

George Paul and Lora Phyllis Cutright McComas

5. **Lora Phyllis CUTRIGHT** (Orla) was born 7 Dec 1926 in Lost Creek, WV.

Phyllis married **George Paul MCCOMAS**[2] on 31 May 1948 in Lost Creek, WV. George was born 20 Nov 1920 in Ottawa, WV. He died 27 Oct 2001 in Ripley, WV and was buried in Jackson County Memory Gardens.

They had the following children:

+   14   F   i.   **Paula Irene MCCOMAS** was born 1 Aug 1948.

+   15   M   ii.   **Mark Alan MCCOMAS** was born 3 Apr 1953.

+   16   M   iii.   **Eric Edward MCCOMAS** was born 25 Feb 1957.

6.   **Rex CUTRIGHT** (Orla) was born 26 Jun 1934.

Rex married **Phyllis Jean DANIELS** on 19 Aug 1955.

Rex and Phyllis Jean Daniels Cutright Family

They had the following children:

     17   M   i.   **Maxwell Kirk CUTRIGHT** was born 9 May 1956.

     18   F   ii.   **Melody Kim CUTRIGHT** was born 23 Aug 1957.

     19   M   iii.   **Timothy Rex CUTRIGHT** was born 2 Feb 1959.

     20   M   iv.   **Jeffrey Lynn CUTRIGHT** was born 20 Jun

1960.

+ 21 F v. **Tammy Rexanne CUTRIGHT** was born 8 Dec 1961.

Third Generation

8. **Richard ROMINE** (Bessie Irene CUTRIGHT, Orla) was born 7 Apr 1943 in Corpus Christi, TX.

Richard married **Georgia CHILDS** on Aug 1995.

They had the following children:

22 M i. **Ronald Wayne ROMINE** was born 23 Nov 1967.

23 M ii. **David ROMINE** was born ~1967.

9. **Renee Lora ROMINE** (Bessie Irene CUTRIGHT, Orla) was born 13 Sep 1952 in McKinley Field, Bermuda.

She had the following child:

24 M i. **Adam ROMINE**.

14. **Paula Irene MCCOMAS** (Lora Phyllis CUTRIGHT, Orla) was born 1 Aug 1948 in Clarksburg, WV.

Paula married (1) **William Steven WHITE**, son of **William WHITE and Roben RUPERT**, on 29 Aug 1967.

They had the following children:

25 F i. **Natalie Irene WHITE** was born 8 Dec 1973.

26 M ii. **Paul Ballard Steven WHITE** was born 10 Mar 1975.

Paula also married (2) **Duane STOWERS** on 1988.

15. **Mark Alan MCCOMAS** (Lora Phyllis CUTRIGHT, Orla) was born 3 Apr 1953 in Clarksburg, WV.

Mark married **Donna ROBINSON**, daughter of **Donald Audrey ROBINSON and Hattie STEELE**.

They had the following children:

163

27 F   i. **Carrie Lee MCCOMAS**.

28 M ii. **Wade Philip MCCOMAS**.

16. **Eric Edward MCCOMAS** (Lora Phyllis CUTRIGHT, Orla) was born 25 Feb 1957 in Clarksburg, WV.

Eric married **April PARSONS**, daughter of **Buddy PARSONS and Donna NOFFINGER.**

They had the following children:

29 M   i. **Richard Aaron MCCOMAS**.

30 F ii. **Erica Lee MCCOMAS**.

21. **Tammy Rexanne CUTRIGHT** (Rex CUTRIGHT, Orla) was born 8 Dec 1961 in Clarksburg, WV.

She had the following children:

31 F   i. **Jean CUTRIGHT**.

32 F ii. **Sara CUTRIGHT**.

"Cousins" of

George D. and Hazel Bowyer Hardman

Descendants of

Irene Cutright Romine Paugh

First Generation

1. **Lora Arvilla HARDMAN** was born 23 Feb 1902 in Fall Run, Braxton Co., WV. She died 1 Apr 1992 in Clarksburg, Harrison Co., WV.

   Lora married **Orla CUTRIGHT Sr.** "Cutty" on 19 Aug 1919 in Oakland, Md.. Cutty died 21 Oct 1969 in Harrison Co., WV.

   They had the following children:

   +   2   F   i.   **Irene CUTRIGHT**[1] was born 11 Apr 1921.

        3   F   ii.   **Vivian Grey CUTRIGHT** was born 20 Sep 1922.

        4   F   iii.   **Lora Phyllis CUTRIGHT** was born 7 Dec 1926.

        5   M   iv.   **Rex CUTRIGHT** was born 26 Jun 1934.

Second Generation

2. **Irene CUTRIGHT** (Lora Arvilla) was born 11 Apr 1921.

   Irene married **Ferrell C. ROMINE** on 20 Apr 1939 in Elkton, Md. Ferrell died 3 Nov 1986.

   They had the following children:

   +   6   M   i.   **Gary ROMINE** was born 8 Sep 1940.

   +   7   M   ii.   **Richard ROMINE** was born 7 Apr 1943.

   +   8   F   iii.   **Lora Renee ROMINE** was born 13 Sep 1952.

   +   9   M   iv.   **Thomas Jay ROMINE** was born 19 May 1956.

   Bessie also married **Howard PAUGH** in 1992.

Third Generation

6. **Gary ROMINE** (Irene CUTRIGHT, Lora Arvilla) was born 8 Sep 1940.

    Gary married **Karen HEDBLOM**.

    They had the following children:

    10 M   i. **Timothy Alan ROMINE** was born 14 Apr 1970.

    Timothy married **Karen TLUSTY** on 29 Dec 2001.

    11 F   ii. **Kathryn Lesa ROMINE** was born 4 Oct 1973.

    12 M   iii. **Scott Alan ROMINE** was born 4 Apr 1979.

7. **Richard ROMINE** (Irene CUTRIGHT, Lora Arvilla) was born 7 Apr 1943.

    Richard married **Georgia** on Aug 1964.

    They had the following children:

    +   13 M   i. **Ronald ROMINE** was born after 1964.

    +   14 M   ii. **David ROMINE** was born 18 Dec 1969.

    Richard also married **Sandy MILEY** on 1 Jun 1995.

8. **Lora Renee ROMINE** (Irene CUTRIGHT, Lora Arvilla) was born 13 Sep 1952.

    Lora married **Steve COLEMAN**.

    They had the following child:

    15 M   i. **Adam COLEMAN**.

    Lora also married **William Terry EDWARDS** on 14 Sep 1988. William was born 15 Sep 1948.

9. **Thomas Jay ROMINE** (Irene CUTRIGHT, Lora Arvilla) was born 19 May 1956.

    Thomas married **Linda Lee SNYDER**. Linda was born 23 Aug 1975. She died 12 Aug 1982.

They had the following child:

+   16 F   i.   **Brandy ROMINE** was born 18 Apr 1977.

Thomas also married **Marsha Lynn GRADY** on 15 Jun 1985.

Fourth Generation

13. **Ronald ROMINE** (Richard ROMINE, Irene CUTRIGHT, Lora Arvilla) was born after 1964.

Ronald married **UNKNOWN**.

He had the following children:

   17 F   i.   **Hannah ROMINE**.

   18 F   ii.   **Sarah ROMINE**.

Ronald also married **Kari TEMPLETON** on Dec 1991.

They had the following child:

   19 M   iii. **Ryan David ROMINE** was born 4 Jun 1992.

14. **David ROMINE** (Richard ROMINE, Irene CUTRIGHT, Lora Arvilla) was born 18 Dec 1969.

David married **Kimberlee GRUBER** on 31 Jul 1998.

They had the following children:

   20 F   i.   **Ashlee Kay ROMINE** was born 9 May 2001.

   21 F   ii.   **Madison Renee ROMINE** was born 9 May 2001.

   22 M   iii. **Dylan Ron ROMINE** was born 17 Jun 2004.

16. **Brandy ROMINE** (Thomas Jay ROMINE, Irene CUTRIGHT, Lora Arvilla) was born 18 Apr 1977.

Brandy married **Adam SPRY** on 15 Feb 2003.

They had the following child:

   23 M   i.   **Cohen Bradshir SPRY** was born 10 Mar 2005.

Descendants of

Ellen Virginia and Enoch George Watson

First Generation

1. **Ellen Virginia BOWYER**[2] (Leonard, Leonard) was born 13 Jul 1840 in Bath Co., Virginia. She died 16 Oct 1898 in Upshur Co., West Virginia.

   Ellen married **Enoch George WATSON**. Enoch was born 2 Jun 1838 in Bath Co., Virginia. He died 16 Feb 1898 in Copen, Gilmer Co., West Virginia.

   They had the following child:

   +   2   M   i.   **Warder W. WATSON** was born 18 Jul 1870 and died 1946.

Second Generation

2. **Warder W. WATSON** (Ellen Virginia, Leonard, Leonard) was born 18 Jul 1870 in Gilmer Co., West Virginia. He died 1946 in Selbyville, Upshur Co., West Virginia.

   Warder married **Ida Mae NIXON**. Ida was born 12 Dec 1881 in Canaan, West Virginia. She died 13 Aug 1932 in Selbyville, Upshur Co., West Virginia.

   They had the following child:

   +   3   F   i.   **Juanita Mae WATSON** was born 25 Apr 1917 and died 4 Feb 1999.

Third Generation

3. **Juanita Mae WATSON** (Warder W. WATSON, Ellen Virginia, Leonard, Leonard) was born 25 Apr 1917 in Dogway, West Virginia. She died 4 Feb 1999 in Tucson, Pima Co., Arizona.

   Juanita married **Verl Kent REGER**. Verl was born 11 Nov 1911 in Lorentz, Upshur Co., West Virginia. He died 17 Aug 1976 in Tucson, Pima Co., Arizona.

   They had the following children:

      4   F   i.   **Verleen REGER** was born 20 Feb 1938 in Buckhannon, West Virginia.

5 M ii. **Leonard K. REGER** was born
21 Sep 1939 in Buckhannon, West
Virginia. He died 30 Apr 2002 in Elfrieda,
Arizona.

6 F iii. **Brenda Sue REGER** was born
16 Sep 1943 in Ft. Wayne, Indiana.

7 M iv. **Lawrence Wayne REGER** was born
31 Oct 1945 in Ft. Wayne, Indiana.

Descendants of

Emory Jackson Bowyer and
Cornelia Stump,
Susan Barnett,
Alberta Spaur

First Generation

Emory Jackson Bowyer

1. **Emory Jackson BOWYER**[3] was born 2 Feb 1873 in Horn Creek, Gilmer County, West Virginia. He died 4 Feb 1957 in Falls Mill, Braxton County, West Virginia.

   Emory married **Fanny Cornelia STUMP**, daughter of Hezekiah STUMP and Lenore PULLIAM, on 25 Nov 1893 in Falls Mill, Braxton County, West Virginia. Fanny was born 6 Oct 1874 in Braxton County, West Virginia. She died 22 Mar 1896 in Braxton County, West Virginia.

   They had the following children:

+   2 F   i.   **Elma Ocie BOWYER** was born 30 Apr 1893 and died 29 May 1966.

      3 F   ii.   **Cornelia Lynn BOWYER** was born 15 Mar 1896. She died 15 Mar 1896.

   Emory was also not married to **Susan BARNETT**. Susan was born 1876. She died 1948.

   They had the following child:

+   4 F   iii.   **Lela Ocie BOWYER** was born 1900 and died Jan 1952.

Alberta Spaur

Emory also married **Alberta SPAUR**, daughter of **John SPAUR** and **Jemina AMOS**, on 25 Jun 1899. Alberta was born 30 Mar 1883 in Gilmer County, West Virginia. She died 27 Aug 1970.

They had the following children:

+   5   F   iv.   **Dochie Eva BOWYER** was born 25 Jun 1900 and died 7 Jan 1966.

+   6   F   v.   **Lochie Mae BOWYER** was born 2 Jul 1902 and died 30 Sep 1993.

+   7   M   vi.   **Everette Guy BOWYER** was born 2 Nov 1904 and died 13 Apr 1988.

+   8   F   vii.   **Reatha Leone BOWYER** was born 29 Oct 1906 and died 1999.

+   9   F   viii.   **Winnie Letalia BOWYER** was born 8 Sep 1908.

+   10   M   ix.   **Delbert Carris BOWYER** was born 3 Oct 1910 and died 16 Sep 1973.

+   11   F   x.   **Loma Ella BOWYER** was born 23 Oct 1912 and died 8 Apr 1992.

+   12   F   xi.   **Wilma Gertrude BOWYER** was born 6 Feb 1915 and died 5 May 1989.

+   13   F   xii.   **Grace Mildred BOWYER** was born 8 Sep 1918 and died 1999.

     14   F   xiii.   **Virginia Etta BOWYER** was born 4 Jul

1921.

Virginia married **Edward SODOSKY**.

Second Generation

2. **Elma Ocie BOWYER** (Emory Jackson) was born 30 Apr 1893 in Braxton County, West Virginia. She died 29 May 1966 in Lewis County, West Virginia.

   Elma married **Franklin Lot EXLINE** on 8 Apr 1914. Franklin was born 14 Apr 1890. He died 4 Jan 1965.

   They had the following children:

   +   15   F   i.   **Wandah EXLINE** was born 23 Jan 1915.

   +   16   F   ii.   **Edna Marie EXLINE** was born 17 Dec 1918 and died 4 Jan 1965.

   +   17   M   iii.   **Roy Dowe EXLINE** was born 7 Feb 1921.

   +   18   F   iv.   **Freda Muriel EXLINE** was born 8 Jul 1925.

4. **Lela Ocie BOWYER** (Emory Jackson) was born 1900. She died Jan 1952.

   Lela married **Roy R. HARRIS**. Roy was born 1900.

   They had the following children:

        19   M   i.   **Boy HARRIS** was born about 1921. He died about 1921.

   +   20   M   ii.   **Wade Cameron HARRIS** was born 7 Apr 1921 and died Jul 1969.

   +   21   F   iii.   **Pearlotha May HARRIS** was born 1924.

   +   22   M   iv.   **Eugene Neuman HARRIS** was born 18 Oct 1926.

        23   M   v.   **Boy HARRIS** was born 1927. He died 1927.

   +   24   M   vi.   **Arthur Paul HARRIS** was born 28 Sep 1928 and died 28 May 1982.

+   25 F   vii. **Margaretta Marie HARRIS** was born 15 Jan 1932.

     26 M   viii. **Freddie Lee HARRIS** was born 15 Jan 1932. He died 15 Apr 1932.

+   27 F   ix.   **Mary Louise HARRIS** was born 15 Apr 1934.

5. **Dochie Eva BOWYER** (Emory Jackson) was born 25 Jun 1900. She died 7 Jan 1966.

    Dochie married **Alva David BARRICKMAN** on 6 Aug 1918. Alva was born 8 May 1898. He died 30 Jun 1990.

    They had the following children:

+   28 F   i.   **Velma Annette BARRICKMAN** was born 6 Feb 1921.

+   29 F   ii.   **Reva Mae BARRICKMAN** was born 2 Sep 1922.

     30 M   iii. **Alva David BARRICKMAN** was born 4 Sep 1924. He died 7 Sep 1924.

+   31 F   iv.   **Melva BARRICKMAN** was born 7 Dec 1927.

+   32 F   v.   **Lounette BARRICKMAN** was born 23 Dec 1929.

+   33 F   vi.   **Hilda Phyllis BARRICKMAN** was born 10 Feb 1933.

     34 M   vii. **Gail BARRICKMAN** was born 5 Jan 1942. He died 5 Jan 1942.

6. **Lochie Mae BOWYER** (Emory Jackson) was born 2 Jul 1902. She died 30 Sep 1993.

    Lochie Mae married **French WILLIAMS** on 26 Jul 1924. French was born 14 Mar 1903. He died 1981.

    They had the following children:

     35 M   i.   **Dana Elvin WILLIAMS** was born 4 May 1925. He died 1989/1990.

36 F   ii. **Vieva Regina WILLIAMS** was born 18 Sep 1927.

37 F   iii. **Eloise Mae WILLIAMS** was born 10 Mar 1933.

38 M   iv. **French Eldon WILLIAMS** was born 10 Mar 1933. He died 5 May 1936.

39 F   v. **Shirley Marie WILLIAMS** was born 2 May 1936.

40 F   vi. **Shelva Annabelle WILLIAMS** was born 17 Dec 1937. She died 20 Jul 1958.

41 F   vii. **Marmel Leigh WILLIAMS** was born 24 Oct 1940. She died 15 Feb 1941.

7. **Everette Guy BOWYER** (Emory Jackson) was born 2 Nov 1904. He died 13 Apr 1988.

Everette married **Gertrude Grabton WHITE** on 5 Aug 1933. Gertrude died 1999.

They had the following children:

42 M   i. **Everette Jackson BOWYER** was born 1934.

43 M   ii. **Williams White BOWYER** was born 1935.

44 F   iii. **Phyllis Ruth BOWYER** was born 1938.

Phyllis married **BUSH**.

45 M   iv. **Edwin Lee BOWYER** was born 1939.

46 M   v. **Dewey Lynn BOWYER** was born 1947.

8. **Reatha Leone BOWYER** (Emory Jackson) was born 29 Oct 1906. She died 1999.

Reatha married **Gordon DYER** on 29 Jul 1923. Gordon was born 19 May 1904. He died 30 Nov 1994.

They had the following children:

+   47 M   i. **Leonard DYER** was born 14 Aug 1924.

+ 48 F ii. **Velda Lee DYER** was born 7 Dec 1926.

+ 49 M iii. **Edsel Verl DYER** was born 14 Aug 1924.

+ 50 F iv. **Opaline Leona DYER** was born 28 Mar 1931.

+ 51 M v. **Ellwood Jackson DYER** was born 19 Jul 1933.

+ 52 F vi. **Ila DYER** was born 13 Jul 1935.

+ 53 F vii. **Freda Belle DYER** was born 24 Dec 1937.

+ 54 F viii. **Wilma Mae DYER** was born 8 Jul 1940.

+ 55 F ix. **Karen DYER** was born 21 Jun 1945.

56 M x. **Terry DYER** was born 2 Oct 1948.

57 M xi. **Gary Lane DYER** was born 20 Apr 1951.

9. **Winnie Letalia BOWYER** (Emory Jackson) was born 8 Sep 1908.

Winnie married **William KERNS** on 11 Apr 1930. William was born 2 Jan 1910. He died 1980.

They had the following children:

58 F i. **Joann Belle KERNS** was born 22 Aug 1932.

Joann married **John LANDFRIED**. John was born 4 Dec 1926.

+ 59 F ii. **Mary Sue KERNS** was born 21 Jan 1936.

+ 60 F iii. **Patricia Leigh KERNS** was born 6 Aug 1941.

10. **Delbert Carris BOWYER** (Emory Jackson) was born 3 Oct 1910. He died 16 Sep 1973.

Delbert married **Nannie Kathleen CASTO** on 15 Jan 1933. Nannie was born 1912.

They had the following children:

61 M i. **Delbert LeRoy BOWYER** was born 5 Jan 1935. He died 10 June 2001.

+ 62 M ii. **James Coy BOWYER** was born 4 Sep 1936.

63 F iii. **Audra Ann BOWYER** was born 30 Aug 1938.

+ 64 M iv. **Chester Duane BOWYER** was born 29 Sep 1940.

+ 65 M v. **Dale Lane BOWYER** was born 26 Oct 1942.

66 M vi. **Ronald Leonard BOWYER** was born 22 Jul 1945.

11. **Loma Ella BOWYER** (Emory Jackson) was born 23 Oct 1912. She died 8 Apr 1992.

Loma married **Vellow Oley GARRISON**. Vellow was born 1903. He died 1973.

They had the following children:

+ 67 F i. **Velloma Mae GARRISON** was born 1936.

+ 68 F ii. **Mozelle GARRISON** was born 1937.

+ 69 F iii. **Avalon Elouise GARRISON** was born 1940.

+ 70 F iv. **Dahline Nadine GARRISON** was born 1941.

+ 71 F v. **Jo La Green GARRISON** was born 1943.

+ 72 M vi. **Lane Lynn GARRISON** was born 1947.

12. **Wilma Gertrude BOWYER** (Emory Jackson) was born 6 Feb 1915. She died 5 May 1989.

Wilma married **Charles Stanley PERKINS**.

They had the following children:

+ 73 F i. **Helen PERKINS**.

+ 74 F ii. **Alberta Bell PERKINS** was born 20 Sep 1941.

75 M iii. **William Jackson PERKINS** was born 2 Mar 1944.

13. **Grace Mildred BOWYER** (Emory Jackson) was born 8 Sep 1918. She died 1999.

Grace married **Okal Burl MOORE**. Okal was born 26 Jul 1917. He died 31 Oct 1987.

They had the following children:

+   76 M   i. **Robert Bowyer MOORE** was born 16 Feb 1943 and died 3 Oct 1975.

+   77 M   ii. **Jeffrey MOORE** was born 20 Nov 1947.

+   78 M   iii. **Gary Bruce MOORE** was born 6 Aug 1949.

Third Generation

15. **Wandah EXLINE** (Elma Ocie BOWYER, Emory Jackson) was born 23 Jan 1915.

Wandah married **George W. WALTERS** on 3 Sep 1932. George was born 19 Aug 1905. He died 12 Jul 1985.

They had the following children:

   79 F   i. **Anna Carol WALTERS** was born 23 Mar 1935. She died 24 Mar 1935.

+   80 F   ii. **Kathryn Elaine WALTERS** was born 19 Mar 1937.

   81 M   iii. **John Franklin WALTERS** was born 21 Mar 1947.

           John married **Joan Christine NEMETH** on 26 Dec 1970.

           John also married **Joan Moberg MCGINNIS** on 27 Oct 1979. Joan was born 15 Mar 1950.

16. **Edna Marie EXLINE** (Elma Ocie BOWYER, Emory Jackson) was born 17 Dec 1918. She died 4 Jan 1965.

Edna married **Vinton Lee BOSLEY** on 1947.

They had the following children:

+ 82 M i. **David Noel BOSLEY** was born 25 Dec 1947.

83 F ii. **Edna Leigh BOSLEY** was born 1956. She died 1957.

17. **Roy Dowe EXLINE** (Elma Ocie BOWYER, Emory Jackson) was born 7 Feb 1921.

Roy married **Opal N. PERRY**. Opal was born 22 Oct 1914.

They had the following children:

84 M i. **Randall Morgan EXLINE** was born 7 Oct 1948. He died 21 June 1993.

+ 85 M ii. **Roy Henry Lott EXLINE** was born 23 Dec 1950.

+ 86 M iii. **Christopher Perry EXLINE** was born 24 Aug 1956.

18. **Freda Muriel EXLINE** (Elma Ocie BOWYER, Emory Jackson) was born 8 Jul 1925.

Freda married **E. E. ROBERTSON**.

They had the following child:

+ 87 F i. **Pamela ROBERTSON** was born Jan 1946.

Freda also married **Paul YOUNG** . Paul died Nov 1989.

20. **Wade Cameron HARRIS** (Lela Ocie BOWYER, Emory Jackson) was born 7 Apr 1921. He died Jul 1969.

Wade married **Lucy (Hayes) BAPP**.

They had the following child:

+ 88 F i. **Susan Marie HARRIS** was born 16 Jun 1953.

21. **Pearlotha May HARRIS** (Lela Ocie BOWYER, Emory Jackson) was born 1924.

Pearlotha married **Walter NAGLE**.

They had the following children:

    89 M   i. **Dennis Wade NAGLE**.

    90 F   ii. **Paula Ann NAGLE**.

Pearlotha also married **Fred BRYSON**.

They had the following children:

    91 M   iii. **Fred Bruce BRYSON**.

    92 M   iv. **Jeffrey BRYSON**.

22. **Eugene Neuman HARRIS** (Lela Ocie BOWYER, Emory Jackson) was born 18 Oct 1926.

Eugene married **Ruby Pearl KING**. Ruby was born 27 Apr 1929.

They had the following children:

+   93 F   i. **Linda L. HARRIS** was born 24 Nov 1946.

+   94 F   ii. **Betty Jean HARRIS** was born 2 Dec 1947.

+   95 M   iii. **Roy E. HARRIS**.

24. **Arthur Paul HARRIS** (Lela Ocie BOWYER, Emory Jackson) was born 28 Sep 1928. He died 28 May 1982.

Arthur married **Eva Delle LEAVETT**.

They had the following children:

+   96 F   i. **Marilyn Kay HARRIS**.

    97 M   ii. **Matthew Paul HARRIS**.

    98 F   iii. **Girl HARRIS** was born 1961.

    99 M   iv. **Brian HARRIS** was born 1964.

Arthur also married **Sandy UNKNOWN**.

25. **Margaretta Marie HARRIS** (Lela Ocie BOWYER, Emory Jackson) was born 15 Jan 1932.

Margaretta married **Eugene KRUSAYNSKI** on 1971. Eugene was born 13 Oct 1925. He died Jun 1991.

Margaretta also married **Gale ROBINSON**.

They had the following children:

+ 100 M i. **William Gale ROBINSON** was born 1949.

+ 101 M ii. **Larry Jo ROBINSON**.

  102 F iii. **Thelma Jean ROBINSON**.

  103 F iv. **Wilma Dean ROBINSON**.

+ 104 F v. **Hope Marie ROBINSON**.

27. **Mary Louise HARRIS** (Lela Ocie BOWYER, Emory Jackson) was born 15 Apr 1934.

Mary married **Admiral D. BUTCHER**.

Mary also married **Jackson Enoch CARTER**.

They had the following children:

+ 105 M i. **Jack Eugene CARTER** was born 11 Jul 1961.

+ 106 F ii. **Tamara Louise CARTER** was born 12 Jun 1962.

  107 F iii. **Brenda Cecile CARTER** was born 17 Apr 1964.

Mary also married **Erich R FISCHER** on 1970.

They had the following child:

  108 F iv. **Mary Lizabeth FISCHER** was born 4 Oct 1971.

28. **Velma Annette BARRICKMAN** (Dochie Eva BOWYER, Emory Jackson) was born 6 Feb 1921.

Velma married **Unknown MURPHY**.

They had the following children:

+ 109 F i. **Scarlett MURPHY** was born 24 Jul 1943.

+ 110 F ii. **Sandra MURPHY** was born 16 Oct 1946.

+ 111 M iii. **Michael James MURPHY** was born 30 Jan 1948.

+ 112 M iv. **Mark Andrew MURPHY** was born 5 Jan 1951 and died 12 Mar 1976.

113 M v. **Paul Edward MURPHY**.

Velma also married **Jack LEWIS**.

29. **Reva Mae BARRICKMAN** (Dochie Eva BOWYER, Emory Jackson) was born 2 Sep 1922.

Reva married **Willie Burton GREGORY** on 12 Apr 1941. Willie died 18 Jan 1945.

Reva also married **Raymond ADKINS** on 24 Feb 1946.

They had the following children:

+ 114 F i. **Jeanie Merea ADKINS** was born 17 Nov 1946.

+ 115 M ii. **Roy Lee ADKINS** was born 16 Apr 1949.

+ 116 F iii. **Janet Faye ADKINS**.

31. **Melva BARRICKMAN** (Dochie Eva BOWYER, Emory Jackson) was born 7 Dec 1927.

Melva married (1) **James Madison HAMRICK**. James was born 17 Oct 1921. He died 10 Sep 1977.

They had the following children:

+ 117 M i. **James M. HAMRICK Jr.** was born 8 Dec 1946 and died 20 Feb 1972.

+ 118 F ii. **Patricia Ann HAMRICK** was born 2 Sep 1948.

+ 119 M iii. **Ken Lawrence HAMRICK** was born 11 Jan 1954.

Melva also married **John F. FUCHS** on 21 Jul 1979. John was born 21 Feb 1922.

32. **Lounette BARRICKMAN** (Dochie Eva BOWYER, Emory Jackson) was born 23 Dec 1929.

Lounette married **Dale CLINTON** on 25 Feb 1950. Dale was born 20 Oct 1929.

They had the following children:

+   120   M   i.   **Dale M. CLINTON** was born 26 Jul 1951.

+   121   M   ii.   **Stuart L. CLINTON** was born 30 Oct 1952.

      122   M   iii.   **Darryl R. CLINTON** was born 4 Oct 1960.

33. **Hilda Phyllis BARRICKMAN** (Dochie Eva BOWYER, Emory Jackson) was born 10 Feb 1933.

Hilda married **James Stephen WILLIAMS**.

They had the following children:

+   123   F   i.   **Diane Sherrill WILLIAMS** was born 30 Sep 1955.

      124   F   ii.   **Debra Jean WILLIAMS** was born 18 Sep 1958.

      125   M   iii.   **Stephen David WILLIAMS** was born 12 Nov 1959.

47. **Leonard DYER** (Reatha Leone BOWYER, Emory Jackson) was born 14 Aug 1924.

Leonard married **Elizabeth CARTER** on Aug 1946.

They had the following children:

      126   M   i.   **Durwin Lee DYER** was born 29 Oct 1950.

      127   M   ii.   **Norris DYER** was born 18 Jun 1953.

      128   M   iii.   **Gordon Leonard DYER**.

Leonard also married **Minnie UNKNOWN**.

48. **Velda Lee DYER** (Reatha Leone BOWYER, Emory Jackson) was born 7 Dec 1926.

Velda married **Kenneth TAYLOR** on 31 Jan 1950. Kenneth was born 20 Dec 1921.

They had the following children:

      129   M   i.   **Kenneth TAYLOR Jr.** was born 27 Nov 1951.

                Kenneth married **Kathryn Lynne**

HERRINGTON.

+   130   M   ii.   **Jeffrey B. TAYLOR** was born 23 Feb 1959.

49. **Edsel Verl DYER** (Reatha Leone BOWYER, Emory Jackson) was born 14 Aug 1924.

Edsel married **Clara June KING** on 31 Jul 1949. Clara was born 29 Jun 1927.

They had the following children:

+   131   M   i.   **Timothy Verl DYER** was born 9 Sep 1951.

+   132   F   ii.   **Julie Ann DYER** was born 21 Feb 1962.

50. **Opaline Leona DYER** (Reatha Leone BOWYER, Emory Jackson) was born 28 Mar 1931.

Opaline married **Earl H. DEAN** on 31 Jan 1950. He died 21 Oct 1996.

They had the following children:

+   133   F   i.   **Brenda Kay DEAN** was born 1 Jun 1951.

+   134   F   ii.   **Joan Denise DEAN** was born 9 Jun 1953.

+   135   M   iii.   **Hermit Earl DEAN** was born 26 Aug 1954.

  136   M   iv.   **Wendell Lee DEAN** was born 27 Mar 1956. He died 27 Mar 1956.

+   137   F   v.   **Sandra Lou DEAN** was born 16 Jun 1957.

+   138   F   vi.   **Darlene Sue DEAN** was born 17 Jan 1959.

  139   M   vii.   **Richard DEAN** "Ricky" was born 7 Dec 1961.

+   140   F   viii.   **Lisa Jean DEAN** was born 1 Nov 1963.

+   141   F   ix.   **Nancy Jane DEAN** was born 2 Feb 1964.

She also married **"Bud" PRINCE** 12 Apr 2002.

51. **Ellwood Jackson DYER** (Reatha Leone BOWYER, Emory Jackson) was born 19 Jul 1933.

Ellwood married **Wilma STULL**.

They had the following children:

142 M   i. **Howard G. DYER.**

+ 143 M ii. **Ellwood J. DYER Jr.** died 5 Nov 1981.

144 M iii. **Robert DYER.**

145 M iv. **Ronald DYER.**

146 M v. **Michael DYER.**

52. **Ila DYER** (Reatha Leone BOWYER, Emory Jackson) was born 13 Jul 1935.

Ila married **Marvin J. QUEEN.**

They had the following children:

147 M i. **George QUEEN** was born 6 May 1951.

148 F ii. **Vickie Lynne QUEEN** was born 17 Nov 1952.

149 M iii. **Alvin QUEEN** was born 5 May 1954.

150 F iv. **Lyanna QUEEN** was born 11 Dec 1956.

151 M v. **Willard QUEEN** was born 15 Sep 1957.

Ila also married **Leslie PATTERSON.**

They had the following child:

152 M vi. **Leslie V. PATTERSON.**

53. **Freda Belle DYER** (Reatha Leone BOWYER, Emory Jackson) was born 24 Dec 1937.

Freda married **Arthur VINCENT.**

54. **Wilma Mae DYER** "Billie" (Reatha Leone BOWYER, Emory Jackson) was born 8 Jul 1940.

Billie married **William F. SANDS** on 25 Jan 1956.

They had the following children:

153 M i. **Michael Eugene SANDS** was born 10 Feb 1957.

154 M ii. **Richard David SANDS** was born 12 Oct

1960.

155　F　　iii.　**Tiffany SANDS** was born 1978.

55. **Karen DYER** (Reatha Leone BOWYER, Emory Jackson) was born 21 Jun 1945.

Karen married **Rondal SLAUGHTER** on Jun 1963.

They had the following child:

156　F　　i.　**Katrina Dawn SLAUGHTER** was born 19 Sep 1966.

59. **Mary Sue KERNS** (Winnie Letalia BOWYER, Emory Jackson) was born 21 Jan 1936.

Mary married **Earl William HANKS** Earl was born 14 Sep 1935.

They had the following child:

157　F　　i.　**Christy Lane HANKS** was born 25 Dec 1963.

Mary also married **Cyril Laking CARR Jr.**. Cyril was born 3 May 1928.

60. **Patricia Leigh KERNS** (Winnie Letalia BOWYER, Emory Jackson) was born 6 Aug 1941.

Patricia married **George Thomas PATE III**.

They had the following child:

158　F　　i.　**Patricia Lynne PATE** was born 23 Jul 1967.

62. **James Coy BOWYER** (Delbert Carris, Emory Jackson) was born 4 Sep 1936.

James married **Patrica Lou ROONEY** on 2 Aug 1958.

They had the following child:

+　159　F　　i.　**Beverly Ann BOWYER** was born 4 Apr 1961.

James also married **Anita Louise TRIBUZIO** on 20 May 1966.

They had the following children:

160　F　ii.　**Linda Sue BOWYER** was born 10 May 1967.

161　M　iii.　**James C. BOWYER** was born 6 May 1968.

162　M　iv.　**Michael John BOWYER** was born 6 Aug 1974.

64. **Chester Duane BOWYER** (Delbert Carris, Emory Jackson) was born 29 Sep 1940.

Chester married **Ronna Lee HUFFMAN** on 12 Dec 1964. Ronna was born 7 Feb 194?.

They had the following children:

163　M　i.　**Brent Duane BOWYER** was born 7 Mar 1973.

164　F　ii.　**Christie Lynn BOWYER** was born 23 Dec 1975.

65. **Dale Lane BOWYER** (Delbert Carris, Emory Jackson) was born 26 Oct 1942.

Dale married **Mary G. COLEMAN** on 11 Jul 1971.

They had the following children:

165　M　i.　**Dale Lane BOWYER** was born 6 Dec 1973.

166　F　ii.　**Lora Lee BOWYER** was born 1 Jan 1975.

167　F　iii.　**Heather Susanne BOWYER** was born 7 Feb 1980.

168　F　iv.　**Summer Ashton BOWYER** was born 21 Sep 1989. She died 21 Sep 1989.

67. **Velloma Mae GARRISON** (Loma Ella BOWYER, Emory Jackson) was born 1936.

Velloma married **Unknown DAVIS**.

They had the following child:

169　F　i.　**Debbie DAVIS**.

68. **Mozelle GARRISON** (Loma Ella BOWYER, Emory Jackson) was born 1937.

Mozelle married **Bob LAMBERT**.

They had the following child:

   170 F   i. **Sherry LAMBERT**.

Mozelle also married **UNKNOWN**.

They had the following children:

   171 M   ii. **Derek DANNER**.

   172 M iii. **Derek DANNER**.

   173 M iv. **Mark DANNER**.

69. **Avalon Elouise GARRISON** (Loma Ella BOWYER, Emory Jackson) was born 1940.

Avalon married **Unknown DUNCAN**.

They had the following children:

   174 M   i. **Charles DUNCAN**.

   175 F   ii. **Josephine DUNCAN**.

   176 F iii. **Tootie DUNCAN**.

70. **Dahline Nadine GARRISON** (Loma Ella BOWYER, Emory Jackson) was born 1941.

Dahline married **Unknown HILTON**.

They had the following children:

   177 F   i. **Audrey HILTON**.

   178 M   ii. **Donny CHURCH**.

71. **Jo La Green GARRISON** (Loma Ella BOWYER, Emory Jackson) was born 1943.

Jo married **Unknown HARRIS**.

They had the following children:

   179 F   i. **Shelly HARRIS**.

180 M ii. **Billy Jo HARRIS**.

72. **Lane Lynn GARRISON "Dewey"** (Loma Ella BOWYER, Emory Jackson) was born 1947.

Dewey married **UNKNOWN**.

They had the following children:

181 M i. **Lane GARRISON "Jr."**.

182 F ii. **Lavonna GARRISON**.

73. **Helen PERKINS** (Wilma Gertrude BOWYER, Emory Jackson).

Helen married **Phillip CONLEY**.

They had the following children:

183 M i. **Roy CONLEY**.

184 F ii. **Rosemarie CONLEY**.

185 F iii. **Wilma Lee CONLEY**.

186 F iv. **Alice Faye CONLEY**.

187 F v. **Amy Rebecca CONLEY**.

74. **Alberta Bell PERKINS** (Wilma Gertrude BOWYER, Emory Jackson) was born 20 Sep 1941.

Alberta married **James ELKINS**.

They had the following children:

188 F i. **Stepheny ELKINS**.

189 F ii. **Regina ELKINS**.

76. **Robert Bowyer MOORE** (Grace Mildred BOWYER, Emory Jackson) was born 16 Feb 1943. He died 3 Oct 1975.

Robert married **Phyliss Ann ROBISON**. Phyliss was born 19 Oct 19??.

They had the following child:

+ 190 M i. **Robert Lane MOORE** was born 7 Jun 1964.

77. **Jeffrey MOORE** (Grace Mildred BOWYER, Emory

Jackson) was born 20 Nov 1947.

Jeffrey married **Irene KANE**. Irene was born 21 Mar 1947.

They had the following children:

  191 M   i. **Jeffrey B. MOORE Jr.** was born 14 Apr 1968.

  192 M   ii. **William Joseph MOORE** was born 9 Aug 1970.

  193 M iii. **Adam Reed MOORE** was born 8 Sep 1980.

78. **Gary Bruce MOORE** (Grace Mildred BOWYER, Emory Jackson) was born 6 Aug 1949.

Gary married **Mary Ellen CHRISTIE**. Mary was born 19 Jul 1949.

Gary also married **Susan Michelle CROY**. Susan was born 24 Jul 1958.

They had the following children:

  194 M   i. **Gary B. MOORE Jr.** was born 3 Jul 1972.

  195 M   ii. **Mark Ashley MOORE** was born 17 May 1976.

Fourth Generation

80. **Kathryn Elaine WALTERS** (Wandah EXLINE, Elma Ocie BOWYER, Emory Jackson) was born 19 Mar 1937.

Kathryn married **Alex Joseph PARACSI** on 21 Dec 1958. Alex was born 20 Jan 1939.

They had the following children:

  196 F   i. **Lisa Lynn PARACSI** was born 19 Feb 1964.

                 Lisa married **Todd HAMMER** on 22 Apr 1989. Todd was born 31 Mar 1962.

  197 M   ii. **Alex Jon PARACSI** was born 6 Jan 1967.

82. **David Noel BOSLEY** (Edna Marie EXLINE, Elma Ocie BOWYER, Emory Jackson) was born 25 Dec 1947.

David married **Lisa UNKNOWN**.

They had the following children:

198 F   i. **Rebeccah BOSLEY**.

199 M ii. **Aaron BOSLEY**.

85. **Roy Henry Lott EXLINE** (Roy Dowe EXLINE, Elma Ocie BOWYER, Emory Jackson) was born 23 Dec 1950.

Roy married **Patricia WHITCHURCH** on 20 Apr 1974. Patricia was born 7 Jul 1954.

They had the following children:

200 M   i. **Michael L. EXLINE** was born 7 May 1975.

201 F   ii. **Jessica Ann EXLINE** was born 10 Dec 1976.

202 M iii. **Jared C. EXLINE** was born 21 Jan 1978.

203 F   iv. **Megan Beth EXLINE** was born 18 Jul 1981.

Roy also married **Karen PATTERSON** on 7 Oct 1989.

86. **Christopher Perry EXLINE** (Roy Dowe EXLINE, Elma Ocie BOWYER, Emory Jackson) was born 24 Aug 1956.

Christopher married **Susan Clair BUCHNER** on 14 Aug 1956. Susan was born 12 Nov 1951.

They had the following children:

204 M   i. **Christopher Allen EXLINE** was born 30 Nov 1983.

205 F   ii. **Laura Nell EXLINE** was born 9 Jul 1985.

206 M iii. **William F. EXLINE** was born 6 Mar 1989.

87. **Pamela ROBERTSON** (Freda Muriel EXLINE, Elma Ocie BOWYER, Emory Jackson) was born Jan 1946.

Pamela married **Jack BOGGS** on 1965.

They had the following children:

207 M i. **Michael BOGGS**.

208 F ii. **Julie BOGGS**.

Pamela also married **Breese BRINEGER**.

88. **Susan Marie HARRIS** (Wade Cameron HARRIS, Lela Ocie BOWYER, Emory Jackson) was born 16 Jun 1953.

Susan married **Charles SMITH**.

They had the following child:

209 F i. **April M. SMITH** was born Apr 1967.

93. **Linda L. HARRIS** (Eugene Neuman HARRIS, Lela Ocie BOWYER, Emory Jackson) was born 24 Nov 1946.

Linda married **Don GARRETTE**.

They had the following child:

210 F i. **Leila D. GARRETTE** was born 23 Dec 1967.

Linda also married **Frank BERGMAN**. Frank was born 2 Feb 1953.

They had the following children:

211 F ii. **Becky L BERGMAN** was born 18 Dec 1981.

212 M iii. **Justin S. BERGMAN** was born 26 Dec 1985.

94. **Betty Jean HARRIS** (Eugene Neuman HARRIS, Lela Ocie BOWYER, Emory Jackson) was born 2 Dec 1947.

Betty married **Eugene J. LICCARDI**. Eugene was born 20 Apr 1946.

They had the following children:

213 F i. **Girl LICCARDI** was born Dec 1963. She died Dec 1963.

+ 214 M ii. **James P. LICCARDI** was born 5 Apr 1968.

+ 215 M iii. **Barry D. LICCARDI**.

95. **Roy E. HARRIS** (Eugene Neuman HARRIS, Lela Ocie BOWYER, Emory Jackson).

Roy married **Kathy M. UNKNOWN**. Kathy was born 20 Dec 1961.

They had the following children:

216 F   i.   **Missie HARRIS** was born 19 Dec 19??.

217 F   ii.   **Malinda HARRIS** was born 13 Oct 1978.

218 F   iii.   **Kirsty HARRIS** was born 8 Jun 1979.

219 M   iv.   **Boy HARRIS** was born 198?.

Roy also married **Gail UNKNOWN**.

96. **Marilyn Kay HARRIS** (Arthur Paul HARRIS, Lela Ocie BOWYER, Emory Jackson).

Marilyn married **UNKNOWN**.

They had the following children:

220 M   i.   **Boy (twins) UNKNOWN**.

221 F   ii.   **Girl UNKNOWN**.

100.   **William Gale ROBINSON** (Margaretta Marie HARRIS, Lela Ocie BOWYER, Emory Jackson) was born 1949.

William married **Nancy KINCADE**.

They had the following children:

222 M   i.   **Michael Allen ROBINSON**.

223 M   ii.   **Patrick Allen ROBINSON**.

224 F   iii.   **Marcy Lyne ROBINSON**.

William also married **Cindy UNKNOWN**.

William also married **Teresa UNKNOWN**.

101.   **Larry Jo ROBINSON** (Margaretta Marie HARRIS, Lela Ocie BOWYER, Emory Jackson).

Larry married **WALTERS**.

They had the following child:

225 M   i.   **Larry Bruce ROBINSON**.

104.   **Hope Marie ROBINSON** (Margaretta Marie HARRIS, Lela Ocie BOWYER, Emory Jackson).

Hope married **James Daniel MCHUGH**.

They had the following children:

226 F   i.   **Stacy Lee MCHUGH** was born 1978.

227 M   ii. **Steven Daniel MCHUGH** was born 1979.

Hope also married **Michael KORAL**.

They had the following children:

228 F   iii. **Sarah Marie KORAL** was born 1984.

229 M   iv. **Joseph Michael KORAL** was born 22 Jan 1987.

230 M   v.   **Michael John KORAL** was born 18 Jun 1988.

231 M   vi. **David Phillip KORAL** was born Oct 1989.

232 M   vii. **Michael KORAL** was born 1990. He died 1990 at birth.

105.   **Jack Eugene CARTER** (Mary Louise HARRIS, Lela Ocie BOWYER, Emory Jackson) was born 11 Jul 1961.

Jack married **Sherrie Lynn LAKE**.

They had the following children:

233 F   i.   **Samantha Marie CARTER** was born 11 May 1988.

234 F   ii. **Brittany Nicole CARTER** was born 23 Feb 1991.

106.   **Tamara Louise CARTER** (Mary Louise HARRIS, Lela Ocie BOWYER, Emory Jackson) was born 12 Jun 1962.

Tamara married **Jason DUTTER**.

Tamara also married **Brian JENNINGS**.

They had the following children:

235 M   i.   **Benjamin David JENNINGS** was born 5

Aug 1985.

236 M ii. **Jonathan Thomas JENNINGS** was born 23 May 1989.

109. **Scarlett MURPHY** (Velma Annette BARRICKMAN, Dochie Eva BOWYER, Emory Jackson) was born 24 Jul 1943.

Scarlett married **Unknown STOUGH**.

They had the following child:

237 M i. **Ryan Adali STOUGH** was born 12 Mar 1971.

110. **Sandra MURPHY** (Velma Annette BARRICKMAN, Dochie Eva BOWYER, Emory Jackson) was born 16 Oct 1946.

Sandra married **Unknown CLARK**.

She had the following child:

238 M i. **Brian Michael FLEMING** was born 15 May 1972.

111. **Michael James MURPHY** (Velma Annette BARRICKMAN, Dochie Eva BOWYER, Emory Jackson) was born 30 Jan 1948.

Michael married **UNKNOWN**.

They had the following children:

239 M i. **Michael Shawn MURPHY** was born 26 May 1969.

240 M ii. **Jason James MURPHY** was born 7 Jul 1976.

112. **Mark Andrew MURPHY** (Velma Annette BARRICKMAN, Dochie Eva BOWYER, Emory Jackson) was born 5 Jan 1951. He died 12 Mar 1976.

Mark married **UNKNOWN**.

They had the following child:

241 M i. **Mark Andrew MURPHY Jr.** was born 14 Dec 1970.

114. **Jeanie Merea ADKINS** (Reva Mae BARRICKMAN, Dochie Eva BOWYER, Emory Jackson) was born 17 Nov 1946.

Jeanie married **Robert H. CANGIALOSI** on 24 Feb 1968.

They had the following children:

+ 242 F i. **Catherine Marie CANGIALOSI** was born 3 Sep 1968.

243 M ii. **Scott Robert CANGIALOSI** was born 5 Feb 1971.

244 M iii. **Alex Gregory CANGIALOSI** was born 25 Jun 1976.

115. **Roy Lee ADKINS** (Reva Mae BARRICKMAN, Dochie Eva BOWYER, Emory Jackson) was born 16 Apr 1949.

Roy married **Mary Ellen MURPHY** on 17 Jun 1978.

They had the following child:

245 F i. **Yvonne Leslie ADKINS** was born 8 Jun 1981.

116. **Janet Faye ADKINS** (Reva Mae BARRICKMAN, Dochie Eva BOWYER, Emory Jackson).

Janet married **Paul SABINA**.

They had the following child:

246 F i. **Tanya SABINA** was born 6 Apr 1972.

Janet also married **N. L. MORRISON** "Pete".

They had the following child:

247 F ii. **Reva Loraine MORRISON** was born 10 Feb 1974.

117. **James M. HAMRICK Jr.** (Melva BARRICKMAN, Dochie Eva BOWYER, Emory Jackson) was born 8 Dec 1946. He died 20 Feb 1972.

James married **Cheryl MCLAVE** on 1969.

They had the following child:

248 M   i. **James M. HAMRICK III** was born 5 Jul 1970.

118. **Patricia Ann HAMRICK** (Melva BARRICKMAN, Dochie Eva BOWYER, Emory Jackson) was born 2 Sep 1948.

Patricia married **Glen William CRAIG** on 8 Mar 1967.

They had the following child:

+ 249 F   i. **Vickie Lee CRAIG** was born 8 Jun 1969.

119. **Ken Lawrence HAMRICK** (Melva BARRICKMAN, Dochie Eva BOWYER, Emory Jackson) was born 11 Jan 1954.

Ken married **Angelika KRELLER** on 30 Jun 1978.

They had the following children:

250 F   i. **Marissa Mary HAMRICK** was born 24 Nov 1981.

251 F   ii. **Vanessa Lynn HAMRICK** was born 8 Aug 1985.

120. **Dale M. CLINTON** "Spyke" (Lounette BARRICKMAN, Dochie Eva BOWYER, Emory Jackson) was born 26 Jul 1951.

Spyke married **Kathryn JOHNSON**. Kathryn was born 15 Aug 1953.

They had the following children:

252 F   i. **Kristine CLINTON** was born 9 Jul 1976.

121. **Stuart L. CLINTON** (Lounette BARRICKMAN, Dochie Eva BOWYER, Emory Jackson) was born 30 Oct 1952.

Stuart married **Angela DOURLEY**. Angela was born 15 Apr 1956.

They had the following children:

253 F   i.   **Laura Elizabeth CLINTON** was born 28 Nov 1981.

254 M   ii.   **Ian Stuart CLINTON** was born 29 Jun 1984.

123.   **Diane Sherrill WILLIAMS** (Hilda Phyllis BARRICKMAN, Dochie Eva BOWYER, Emory Jackson) was born 30 Sep 1955.

Diane married **Donald Lee MOUNT** on 2 Feb 1974.

They had the following child:

255 F   i.   **Bonnie Shenill MOUNT** was born 21 Jun 1982.

130.   **Jeffrey B. TAYLOR** (Velda Lee DYER, Reatha Leone BOWYER, Emory Jackson) was born 23 Feb 1959.

Jeffrey married **Sherry Lee ARMSTEAD**.

They had the following children:

256 F   i.   **Stephanie Lynn TAYLOR**.

257 F   ii.   **Theresa Marie TAYLOR**.

258 M   iii.   **Clifton Charles TAYLOR**.

131.   **Timothy Verl DYER** (Edsel Verl DYER, Reatha Leone BOWYER, Emory Jackson) was born 9 Sep 1951.

Timothy married **Susan Carol PUGH**.

They had the following child:

259 M   i.   **Timothy Verl DYER Jr.** was born 1951.

132.   **Julie Ann DYER** (Edsel Verl DYER, Reatha Leone BOWYER, Emory Jackson) was born 21 Feb 1962.

Julie married **Baisil Monroe ROLAND**.

They had the following children:

260 M   i.   **Jeremy Allen ROLAND** was born 14 Aug 1983.

261 F   ii.   **Mendy Lee ROLAND** was born 7 Jun 1986.

133.   **Brenda Kay DEAN** (Opaline Leona DYER, Reatha

Leone BOWYER, Emory Jackson) was born 1 Jun 1951.

Brenda married **John TATER**.

They had the following child:

262　F　　i.　**Tammy TATER**.

Brenda also married **Michael KISH**.

134.　**Joan Denise DEAN** (Opaline Leona DYER, Reatha Leone BOWYER, Emory Jackson) was born 9 Jun 1953.

Joan married **Jerry MCMILLION**.

They had the following children:

263　M　　i.　**Eric MCMILLION**.

264　M　　ii.　**Regus MCMILLION**.

265　M　　iii.　**Joshua MCMILLION**.

135.　**Hermit Earl DEAN** (Opaline Leona DYER, Reatha Leone BOWYER, Emory Jackson) was born 26 Aug 1954.

Hermit married **Judy ARMSTRONG**.

They had the following child:

266　F　　i.　**Amber DEAN**.

137.　**Sandra Lou DEAN** (Opaline Leona DYER, Reatha Leone BOWYER, Emory Jackson) was born 16 Jun 1957.

Sandra married **Ellwood J. DYER Jr.**, son of Ellwood Jackson DYER and Wilma STULL, on 30 Jan 1976. Ellwood died 5 Nov 1981.

They had the following child:

267　M　　i.　**Richard DYER**.

138.　**Darlene Sue DEAN** (Opaline Leona DYER, Reatha Leone BOWYER, Emory Jackson) was born 17 Jan 1959.

Darlene married **Kenneth Lee SHEW**.

They had the following children:

268　　　i.　**Jessie SHEW**.

269 F   ii. **Amanda SHEW**.

270 F   iii. **Christy SHEW**.

140.   **Lisa Jean DEAN** (Opaline Leona DYER, Reatha Leone BOWYER, Emory Jackson) was born 1 Nov 1963.

Lisa married **Unknown BROWN**.

They had the following child:

271 M   i. **Shannon BROWN**.

141.   **Nancy Jane DEAN** (Opaline Leona DYER, Reatha Leone BOWYER, Emory Jackson) was born 2 Feb 1964.

Nancy married **Wayne VARWIG Sr**.

They had the following child:

272 M   i. **Wayne VARWIG Jr**.

143.   **Ellwood J. DYER Jr.** (Ellwood Jackson DYER, Reatha Leone BOWYER, Emory Jackson) died 5 Nov 1981.

Ellwood married **Sandra Lou DEAN**, daughter of Earl H. DEAN and Opaline Leona DYER, on 30 Jan 1976. Sandra was born 16 Jun 1957.

They had the following child:

273 M   i. **Richard DYER** is printed as #269 is the same child. The parents were first cousins.

159.   **Beverly Ann BOWYER** (James Coy, Delbert Carris, Emory Jackson) was born 4 Apr 1961.

Beverly married **Tony FALSETTA**.

They had the following child:

274 F   i. **Leah Justine WICKSTRON** was born 11 Feb 1987.

190.   **Robert Lane MOORE** (Robert Bowyer MOORE, Grace Mildred BOWYER, Emory Jackson) was born 7 Jun 1964.

Robert married **Rebecca Lynn JOHNS** on 1 Nov 1988.

They had the following child:

275　F　　i.　**Amber MOORE** was born 12 Sep 1989.

Fifth Generation

214.　**James P. LICCARDI** (Betty Jean HARRIS, Eugene Neuman HARRIS, Lela Ocie BOWYER, Emory Jackson) was born 5 Apr 1968.

James married **UNKNOWN**.

They had the following child:

276　M　　i.　**Aimie E. LICCARDI** was born 18 May 1986.

215.　**Barry D. LICCARDI** (Betty Jean HARRIS, Eugene Neuman HARRIS, Lela Ocie BOWYER, Emory Jackson).

Barry married **Kerry L. UNKNOWN**. Kerry was born 1 Aug 1971.

They had the following child:

277　M　　i.　**Nicholas A. LICCARDI** was born 17 Dec 1990.

242.　**Catherine Marie CANGIALOSI** (Jeanie Merea ADKINS, Reva Mae BARRICKMAN, Dochie Eva BOWYER, Emory Jackson) was born 3 Sep 1968.

Catherine married **UNKNOWN**.

They had the following children:

278　M　　i.　**Caine William CANGIALOSI** was born 25 Oct 1987.

279　F　　ii.　**Amber Marie CANGIALOSI** was born 25 Feb 1989.

249.　**Vickie Lee CRAIG** (Patricia Ann HAMRICK, Melva BARRICKMAN, Dochie Eva BOWYER, Emory Jackson) was born 8 Jun 1969.

Vickie married **UNKNOWN**.

Vickie also married **UNKNOWN**.

They had the following child:

280 F   i. **Teia Marie MOORE** was born 3 Feb 1987.

Descendants of

Washington Cicero Bowyer,
Mary Lowry and Eliza Queen

First Generation

1. **Washington Cicero BOWYER**[4] was born 1835 in Bath Township, Va. He died in Parkersburg, WV.

   Washington married **Mary J. LOWRY** on 12 Mar 1856 in Highland Co., Va. Mary was born 1838 in Highland Co., Va. She died ~1860.

   They had the following children:

      2 F   i. **Sarah S. J. BOWYER** was born 28 May 1857 in Back Creek, Highland Co., Va.. She died 11 Apr 1859 in Back Creek, Highland Co., Va.

      3 M   ii. **William O. BOWYER** was born 1860 in Highland Co., Va. He died before 1870.

   Washington also married **Eliza QUEEN** on 30 Jan 1862 in Harrison Co., (W)V. Eliza was born 1840 in Lewis Co., (W)V. She died ~1882.

James Benton and Charles Leonard Boyer

   They had the following children:

   +   4 M   iii. **James Benton BOYER** was born 5 Jan 1863 and died 3 Mar 1950.

   +   5 F   iv. **Rebecka BOWYER** was born 1866.

+   6 M   v.   **Charles Leonard BOYER** was born 2 Nov 1870 and died 12 Jul 1951.

+   7 F   vi.   **Virginia Ann BOWYER** was born 1872.

+   8 F   vii.   **Cora Beatrice BOWYER** was born 1876.

     9 F   viii.   **Docia Elizabeth BOWYER** was born 1878.

               Docia married **Eugene Augustus ALLEN** on 4 Jun 1901 in Wood Co., WV.

   10 M   ix.   **Edran E. BOWYER** was born 1882 in Horn Creek, Gilmer Co., WV. He died 12 Jan 1882 in Horn Creek, Gilmer Co., WV.

Second Generation

4. **James Benton BOYER** (Washington Cicero) was born 5 Jan 1863 in Clarksburg, (W)V. He died 3 Mar 1950 in Casper, Natrona, Wyoming.

James married **Ida Matilda BLANKENSHIP**, daughter of John BLANKENSHIP and Jane SARILDA, on 19 Jun 1889 in Cawker City, Mitchell, Kansas. Ida was born 23 Aug 1867 in Easton, Missouri. She died 25 Jun 1943 in Casper, Natrona, Wyoming.

They had the following children:

+   11 F   i.   **Stella Chloe BOYER** was born 15 Mar 1890.

+   12 M   ii.   **John Blankenship BOYER** was born 5 Aug 1892 and died 6 Mar 1939.

+   13 M   iii.   **Emile James BOYER** was born 18 Dec 1895.

+   14 M   iv.   **Stacy Everett BOYER** was born 8 Dec 1901 and died 12 Apr 1992.

   15 M   v.   **Dean Edward BOYER** was born 10 Oct 1905 in Wheatland, Platte, Wyoming. He

died 5 Jun 1928 in Rapid City, Pennington, South Dakota and was buried in Highland Park Cemetery, Casper, Wyoming.

James also married **May V. RUSH** on 1920 in Golden, Jefferson, Colorado. May was born 23 Jul 1888 in Crawford, Dawes, Nebraska. She died 1959 in Casper, WY.

5. **Rebecka BOWYER** (Washington Cicero) was born 1866 in WV.

Rebecka married **John WILLIAMS**.

They had the following children:

   16   F   i.   **Beatrice WILLIAMS**.

   17   F   ii.   **Nellie WILLIAMS**.

   18   F   iii.   **Dell Chloe WILLIAMS**.

   Dell married **C. BROOKOVER**.

   19   F   iv.   **Roma Eliza WILLIAMS**.

   Roma married **Ray MORRISON**.

   20   F   v.   **Mable Garnett WILLIAMS**.

   Mable married **Harry GUINN**.

6. **Charles Leonard BOYER** (Washington Cicero) was born 2 Nov 1870 in Parkersburg, WV. He died 12 Jul 1951 in Salina, Kansas and was buried 16 Jul 1951 in Gypsum Hill Cemetery, Salina, Kansas.

Charles married **Josephine Viola LOCKE**, daughter of Joseph LOCKE and Mary CLAMPETT. Josephine was born 10 Mar 1875 in Stockton, Seneca, Kansas. She died 24 Aug 1959 in Evergreen, Colorado and was buried in Gypsum Hill Cemetery, Salina, Kansas.

Josephine Locke and Charles Leonard Boyer

They had the following children:

Errol, Ethel, Cecil, Myrtle, Louise, Cleo   *Front row: Errol, Josephine, Cleo*

Second Row: Ethel, Cecil, Louise

21 F i. **Edith May BOYER** was born 24 Sep 1893 in Plainville, Kansas. She died 13 Oct 1893 in Plainville, Kansas and was buried in Mt. Vernon Cemetery.

22 M ii. **James Eustace BOYER** was born 5 May 1895 in Rooks Co., Webster (Stockton) Kansas. He died 18 Jan 1908 in Rooks Co., Webster (Stockton) Kansas and was buried 19 Jan 1908 in Mt Vernon Cemetery.

210

23 M iii. **Loydess Leonard BOYER** was born 1 Jan 1897 in Plainville, Kansas. He died 11 Jan 1897 in Plainville, Kansas.

+ 24 M iv. **Cleo Dewey BOYER** was born 7 Jul 1899 and died 29 May 1970.

+ 25 M v. **Erroll Ray BOYER** was born 18 Jul 1902 and died 19 Feb 1961.

+ 26 F vi. **Ethel Marie BOYER** was born 9 Jun 1905 and died 8 Jan 2001.

+ 27 F vii. **Cecil Beatrice BOYER** was born 16 Oct 1907 and died 9 Apr 2001.

28 M viii. **Charles Lee BOYER** was born 11 Jan 1910 in Rooks Co., Webster (Stockton) Kansas. He died 21 Jul 1956 in Hammond, Indiana and was buried in Roselawn Cemetery, Salina, Kansas.

Charles married **Opal Francis SCHAFF** on 5 May 1937 in Waukegan, Illinois. Opal was born 5 Jun 1915 in Chicago, Illinois. She died in Albany, Oregon and was buried 10 Oct 2001 in Roselawn Memorial Park, Salina, Kansas.

+ 29 F ix. **Myrtle Irene BOYER** was born 12 May 1913 and died 23 Mar 1990.

30 M x. **Wilber Muriele BOYER** was born 27 Jan 1916 in Plainville, Kansas. He died 27 Jan 1916.

+ 31 F xi. **Mary Louise BOYER**.

7. **Virginia Ann BOWYER** (Washington Cicero) was born 1872.

Virginia married **Alonzo MCCOY**.

They had the following children:

32 M i. **William R. MCCOY**.

33 F   ii. **Anna Marie MCCOY**.

Virginia also married **Earl PICKENS** on 4 Jun 1901.

They had the following child:

34 F   iii. **Ada May PICKENS**.

8. **Cora Beatrice BOWYER** (Washington Cicero) was born 1876.

Cora married **Andrew GIGER**.

They had the following children:

35 F   i. **Eleanor GIGER**.

36 F   ii. **Beatrice GIGER**.

Third Generation

11. **Stella Chloe BOYER** (James Benton BOYER, Washington Cicero) was born 15 Mar 1890 in Cawker City, Mitchell, Kansas.

Stella married **Marion Nye WHEELER**, son of Marion P. WHEELER, on 20 Jan 1914 in Gering, Scottsbluff, Nebraska. Marion was born 16 Jun 1889 in Johnstown, Brown, Nebraska. He died 23 Nov 1971 in Casper, Natrona, Wyoming.

They had the following child:

37 M   i. **Marion Bowyer WHEELER**.

12. **John Blankenship BOYER** (James Benton BOYER, Washington Cicero) was born 5 Aug 1892 in Stockton, Seneca, Kansas. He died 6 Mar 1939 in Laramie, Albeny, Wyoming and was buried 11 Mar 1939 in Casper, Natrona, Wyoming.

John married **Josephine WESTOVER**.

They had the following children:

38 F   i. **Elizabeth BOYER**.

39 F ii. **Stella BOYER**.

40 F iii. **Joanna BOYER**.

13. **Emile James BOYER** (James Benton BOYER, Washington Cicero) was born 18 Dec 1895 in Plainville, Kansas.

Emile married **Cora Leome HILL**. Cora was born 24 Apr 1905 in Buffalo, Johnson, Wyoming. She died 10 Sep 1952 in Imperial Beach, San Diego, California and was buried 15 Sep 1952 in Casper, Natrona, Wyoming.

Emile also married **Mary Louise GAMBRELL**, daughter of William GAMBRELL and Alice SIDDALL. Mary was born 15 Oct 1901 in Dallas, Texas.

They had the following child:

41 F i. **Mary Louise BOYER**.

14. **Stacy Everett BOYER** (James Benton BOYER, Washington Cicero) was born 8 Dec 1901 in Wheatland, Platte, Wyoming. He died 12 Apr 1992 in Casper, Natrona, Wyoming and was buried in Highland Park Cemetery, Casper, Wyoming.

Stacy married **Cornelia Abercrombia PRIVATE**.

They had the following children:

+ 42 F i. **Donna Jean BOYER** was born 19 Jul 1948 and died 2 Dec 1991.

+ 43 M ii. **Stacy James BOYER**.

Stacy also married **Mildred H. MORFORD** on 8 Sep 1923 in Casper, Natrona, Wyoming.

Stacy also married **Imogene Cora FIELDS** on 16 Jul 1946 in Douglas, Converse, Wyoming. Imogene was born 21 Jul 1920 in Garber, Garfield, Oklahoma. She died 4 Mar 1990 in Casper, Natrona, Wyoming and was buried in Highland Park Cemetery, Casper, Wyoming.

They had the following children:

44 F iii. **Donna Jean BOYER** was born 19 Jul 1948 in Casper, Natrona, Wyoming. She died 2 Dec 1991 in Casper, Natrona, Wyoming.

45 M iv. **Stacy James BOYER**.

24. **Cleo Dewey BOYER** (Charles Leonard BOYER, Washington Cicero) was born 7 Jul 1899 in Stockton, Seneca, Kansas. He died 29 May 1970 in Wichita, Kansas.

Cleo married **Ethel R. WOODARD**. Ethel was born 24 Apr in Illinois.

They had the following children:

+ 46 F i. **Geneva BOYER** was born 25 Jul 1912.

47 F ii. **Viola BOYER**.

48 F iii. **Katheryn BOYER**.

25. **Erroll Ray BOYER** (Charles Leonard BOYER, Washington Cicero) was born 18 Jul 1902 in Stockton, Seneca, Kansas. He died 19 Feb 1961 in Salina, Kansas and was buried in Roselawn Cemetery, Salina, Kansas.

Erroll married **Bessie L. HERRINGTON** on Aug 1924 in Abilene, Kansas. Bessie was born 14 Jun 1908 in Culver, Kansas. She died 1984 in Salina, Kansas and was buried in Roselawn Cemetery, Salina, Kansas.

They had the following children:

49 M i. **Erroll Ray BOYER** was born 5 Jan 1925 in Salina, Kansas. He died 24 May 1972 in Salina, Kansas and was buried in Roselawn Cemetery, Salina, Kansas.

Erroll married **Dolores KAMPE**.

26. **Ethel Marie BOYER** (Charles Leonard BOYER, Washington Cicero) was born 9 Jun 1905 in Stockton, Seneca, Kansas. She died 8 Jan 2001 in Carrollton, Texas and was buried 10 Oct 2001 in Roselawn Cemetery, Salina, Kansas.

Ethel married **Harry William HAGLER** on 3 Jul 1923 in Salina, Kansas. Harry was born 5 Jun 1901 in Salina, Kansas. He died 25 May 1960 in Salina, Kansas and was buried 28 May 1960 in Roselawn Cemetery, Salina, Kansas.

They had the following children:

+   50   M   i.   **Charles William HAGLER** was born 2 Mar 1924 and died 22 Mar 1971.

+   51   M   ii.   **Harry Robert HAGLER**.

27. **Cecil Beatrice BOYER** (Charles Leonard BOYER, Washington Cicero) was born 16 Oct 1907 in Seneca, Kansas. She died 9 Apr 2001 in Avery, North Carolina.

Cecil married **Victor Lyle FARTHING** on 29 Oct 1928 in Chicago, Illinois. Victor was born 2 Mar 1888. He died 28 Nov 1973 in Boone, North Carolina.

They had the following children:

+   52   M   i.   **Richard Lyle FARTHING** was born 3 Oct 1929 and died 11 Jun 1984.

     53   M   ii.   **Eugene Dewey FARTHING**.

29. **Myrtle Irene BOYER** (Charles Leonard BOYER, Washington Cicero) was born 12 May 1913 in Plainville, Kansas. She died 23 Mar 1990 in Tuson, Arizona.

Myrtle married **Edmund Dayhl SOPER** on 22 Mar 1931 in North Bend, Oregon. Edmund was born 13 Dec 1907 in Bay City, Oregon.

They had the following children:

+   54   M   i.   **Rex Dayhl SOPER**.

+   55   M   ii.   **George William SOPER**.

+   56   M   iii.   **Donald Lee SOPER**.

+   57   M   iv.   **Eulie Albert SOPER**.

31. **Mary Louise BOYER** (Charles Leonard BOYER, Washington Cicero).

Mary married **Edward MCCOLL**. Edward was born 8 Jun 1908 in Osborne, Kansas. He died 1990 in Oregon.

They had the following child:

+   58 F   i. **Joanna LaMarquis MCCOLL**.

Fourth Generation

42. **Donna Jean BOYER** (Stacy Everett BOYER, James Benton BOYER, Washington Cicero) was born 19 Jul 1948 in Casper, Natrona, Wyoming. She died 2 Dec 1991 in Casper, Natrona, Wyoming.

Donna married **Layman Ray CHRISTAIN Sr.** on 20 Sep 1974 in Casper, Natrona, Wyoming. Layman was born 19 Feb 1942 in Huntington, Cabell Co., West Virginia. He died 24 Aug 2000 in Elyria, Lorain, Ohio.

They had the following children:

    59 M   i. **James CHRISTAIN**.

    60 M   ii. **Daniel Ray CHRISTAIN**.

43. **Stacy James BOYER** (Stacy Everett BOYER, James Benton BOYER, Washington Cicero).

Stacy married **Linda Loann POKING**.

They had the following children:

+   61 M   i. **Stacy Allen BOYER**.

+   62 M   ii. **Sean Keith BOYER**.

46. **Geneva BOYER** (Cleo Dewey BOYER, Charles Leonard BOYER, Washington Cicero) was born 25 Jul 1912 in Moline, Illinois. She died in Salina, Kansas and was buried in Roselawn Cemetery, Salina, Kansas.

Geneva married **HOGAN**.

They had the following child:

    63 F   i. **Sandra HOGAN**.

Sandra married **GILBERT**.

50. **Charles William HAGLER** (Ethel Marie BOYER, Charles Leonard BOYER, Washington Cicero) was born 2 Mar 1924 in Salina, Kansas. He died 22 Mar 1971 in Hammond, Indiana.

Charles married **Marie JENNINGS**.

They had the following children:

+   64   M   i.   **Charles William HAGLER Jr.**.

+   65   M   ii.   **Richard HAGLER**.

+   66   F   iii.   **Cathryn HAGLER**.

51. **Harry Robert HAGLER** (Ethel Marie BOYER, Charles Leonard BOYER, Washington Cicero).

Harry married **Ailene June WOODRING**.

They had the following children:

   67   M   i.   **Michael Robert HAGLER** was born 26 Jul 1948 in Wichita, Kansas. He died 3 Apr 1990 in Kansas City, Missouri and was buried 6 Apr 1990 in Gypsum Hill Cemetery, Salina, Kansas.

   68   F   ii.   **Janette Lee HAGLER**.

       Janette married **Charles Calvin COLE**.

+   69   M   iii.   **Douglas Allen HAGLER**.

52. **Richard Lyle FARTHING** (Cecil Beatrice BOYER, Charles Leonard BOYER, Washington Cicero) was born 3 Oct 1929 in Chicago, Illinois. He died 11 Jun 1984 in Banner Elk, North Carolina and was buried 14 Jun 1984 in Mountlawn Memorial Park and Gardens.

Richard married **Jeanette WATSON**.

They had the following children:

   70   M   i.   **Rodney FARTHING**.

   71   M   ii.   **Steven FARTHING**.

54. **Rex Dayhl SOPER** (Myrtle Irene BOYER, Charles Leonard BOYER, Washington Cicero).

Rex married **Doris Dean HARPER**.

They had the following child:

    72 F   i. **Sean Elaine O'Neil SOPER**.

55. **George William SOPER** (Myrtle Irene BOYER, Charles Leonard BOYER, Washington Cicero).

George married **Gladys Rae SIMMONS**.

They had the following child:

    73 M   i. **John Edmund SOPER**.

George also married **Gloria Jean JOHNSON**.

They had the following children:

    74 M   ii. **Douglas William SOPER**.

    75 F   iii. **Belinda Jeanette SOPER**.

56. **Donald Lee SOPER** (Myrtle Irene BOYER, Charles Leonard BOYER, Washington Cicero).

Donald married **Darlene May CARTER**.

They had the following children:

    76 M   i. **Donald Lee SOPER Jr.**

    77 F   ii. **Deborah Ann SOPER**.

57. **Eulie Albert SOPER** (Myrtle Irene BOYER, Charles Leonard BOYER, Washington Cicero).

Eulie married **Gloria Marie DUNDING**.

They had the following children:

    78 M   i. **Edmund John SOPER**.

    79 F   ii. **Margaret Susanne SOPER**.

58. **Joanna LaMarquis MCCOLL** (Mary Louise BOYER, Charles Leonard BOYER, Washington Cicero).

Joanna married **Jack Wayne SCHROCK**.

They had the following children:

+ 80 F   i.   **Jody Ailene SCHROCK**.

+ 81 M   ii.   **John McColl SCHROCK**.

+ 82 M   iii.   **Joel Peter SCHROCK**.

Fifth Generation

61. **Stacy Allen BOYER** (Stacy James BOYER, Stacy Everett BOYER, James Benton BOYER, Washington Cicero).

Stacy married **Romona Joyce PRODUIT**.

They had the following children:

83 M   i.   **Jacob Dean BOYER**.

84 F   ii.   **Jada Daliene BOYER**.

62. **Sean Keith BOYER** (Stacy James BOYER, Stacy Everett BOYER, James Benton BOYER, Washington Cicero).

Sean married **Ashlee ROWLAND**.

They had the following child:

85 F   i.   **Cheleighn Breanne BOYER**.

64. **Charles William HAGLER Jr.** (Charles William HAGLER, Ethel Marie BOYER, Charles Leonard BOYER, Washington Cicero).

Charles married **Diane Emeline KAMRATH**.

They had the following child:

86 M   i.   **David Charles HAGLER**.

David married **Julie Anne SCOTT**.

65. **Richard HAGLER** (Charles William HAGLER, Ethel Marie BOYER, Charles Leonard BOYER, Washington Cicero).

Richard married **Nancy BROWN**.

They had the following child:

+   87 F   i. **Julie Ann HAGLER**.

Richard also married **Terri L. JONES.**

They had the following children:

    88 F   ii. **Dorothy Ann HAGLER** was born 12 Sep 1979. She died 13 Sep 1979.

    89 M iii. **Steven HAGLER**.

    90 M iv. **Robert HAGLER**.

66. **Cathryn HAGLER** (Charles William HAGLER, Ethel Marie BOYER, Charles Leonard BOYER, Washington Cicero).

Cathryn married **Robert B. LEOPOLD.**

They had the following child:

    91 F   i. **Maureen Ann LEOPOLD**.

69. **Douglas Allen HAGLER** (Harry Robert HAGLER, Ethel Marie BOYER, Charles Leonard BOYER, Washington Cicero).

Douglas married **Penny Lou WARD.**

They had the following children:

    92 F   i. **Candace Lee HAGLER**.

    93 F   ii. **Mindy Lou HAGLER**.

    94 F iii. **Ashley Marie HAGLER**.

    95 F   iv. **Lindsey Ann HAGLER**.

    96 F   v. **Grace Ailene HAGLER**.

80. **Jody Ailene SCHROCK** (Joanna LaMarquis MCCOLL, Mary Louise BOYER, Charles Leonard BOYER, Washington Cicero).

Jody married **James DAVIS.**

They had the following children:

    97 F   i. **Jessica Louise DAVIS**.

    98 M ii. **Joshua DAVIS**.

81. **John McColl SCHROCK** (Joanna LaMarquis MCCOLL, Mary Louise BOYER, Charles Leonard BOYER, Washington Cicero).

John married **Bobbi Jo HOLT.**

They had the following children:

99 F   i.   **Paige Elizabeth SCHROCK.**

100 F   ii.   **Andi Alese SCHROCK.**

John also married **Mary Lou MARTINEZ.**

82. **Joel Peter SCHROCK** (Joanna LaMarquis MCCOLL, Mary Louise BOYER, Charles Leonard BOYER, Washington Cicero).

Joel married **Katherine EVERSOLE.**

They had the following children:

101 F   i.   **Kirsten Brittany SCHROCK.**

102 M   ii.   **Jack Legare SCHROCK.**

Sixth Generation

87. **Julie Ann HAGLER** (Richard HAGLER, Charles William HAGLER, Ethel Marie BOYER, Charles Leonard BOYER, Washington Cicero).

Julie married **Douglas Michael CARPENTER.**

They had the following child:

103 M   i.   **Blake Michael CARPENTER.**

Descendants of

John and Nancy Bowyer Sholes

First Generation

1. **John Randolph SHOLES**[5] was born 1878. He died 1951.

Nancy Elizabeth Bowyer

John married **Nancy Elizabeth BOWYER**. She was born 13 Mar 1886. She died 8 Oct 1975.

They had the following children:

+   2   F   i.   **Minnie SHOLES** was born 22 Aug 1905 and died 1979.

+   3   M   ii.   **Okey Frank SHOLES** was born 1908 and died 1974.

     4   M   iii.   **Roy SHOLES** was born 1912.

          Roy married **Barbara Lee BERRY**. Barbara was born 1910. She died 1999.

+   5   F   iv.   **Juanita Mae SHOLES** was born 1924 and died 1994.

Second Generation

2. **Minnie SHOLES** (John Randolph) was born 22 Aug 1905. She died 1979.

Minnie married **Paul Davidson SANDS**. Paul was born 1904. He died 1968.

They had the following children:

+   6   F   i.   **Pauline SANDS** was born 1924 and died 2003.

+   7   M   ii.   **Richard Gene SANDS** was born 1929.

3. **Okey Frank SHOLES** (John Randolph) was born 1908. He died 1974.

Okey married **Ila Marie STOCKERT**. Ila was born 1913. She died 1994.

They had the following children:

+   8   M   i.   **James Robert SHOLES** was born 1931 and died 1984.

+   9   M   ii.   **John Edward SHOLES** was born 1935.

5. **Juanita Mae SHOLES** (John Randolph) was born 1924. She died 1994.

Juanita married **Conrad STINOGLE** "Connie". Connie was born 1914. He died 1967.

They had the following children:

+   10   M   i.   **Conrad John STINOGLE** was born 1945.

+   11   F   ii.   **Joyce Ann STINOGLE** was born 1951.

     12   F   iii.   **Nancy Jane STINOGLE** was born 1953.

            Nancy married **Jon HOUDYSCHELL**.

     13   F   iv.   **Barbara Elizabeth STINOGLE** was born 1955.

            Barbara married **David PETERS**. David was born 1955.

Third Generation

6. **Pauline SANDS** (Minnie SHOLES, John Randolph) was born 1924. She died 2003.

Pauline married **James Adrienne ROWELL**. James was born 1925.

They had the following children:

+   14 F   i. **Paula Adrienne ROWELL** was born 1957 and died 1982.

     15 M ii. **Robert J ROWELL** was born 1961.

             Robert married **Kim DALTON**.

7. **Richard Gene SANDS** (Minnie SHOLES, John Randolph) was born 1929.

Richard married **Blanche Marie SCHLATER**. Blanche was born 1928.

They had the following children:

+   16 M   i. **Michael Paul SANDS** was born 1951.

+   17 M ii. **Donald Richard SANDS** was born 1953.

     18 M iii. **Roy James SANDS** was born 1957.

+   19 F   iv. **Lee Ann SANDS** was born 1962.

+   20 M   v. **Mark Andrew SANDS** was born 1964.

+   21 F vi. **Lesa Marie SANDS** was born 1968.

8. **James Robert SHOLES** (Okey Frank, John Randolph) was born 1931. He died 1984.

James married **Catherine Grace MURPHY**. Catherine was born 1933.

They had the following children:

+   22 M   i. **Robert Perry SHOLES** was born 1950.

+   23 M ii. **Frank Dale SHOLES** was born 1952.

+   24 F iii. **Cathy Marie SHOLES** was born 1954.

James also married **Marie LNU**.

James also married **Charon LNU**.

James also married **Dorothy SMITH**. Dorothy was born

1932.

James also married **Sharon UNKNOWN**.

James also married **Sharon HARDEN**.

James also married **Sharon UNKNOWN**.

James also married **Sherry "HARDEN"**.

They had the following child:

+   25 M iv. **James Roland SHOLES** was born 1963.

9. **John Edward SHOLES** (Okey Frank, John Randolph) was born 1935.

John married **Katherine Edna MULLER**. Katherine was born 1936.

They had the following children:

+   26 F   i. **Dorothy Marie SHOLES** was born 1958.

+   27 F   ii. **Katherine Luellen SHOLES** was born 1961.

+   28 F   iii. **Patricia Ann SHOLES** was born 1962.

+   29 M iv. **John Edward SHOLES Jr.** was born 1964.

10. **Conrad John STINOGLE** (Juanita Mae SHOLES, John Randolph) was born 1945.

Conrad married **Sandra Lee VAN BREMAN**.

They had the following children:

+   30 F   i. **Dyana Renee STINOGLE** was born 1974.

     31 F   ii. **Karyn Anne STINOGLE** was born 1982.

11. **Joyce Ann STINOGLE** (Juanita Mae SHOLES, John Randolph) was born 1951.

Joyce married **Charles Eugene LIVINGSTON**. Charles was born 1948.

They had the following children:

+   32 F   i. **Tracie Jo LIVINGSTON** was born 1968.

+   33 M ii. **David Conrad LIVINGSTON** was born

1969.

+   34   F   iii.   Kimberly Ann LIVINGSTON was born 1971.

Fourth Generation

14. **Paula Adrienne ROWELL** (Pauline SANDS, Minnie SHOLES, John Randolph) was born 1957. She died 1982.

Paula married **Carey BURNS**.

They had the following child:

     35   M   i.   **James Westley BURNS** was born 1980.

16. **Michael Paul SANDS** (Richard Gene SANDS, Minnie SHOLES, John Randolph) was born 1951.

Michael married **Sylvia Ann DUCHAMP**. Sylvia was born 1953.

They had the following child:

     36   F   i.   **Michelle Marie SANDS** was born 1988.

17. **Donald Richard SANDS** (Richard Gene SANDS, Minnie SHOLES, John Randolph) was born 1953.

Donald married **Pennelope POLOMBO**. Pennelope was born 1953.

They had the following children:

     37   M   i.   **John Paul SANDS** was born 1979.

     38   M   ii.   **Bryan Richard SANDS** was born 1981.

19. **Lee Ann SANDS** (Richard Gene SANDS, Minnie SHOLES, John Randolph) was born 1962.

Lee married **Windell B. PHILLIPS**.

They had the following children:

     39   M   i.   **Windell Boughton PHILLIPS** was born 1982.

     40   M   ii.   **Richard PHILLIPS** was born 1983.

20. **Mark Andrew SANDS** (Richard Gene SANDS, Minnie SHOLES, John Randolph) was born 1962.

Mark married **Tandra HOLLIER**. Tandra was born 1966.

They had the following child:

    41 F   i. **Ashlee Elice SANDS** was born 1990.

21. **Lesa Marie SANDS** (Richard Gene SANDS, Minnie SHOLES, John Randolph) was born 1968.

Lesa married **John Mark OTTEN** "Jack". Jack was born 1968.

They had the following children:

    42 M   i. **John Mark OTTEN** was born 1998.

    43 M   ii. **Jacob Matthew OTTEN** was born 2002.

22. **Robert Perry SHOLES** (James Robert, Okey Frank, John Randolph) was born 1950.

Robert married **Sharon Marie PARNELL**. Sharon was born 1950.

They had the following children:

+   44 F   i. **Christi Renee SHOLES** was born 1970.

+   45 M   ii. **Cameron Wyatt SHOLES** was born 1972.

+   46 F   iii. **Amanda Alice SHOLES** was born 1976.

23. **Frank Dale SHOLES** (James Robert, Okey Frank, John Randolph) was born 1952.

Frank married **Shirley Mae PAGER**.

They had the following children:

+   47 M   i. **Frank Rocco SHOLES** was born 1974.

    48 M   ii. **Brandon Lee SHOLES** was born 1977.

Frank also married **Lorraine Alvina CLARK**. Lorraine was born 1953.

24. **Cathy Marie SHOLES** (James Robert, Okey Frank, John Randolph) was born 1954.

Cathy married **Steve Glen STANLEY**. Steve was born 1954.

They had the following children:

+   49   M   i.   **Jared Wayne STANLEY** was born 1973.

      50   F   ii.   **Nichole Lynne STANLEY** was born 1975.

      51   F   iii.   **Erin Marie STANLEY** was born 1979.

25. **James Roland SHOLES** (James Robert, Okey Frank, John Randolph) was born 1963.

James married **Kelly DESANTO**.

They had the following children:

      52   F   i.   **Madeline SHOLES** was born 1988.

      53   M   ii.   **Travis James SHOLES** was born 1990.

James also married **Stephanie EDGELL**. Stephanie was born 1963.

26. **Dorothy Marie SHOLES** (John Edward, Okey Frank, John Randolph) was born 1958.

Dorothy married **Eric Bruce WHIDDEN**.

Dorothy also married **Erwin John FRITZ** .

They had the following children:

      54   F   i.   **Gabrielle LeAnn FRITZ** was born 1984.

      55   F   ii.   **Tabitha Kristi FRITZ** was born 1986.

      56   M   iii.   **Joshua John FRITZ** was born 1988.

      57   M   iv.   **Jeremy Michael FRITZ** was born 1991.

27. **Katherine Luellen SHOLES** (John Edward, Okey Frank, John Randolph) was born 1961.

Katherine married **Paul Arthur PARKER**. Paul was born 1961.

They had the following children:

      58   M   i.   **Stephen Michael PARKER** was born 1987.

59 M ii. **Christopher Paul PARKER** was born 1992.

28. **Patricia Ann SHOLES** (John Edward, Okey Frank, John Randolph) was born 1962.

Patricia married **Charles Matthew ZEH**. Charles was born 1960.

They had the following children:

60 M i. **Matthew Charles ZEH** was born 1989.

61 F ii. **Elizabeth Kathryn ZEH** was born 1992.

Patricia also married **John Douglas STEWART**. John was born 1942.

29. **John Edward SHOLES Jr.** (John Edward, Okey Frank, John Randolph) was born 1964.

John married **Kimberly Carol LININGER**. Kimberly was born 1966.

They had the following children:

62 M i. **Tyler John SHOLES** was born 1997.

63 M ii. **Kyle Robert SHOLES** was born 1999.

30. **Dyana Renee STINOGLE** (Conrad John STINOGLE, Juanita Mae SHOLES, John Randolph) was born 1974.

She had the following child:

64 M i. **Kobie STINOGLE**.

32. **Tracie Jo LIVINGSTON** (Joyce Ann STINOGLE, Juanita Mae SHOLES, John Randolph) was born 1968.

Tracie married **James C. FITZWATER**.

They had the following children:

65 F i. **Tiffany Marie FITZWATER** was born 1990.

66 F ii. **Jamie Lynn FITZWATER** was born 1993.

33. **David Conrad LIVINGSTON** (Joyce Ann STINOGLE, Juanita Mae SHOLES, John Randolph) was born 1969.

David married **Leslie PURCIO**.

They had the following child:

    67 M   i. **David Conrad LIVINGSTON "II"** was born 1993.

34. **Kimberly Ann LIVINGSTON** (Joyce Ann STINOGLE, Juanita Mae SHOLES, John Randolph) was born 1971.

Kimberly married **Richard PARENTE**.

They had the following child:

    68 M   i. **Justin Anthony Lohr PARENTE** was born 2001.

Fifth Generation

44. **Christi Renee SHOLES** (Robert Perry, James Robert, Okey Frank, John Randolph) was born 1970.

Christi married **UNKNOWN**.

They had the following child:

    69 F   i. **Deanna Megan Tyler SHOLES** was born 1993.

Christi also married **UNKNOWN**.

They had the following children:

    70 M   ii. **Evan Blaine William SHOLES** was born 1990.

    71 M   iii. **Christopher Charles SHOLES** was born 1996.

45. **Cameron Wyatt SHOLES** (Robert Perry, James Robert, Okey Frank, John Randolph) was born 1972.

Cameron married (1) **Georgianna LNU**.

They had the following child:

    72 F   i. **Kyani Lorae SHOLES** was born 1992.

Cameron also married (2) **Candy LNU**.

They had the following child:

73 M ii. **Justin Edward Douglas SHOLES** was born 1990.

Cameron also married (3) **Deborah Kay MORGAN**. Deborah was born 1973.

They had the following child:

74 F iii. **Lacey Rae SHOLES** was born 1999.

46. **Amanda Alice SHOLES** (Robert Perry, James Robert, Okey Frank, John Randolph) was born 1976.

Amanda married **Laben STOUT**.

They had the following children:

75 F i. **Sherry Alice (Sholes) STOUT** was born 1997.

76 M ii. **Matthew Kane STOUT** was born 1999.

47. **Frank Rocco SHOLES** (Frank Dale, James Robert, Okey Frank, John Randolph) was born 1974.

Frank married **Yeoryia Athanasios TSIANOS**. Yeoryia was born 1972.

They had the following children:

77 F i. **Anastasia Julia SHOLES** was born 1994.

78 F ii. **Eleni Katherine SHOLES** was born 1997.

49. **Jared Wayne STANLEY** (Cathy Marie SHOLES, James Robert, Okey Frank, John Randolph) was born 1973.

Jared married (1) **Staci DARK**.

Jared also married (2) **Anna LOYD**. Anna was born 1970.

They had the following children:

79 F i. **Elizabeth Ashley STANLEY** was born 1996.

80 F ii. **Jillian Grace STANLEY** was born 1998.

81 F iii. **Vivian Blair STANLEY** was born 2001.

82 M iv. **Devon Glen STANLEY** was born 2002.

Descendants of

Harrison and Seba Brown Lowther

First Generation

1. **Harrison LOWTHER**[6] was born 21 Sep 1875. He died 13 Feb 1964.
   Harrison married **Seba Hester BROWN** the daughter of John Henry and Martha Jane Prince Brown.
   They had the following children:

   2 M   i.   **Harley Bestes LOWTHER** born 7 Apr 1904.
   He died Fall 1969.

   3 F   ii.   **Carrie Edith LOWTHER** born 21 Jan 1905. She died ~1995.

   4 F   iii.   **Erma Virginia LOWTHER** born 5 Oct 1907. She died ~1999.

   5 F   iv.   **Mary Eva LOWTHER** born 14 Feb 1908. She died 1930.

   6 F   v.   **Mabel Leola LOWTHER** born 16 Oct 1910. She died May 1968.

   7 M   vi.   **Unnamed infant** born 5 Dec 1911. He died 11 Dec 1911.

   8 F   vii.   **Marbie Edra LOWTHER** born 15 June 1917. She married **Felix R. TONKIN** 29 June 1949.

   9 M   vii.   **Ramey Harold LOWTHER** born 28 July 1919.

   10 F   viii.   **Martha Juanita LOWTHER** born 5 Oct 1921.

Descendants of

Peter Hardman II of
Peterman, Nicholas Hardman

First Generation

1. **Peter HARDMAN II**[7] (Peterman HARDMAN, Nicholas) was born 23 Jul 1776 in Harrison Co, (W)V. He died 30 Jul 1859 in Greene Co., Ohio.

Peter married **Margaret HACKER** on 5 Dec 1797/1798. Margaret was born 2 Nov 1776 in Harrison Co., (W)V. She died 5 Jul 1815 in Greene Co., Ohio.

They had the following children:

 2 F   i. **Sarah HARDMAN** was born 16 Sep 1798. She died 1833.

 3 F   ii. **Catherine HARDMAN** was born 16 Sep 1798.

 4 M   iii. **John HARDMAN** was born 20 Jan 1800. He died 3 May 1848.

+ 5 M   iv. **Henry HARDMAN** was born 10 Mar 1801 and died 14 Nov 1879.

 6 M   v. **Jonathan HARDMAN** was born 25 Jan 1803. He died 21 Jul 1886.

 7 M   vi. **Jacob W. HARDMAN** was born 25 Jan 1803. He died 21 Jul 1886.

 8 F   vii. **Elizabeth HARDMAN** was born 14 Mar 1806. She died 28 Dec 1878.

 9 F   viii. **Eliza HARDMAN** was born 21 Feb 1808. She died 16 Aug 1849.

 10 F   ix. **Margaret HARDMAN** was born 10 Nov 1810. She died 27 Jul 1847.

 11 M   x. **Nelson HARDMAN** was born 3 Jan 1813.

Second Generation

5. **Henry HARDMAN** (Peter, Peterman, Nicholas) was born 10 Mar 1801 in Harrison Co, (W)V. He died 14 Nov 1879 in Cedar Co., Iowa.

Henry married **Mary SEARLES** on 27 Nov 1821. Mary was born 18 Feb 1803 in Stuben Co., NY. She died 15 Sep 1872 in Cedar Co., Iowa.

They had the following children:

   12 F   i.   **Cynthia HARDMAN** was born 17 May 1823. She died 24 Apr 1867.

+ 13 M   ii. **Cordis HARDMAN** was born 29 Apr 1825 and died 25 Jan 1876.

   14 M   iii. **Cain HARDMAN** was born 22 Nov 1826. He died 1890.

   15 F   iv. **Sarah HARDMAN** was born 22 Oct 1832.

   16 M   v.   **Silas HARDMAN** was born 27 Mar 1839.

   17 F   vi. **Samantha HARDMAN** was born 31 Mar 1844. She died 27 Mar 1888.

Third Generation

13. **Cordis HARDMAN** (Henry, Peter, Peterman, Nicholas) was born 29 Apr 1825 in Clark Co., Ohio. He died 25 Jan 1876 in Cedar Co., Iowa.

Cordis married **Sarah Ann WISE** on 10 Apr 1845. Sarah was born 10 Mar 1827 in Union Co., Pennsylvania. She died 6 Jul 1909 in Iowa.

They had the following children:

+ 18 M   i.   **Nathaniel Marion HARDMAN** was born 5 Feb 1846 and died 22 Sep 1882.

   19 M   ii. **Henry HARDMAN**.

Henry married **Jane CANAAR**.

20 F iii. **Sophia HARDMAN** was born 13 Jul 1851 in Rochester, Cedar, Iowa. She died 20 Jun 1931 in Palto Alto, Mallard, Iowa.

Sophia married **Alexander Russel PEDEN** on 23 Nov 1869. Alexander was born 22 Feb 1844 in Somerset Co., Pennsylvania. He died 15 Jan 1927.

21 M iv. **Owen HARDMAN**.

Owen married **Ella CANAAR**.

Fourth Generation

18. **Nathaniel Marion HARDMAN** (Cordis Hardman, Henry, Peter, Peterman, Nicholas) was born 5 Feb 1846 in Rochester, Dedar, Iowa. He died 22 Sep 1882 in Downs, Osbourne, Kansas.

Nathaniel married **Ellen WILLFORD** on 1 Jan 1868. Ellen was born 26 Dec 1851 in Beloit, Greene Co., Wisconsin. She died 25 Mar 1917 in Downs, Osbourne, Kansas.

They had the following children:

+ 22 M i. **Marion Willford HARDMAN** was born 26 Aug 1869 and died 22 Mar 1945.

+ 23 F ii. **Ella May HARDMAN** died 16 Mar 1871.

24 F iii. **Jessie Blanche HARDMAN** was born 17 Jul 1873.

Jessie married **William E. HATCHER**.

+ 25 M iv. **Arthur Guy HARDMAN** was born 31 Jan 1875.

+ 26 M v. **Claude Leroy HARDMAN** was born 12 Aug 1877 and died 24 Dec 1942.

+ 27 F vi. **Suza Louise HARDMAN** was born 1 Sep

1879 and died 2 Sep 1945.

+ 28 F vii. **Leslye HARDMAN** was born 14 Jan 1882 and died 10 Aug 1974.

Fifth Generation

22. **Marion Willford HARDMAN** (Nathaniel Marion, Cordis Hardman, Henry, Peter, Peterman, Nicholas) was born 26 Aug 1869 in Cedar Co., Iowa. He died 22 Mar 1945 in Downs, Osbourne, Kansas.

Marion married **Geme EDICK** on 6 Mar 1895.

They had the following children:

29 M i. **Dwight Harrison HARDMAN** was born 19 Feb 1897. He died 29 Apr 1955.

Dwight married **Mabel PARKER**.

30 M ii. **Marion Willkins HARDMAN** was born 29 May 1900.

31 F iii. **Mary Isabel HARDMAN** was born 22 Sep 1906.

Mary married **Clarence SUTTER**.

Mary also married **Carl OGREN**.

23. **Ella May HARDMAN** (Nathaniel Marion, Cordis Hardman, Henry, Peter, Peterman, Nicholas) died 16 Mar 1871 in Downs, Osbourne, Kansas.

Ella married **John W. POISAL** on 1889.

They had the following children:

32 M i. **Lloyd Marion POISAL** was born 15 Mar 1891. He died 1906.

+ 33 F ii. **Dorothy Ellen POISAL** was born 18 Feb 1893.

+ 34 M iii. **Leland Stanford POISAL** was born 15 Feb

1896.

+   35 M iv. **Henry Dean POISAL** was born 23 Feb 1899.

    36 M v. **John Wilford POISAL** was born 27 Apr 1901.

John married **Ruth FOWLER**.

Ella also married **Oliver D. AYER**.

25. **Arthur Guy HARDMAN** (Nathaniel Marion, Cordis Hardman, Henry, Peter, Peterman, Nicholas) was born 31 Jan 1875 in Downs, Osbourne, Kansas.

Arthur married **Millie Lou HUFF**.

They had the following children:

+   37 F i. **Mildred Elizabeth HARDMAN** was born 8 Sep 1903.

+   38 M ii. **Lewis Arthur HARDMAN** was born 24 Oct 1908.

26. **Claude Leroy HARDMAN** (Nathaniel Marion, Cordis Hardman, Henry, Peter, Peterman, Nicholas) was born 12 Aug 1877 in Downs, Osbourne, Kansas. He died 24 Dec 1942 in Wakeeney, Trego, Kansas.

Claude married **Blanchie Margaret JOHNSTON**. Blanchie was born 27 Nov 1879. She died 1973.

They had the following children:

+   39 M i. **Robert Arthur HARDMAN** was born 4 Feb 1922 and died 12 Oct 1944.

+   40 F ii. **Margaret HARDMAN** was born 13 Aug 1901.

+   41 M iii. **John Marion HARDMAN** was born 13 Jun 1906.

+   42 M iv. **Claude Wilford HARDMAN** was born Oct 1909.

+ 43 M v. **Charles HARDMAN** was born 4 Feb 1922.

27. **Suza Louise HARDMAN** (Nathaniel Marion, Cordis Hardman, Henry, Peter, Peterman, Nicholas) was born 1 Sep 1879 in Downs, Osbourne, Kansas. She died 2 Sep 1945 in Downs, Osbourne, Kansas.

Suza married **Charles ARNOLD**.

They had the following children:

+ 44 F i. **Helen Louise ARNOLD** was born 17 Oct 1909.

+ 45 F ii. **Florence ARNOLD** was born 5 Oct 1911.

46 F iii. **Margaret ARNOLD** was born 24 Dec 1913. She died 1932.

+ 47 F iv. **Josephine ARNOLD** was born 28 Jun 1916.

+ 48 M v. **James Marion ARNOLD** was born 15 Jun 1919.

28. **Leslye HARDMAN** (Nathaniel Marion, Cordis Hardman, Henry, Peter, Peterman, Nicholas) was born 14 Jan 1882 in Downs, Osbourne, Kansas. She died 10 Aug 1974.

Leslye married **Leonard Edward WOMER**.

They had the following children:

49 F i. **Eleanor WOMER** was born 12 May 1912.

50 F ii. **Elizabeth Hulda WOMER** was born 27 Jul 1912 in Agra, Kansas. She died 8 Sep 2002 in Wichita, Kansas.

+ 51 F iii. **Virginia Dorothy WOMER** was born 27 May 1917.

Sixth Generation

33. **Dorothy Ellen POISAL** (Ella May HARDMAN, Nathaniel Marion, Cordis Hardman, Henry, Peter, Peterman, Nicholas) was born 18 Feb 1893.

Dorothy married **Hyrum TAYLOR**.

They had the following child:

> 52 M i. **Hyrum Douglas TAYLOR** was born 30 Aug 1932.

34. **Leland Stanford POISAL** (Ella May HARDMAN, Nathaniel Marion, Cordis Hardman, Henry, Peter, Peterman, Nicholas) was born 15 Feb 1896.

Leland married **Hazel WILDER**.

They had the following children:

+ 53 F i. **Doris LaVerne POISAL** was born 26 Jul 1920.

+ 54 F ii. **Grenice POISAL** was born Nov 1924.

35. **Henry Dean POISAL** (Ella May HARDMAN, Nathaniel Marion, Cordis Hardman, Henry, Peter, Peterman, Nicholas) was born 23 Feb 1899.

Henry married **Elsie PETERSON**.

They had the following children:

+ 55 F i. **Linda Mae POISAL** was born 18 Feb 1928.

56 F ii. **Marilyn Joyce POISAL** was born 21 Jul 1932.

37. **Mildred Elizabeth HARDMAN** (Arthur Guy, Nathaniel Marion, Cordis Hardman, Henry, Peter, Peterman, Nicholas) was born 8 Sep 1903.

Mildred married **Richard RANEY**.

They had the following child:

+ 57 M i. **Richard Hardman RANEY** was born 3 Jul 1928.

38. **Lewis Arthur HARDMAN** (Arthur Guy, Nathaniel Marion, Cordis Hardman, Henry, Peter, Peterman, Nicholas) was born 24 Oct 1908.

Lewis married **Marian RYAN**.

They had the following children:

+   58 F   i.   **Mary Lew HARDMAN** was born 28 Jul 1932.

    59 M   ii.   **Charles Arthur HARDMAN** was born 12 Dec 1937.

39. **Robert Arthur HARDMAN** (Claude Leroy, Nathaniel Marion, Cordis Hardman, Henry, Peter, Peterman, Nicholas) was born 4 Feb 1922 in Topeka, Kansas. He died 12 Oct 1944 in HCL, Belgium.

Robert married **June Maxine HARRIES** on Sep 1943. June was born 1 Jun 1922 in Wakeeney, Trego, Kansas. She died 26 Jun 1979.

They had the following child:

+   60 M   i.   **Robert Alan HARDMAN** was born 29 Jun 1944.

40. **Margaret HARDMAN** (Claude Leroy, Nathaniel Marion, Cordis Hardman, Henry, Peter, Peterman, Nicholas) was born 13 Aug 1901.

Margaret married **John KINKEL**.

They had the following children:

    61 M   i.   **John Franklin KINKEL** was born 20 Apr 1927.

              John married **Estelle HERBERT**.

    62 M   ii.   **Paul Douglas KINKEL** was born 24 Jul 1954.

41. **John Marion HARDMAN** (Claude Leroy, Nathaniel Marion, Cordis Hardman, Henry, Peter, Peterman, Nicholas) was born 13 Jun 1906.

John married **Merian BLANKENSHIP**.

They had the following children:

    63 F   i.   **Suzanne HARDMAN** was born 6 Oct 1934.

Suzanne married **Arthur Edward PETERSON**.

   64 F   ii. **Barbara HARDMAN** was born 8 Jan 1938.

42. **Claude Wilford HARDMAN** (Claude Leroy, Nathaniel Marion, Cordis Hardman, Henry, Peter, Peterman, Nicholas) was born Oct 1909.

Claude married **Marie SCHEIDER**.

They had the following children:

+   65 M   i. **Donald HARDMAN**.

43. **Charles HARDMAN** (Claude Leroy, Nathaniel Marion, Cordis Hardman, Henry, Peter, Peterman, Nicholas) was born 4 Feb 1922.

Charles married **June STEEPER**.

They had the following children:

   66 F   i. **Judy HARDMAN** was born 29 Jul 1948.

   67 M   ii. **Eric Robert HARDMAN** was born 20 Feb 1951.

   68 M iii. **Gary David HARDMAN** was born 30 Sep 1955.

44. **Helen Louise ARNOLD** (Suza Louise HARDMAN, Nathaniel Marion, Cordis Hardman, Henry, Peter, Peterman, Nicholas) was born 17 Oct 1909.

Helen married **Elmer ROUSEK**.

They had the following children:

+   69 F   i. **Rae Florence ROUSEK** was born 18 Jan 1931.

45. **Florence ARNOLD** (Suza Louise HARDMAN, Nathaniel Marion, Cordis Hardman, Henry, Peter, Peterman, Nicholas) was born 5 Oct 1911.

Florence married **Gordon BORCHERDING**.

They had the following child:

    70 M   i. **Dennis Doyle BORCHERDING** was born 24 Feb 1942.

47. **Josephine ARNOLD** (Suza Louise HARDMAN, Nathaniel Marion, Cordis Hardman, Henry, Peter, Peterman, Nicholas) was born 28 Jun 1916.

Josephine married **Paul ANGELL**.

They had the following children:

    71 M   i. **Lawrence Dean ANGELL** was born 10 Jul 1940.

    72 M   ii. **Roger Kent ANGELL** was born 24 Jul 1942.

    73 F   iii. **Margaret Dianne ANGELL** was born 22 Aug 1944.

    74 F   iv. **Paula Jo ANGELL** was born 6 Feb 1949.

    75 F   v. **Paulette Sue ANGELL** was born 23 Sep 1953.

48. **James Marion ARNOLD** (Suza Louise HARDMAN, Nathaniel Marion, Cordis Hardman, Henry, Peter, Peterman, Nicholas) was born 15 Jun 1919.

James married **Evelyn YOST** .

They had the following children:

    76 F   i. **Cheryl Lynne ARNOLD** was born 18 Jan 1947.

    77 M   ii. **James Stephen ARNOLD** was born 21 Apr 1949.

51. **Virginia Dorothy WOMER** (Leslye HARDMAN, Nathaniel Marion, Cordis Hardman, Henry, Peter, Peterman, Nicholas) was born 27 May 1917.

Virginia married **Harry GREGORY**.

They had the following children:

    78 M   i. **Lewis Dean GREGORY** was born 13 May

1953.

79 F   ii. **Charlotte Ann GREGORY** was born 15 May 1955.

Seventh Generation

53. **Doris LaVerne POISAL** (Leland Stanford POISAL, Ella May HARDMAN, Nathaniel Marion, Cordis Hardman, Henry, Peter, Peterman, Nicholas) was born 26 Jul 1920.

Doris married **Carl SALEEN**.

They had the following child:

80 M   i. **Kenneth Carl SALEEN** was born 18 Mar 1942.

54. **Grenice POISAL** (Leland Stanford POISAL, Ella May HARDMAN, Nathaniel Marion, Cordis Hardman, Henry, Peter, Peterman, Nicholas) was born Nov 1924.

Grenice married **Larry DISHER**.

They had the following children:

81 F   i. **Cheryl Ann DISHER** was born 27 Apr 1944.

82 M   ii. **Gary Morris DISHER** was born 11 Mar 1947.

83 M   iii. **Gregory Charles DISHER** was born 9 Mar 1948.

55. **Linda Mae POISAL** (Henry Dean POISAL, Ella May HARDMAN, Nathaniel Marion, Cordis Hardman, Henry, Peter, Peterman, Nicholas) was born 18 Feb 1928.

Linda married **Thomas NISSEN**.

They had the following children:

84 F   i. **Cynthia Ann NISSEN** was born 16 Apr 1950.

85 M   ii. **Dean Thomas NISSEN** was born 8 Dec

1952.

86   M   iii.   **Rory Shean NISSEN** was born 15 Apr 1955.

57. **Richard Hardman RANEY** (Mildred Elizabeth HARDMAN, Arthur Guy, Nathaniel Marion, Cordis Hardman, Henry, Peter, Peterman, Nicholas) was born 3 Jul 1928.

Richard married **Katherine LARSON**.

They had the following children:

87   F   i.   **Michelle RANEY** was born 5 Feb 1954.

88   M   ii.   **Richard Biscoe RANEY** was born 26 Nov 1955.

58. **Mary Lew HARDMAN** (Lewis Arthur, Arthur Guy, Nathaniel Marion, Cordis Hardman, Henry, Peter, Peterman, Nicholas) was born 28 Jul 1932.

Mary married **George CARNAHAN**.

They had the following child:

89   M   i.   **Stephen Gilbert CARNAHAN** was born 6 May 1956.

60. **Robert Alan HARDMAN** (Robert Arthur, Claude Leroy, Nathaniel Marion, Cordis Hardman, Henry, Peter, Peterman, Nicholas) was born 29 Jun 1944 in Hays, Ellis, Kansas.

Robert married **Neva Jean HILLMAN** on 1 May 1971. Neva was born 11 May 1949 in Wakeeney, Trego, Kansas.

They had the following children:

+   90   F   i.   **Cori HARDMAN** was born 17 Aug 1972.

+   91   F   ii.   **Rebecca Jo Rae HARDMAN** was born 29 Apr 1974.

+   92   M   iii.   **Mark Alan HARDMAN** was born 29 Apr 1976.

65. **Donald HARDMAN** (Claude Wilford, Claude Leroy, Nathaniel Marion, Cordis Hardman, Henry, Peter,

Peterman, Nicholas).

Donald married **UNKNOWN**.

They had the following children:

    93 M   i. **Christopher HARDMAN**.

    94   ii. **Living HARDMAN**.

69. **Rae Florence ROUSEK** (Helen Louise ARNOLD, Suza Louise HARDMAN, Nathaniel Marion, Cordis Hardman, Henry, Peter, Peterman, Nicholas) was born 18 Jan 1931.

Rae married **Gayle SPURGEON**.

They had the following children:

    95 M   i. **Terry Lee SPURGEON** was born 12 Feb 1948.

    96 M   ii. **Michael Patrick SPURGEON** was born 12 Dec 1949.

    97 M   iii. **Rory Marc SPURGEON** was born 6 Dec 1954.

Eighth Generation

90. **Cori HARDMAN** (Robert Alan, Robert Arthur, Claude Leroy, Nathaniel Marion, Cordis Hardman, Henry, Peter, Peterman, Nicholas) was born 17 Aug 1972 in Olathe, Johnson, Kansas.

Cori married **John SCRIVO**. John was born 14 Feb 1969.

They had the following children:

    98 F   i. **Nicole Marie SCRIVO** was born 16 Mar 1993 in Olathe, Johnson, Kansas.

    99 M   ii. **Anthony Dylan SCRIVO** was born 14 Apr 1994.

91. **Rebecca Jo Rae HARDMAN** (Robert Alan, Robert Arthur, Claude Leroy, Nathaniel Marion, Cordis Hardman, Henry,

Peter, Peterman, Nicholas) was born 29 Apr 1974 in Olathe, Johnson, Kansas.

Rebecca was not married to **John SHAW**. John was born 21 Jul 1967.

They had the following children:

100 M   i. **Matthew Alan Andrew HARDMAN** was born 23 Nov 1990 in Olathe, Johnson, Kansas.

Rebecca also married **Christopher Michael BUCKLEY** on 15 May 1993. The marriage ended in divorce. Christopher was born 24 Dec 1971.

They had the following children:

101 M   ii. **Jonathon August Frazier BUCKLEY** was born 28 Jul 1994 in Shawnee, Johnson, Kansas.

102 F   iii. **Allison Jo Rae BUCKLEY** was born 26 Oct 1995.

Rebecca also married **Phillip Joseph FIX** on 20 Oct 2001. Phillip was born 9 Dec 1970 in Ruislip, England.

92. **Mark Alan HARDMAN** (Robert Alan, Robert Arthur, Claude Leroy, Nathaniel Marion, Cordis Hardman, Henry, Peter, Peterman, Nicholas) was born 29 Apr 1976 in Olathe, Johnson, Kansas.

Mark married **Angela Sue DICKS**. Angela was born 30 Sep 1976.

They had the following child:

103 M   i. **Aiden Alan Glenn HARDMAN** was born 21 Jul 2003.

Descendants of

Earl and Lena Hamilton Hardman

First Generation

1. **Earl HARDMAN**[8] was born 26 Jul 1896. He died 25 Oct 1951.

   Earl married **Salena HAMILTON** "Lena". Lena was born 23 Mar 1900. She died 22 Nov 1992.

   They had the following children:

   +   2 F   i.   **Lola Jane HARDMAN** was born 10 Mar 1919 and died 25 Feb 1961.

   +   3 F   ii.   **Opal HARDMAN** was born 15 Oct 1920.

        4 M   iii.   **Gerald Hardman HARDMAN** was born 27 Aug 1922.

                    Gerald married **Carmel SHEPHERD** on 17 Oct 1947. Carmel died 5 Dec 2001.

   +   5 M   iv.   **Virgil HARDMAN** was born 13 Dec 1924.

   +   6 M   v.   **William HARDMAN** was born 30 Apr 1928.

   +   7 M   vi.   **Sylvester HARDMAN** was born 28 May 1930.

   +   8 F   vii.   **Eileen HARDMAN** was born 12 Nov 1935.

   +   9 F   viii.   **Athleen HARDMAN** was born 12 Nov 1935 and died 13 Sep 1996.

Second Generation

2. **Lola Jane HARDMAN** (Earl) was born 10 Mar 1919. She died 25 Feb 1961.

   Lola married **Ray MARSH** about 1937.

   They had the following children:

        10 M   i. **Larry MARSH**.

        11 M   ii. **William Rondell MARSH**.

        12 M   iii. **Michael MARSH**.

        13 F   iv. **Shanda MARSH**.

3. **Opal HARDMAN** (Earl) was born 15 Oct 1920.
Opal married **Warren FELTON** on 22 Jun 1941.
They had the following children:

        14 F   i. **Beverly FELTON**.

        15 M   ii. **David FELTON**.

5. **Virgil HARDMAN** (Earl) was born 13 Dec 1924.
Virgil married **Dorothy CURTIS** on 5 Jan 1946.
They had the following children:

        16 M   i. **Jerry HARDMAN**.

        17 F   ii. **Linda HARDMAN**.

        18 M   iii. **Eddy HARDMAN**.

6. **William HARDMAN** (Earl) was born 30 Apr 1928.
William married **Ann Ree WEST** about 1950.
They had the following children:

        19 F   i. **Cyrie HARDMAN**.

        20 F   ii. **Ila Ree HARDMAN**.

        21 M   iii. **Billy HARDMAN**.

        22 M   iv. **Timothy HARDMAN**.

7. **Sylvester HARDMAN** (Earl) was born 28 May 1930.
Sylvester married **Ann UNKNOWN** about 1950.
They had the following children:

        23 F   i. **Regina HARDMAN**.

        24 F   ii. **Ann HARDMAN**.

8. **Eileen HARDMAN** (Earl) was born 12 Nov 1935.

   Eileen married **Raymond THIBAUT** on 17 Nov 1956.

   They had the following children:

+   25   M   i.   **Raymond David THIBAUT** was born 4 Aug 1958.

+   26   F   ii.   **Linda Eileen THIBAUT** was born 14 Feb 1962.

     27   M   iii.   **Douglas Michael THIBAUT** was born 30 Apr 1968.

9. **Athleen HARDMAN** (Earl) was born 12 Nov 1935. She died 13 Sep 1996.

   Athleen married **Bernard FRAZIER**. Bernard died 25 May 1983.

   They had the following children:

+   28   F   i.   **Cherry Denise FRAZIER**.

+   29   F   ii.   **Deborah Ann FRAZIER**.

+   30   M   iii.   **Eric Andrew FRAZIER**.

11, **William Rondall MARSH**[9] (Lola MARSH, Earl) was born 1 Jan 1943.

   He married **Cynthia Renee TOOTHMAN** 30 Sep 1967. She was born 25 Dec 1968.

   They had the following children:

     31   M   i.   **Bryan Scott MARSH** was born 25 Dec 1968.

     32   M   ii.   **Michael Todd MARSH** was born 25 Dec 1970.

Third Generation

25. **Raymond David THIBAUT** (Eileen HARDMAN, Earl) was born 4 Aug 1958.

   Raymond married **Deborah WHITE** on 14 Aug 1984.

They had the following children:

 33 F i. **Katy THIBAUT**.

 34 F ii. **Molly THIBAUT**.

26. **Linda Eileen THIBAUT** (Eileen HARDMAN, Earl) was born 14 Feb 1962.

Linda married **John MCBRIDE** on 5 Oct 1985.

They had the following children:

 35 M i. **J. P. MCBRIDE**.

 36 F ii. **Meredith MCBRIDE**.

 37 M iii. **Daniel MCBRIDE**.

 38 F iv. **Laura MCBRIDE**.

28. **Cherry Denise FRAZIER** (Athleen HARDMAN, Earl).

Cherry married (1) **James PARSONS** on 6 Dec 1980.

They had the following children:

 39 F i. **Sheena PARSONS** was born 2 Sep 1982.

 40 F ii. **Marisa PARSONS** was born 15 Sep 1983.

Cherry also married (2) **David MOSER** on Jan 1987.

29. **Deborah Ann FRAZIER** (Athleen HARDMAN, Earl).

Deborah married (1) **John RICHARDS** on 1 Sep 1978.

They had the following children:

 41 M i. **Joshua RICHARDS** was born 26 May 1979.

 42 F ii. **Cherra RICHARDS** was born 19 Mar 1981.

Deborah also married (2) **Kelly RORICK**.

They had the following children:

 43 F iii. **Sydnie RORICK** was born 12 Aug 1992.

30. **Eric Andrew FRAZIER** (Athleen HARDMAN, Earl).

Eric married **Tammy PALMER** on 30 Oct 1982.

They had the following children:

   44 M   i. **Dustin FRAZIER** was born 19 Apr 1983.

   45 F   ii. **Selena FRAZIER**.

   46 F   iii. **Carley FRAZIER**.

Descendants of

Frank and Leatha Hardman Williams

First Generation

1. **Leatha Carrie HARDMAN**[10] was born 12 Jun 1901 in Fall Run, Braxton County, WV. She died 24 Dec 1955 in Benwood, WV and was buried in Riverview Cemetery, Marshall Co., WV.

Leatha married **Frank C. WILLIAMS** on 2 Nov 1922. Frank died Jun 1955 in Riverview Cemetery, Marshall Co., WV.

They had the following children:

> 2 F   i.   **Amelia WILLIAMS** was born 23 Feb 1924. She died 23 Feb 1924.
>
> 3 F   ii.   **Alta May WILLIAMS** was born 11 Mar 1925. She died before 1976.
>
> +   4 F   iii.   **Agnes WILLIAMS** was born 16 Oct 1926.
>
> +   5 M   iv.   **Carl WILLIAMS** was born 6 Jan 1934 and died 8 Jul 1975.
>
> +   6 M   v.   **George WILLIAMS** was born 15 May 2002.
>
> +   7 F   vi.   **Hazel WILLIAMS** was born 1 Nov 1935.

Second Generation

4. **Agnes WILLIAMS** (Leatha Carrie) was born 16 Oct 1926.

Agnes married **Charles TRACY**. Charles was born 20 Jan 1911.

They had the following children:

> 8 M   i.   **Samuel TRACY** was born 27 Feb 1947. He died 20 Feb 2005.
>
> 9 M   ii.   **Michael TRACY** "Mike" was born 21 Mar

1950.

    10 M   iii. **Charles TRACY** was born 1 Jul 1953.

+   11 F   iv. **Mary TRACY** was born 15 Apr 1955.

    12 M   v. **Jack TRACY** was born 21 Sep 1957. He died 13 Feb 2002.

+   13 F   vi. **Alta TRACY** was born 26 Apr 1963 and died 16 Jun 2000.

5. **Carl WILLIAMS** (Leatha Carrie) was born 6 Jan 1934. He died 8 Jul 1975.

Carl married **Lorena MCKENNAN** on 10 Jun 1955. Lorena was born 12 Sep 1936.

They had the following children:

+   14 F   i. **Carla Jo WILLIAMS** was born 7 Jan 1957.

+   15 F   ii. **Patricia Anne WILLIAMS** was born 27 Feb 1958.

+   16 F   iii. **Christy Lynn WILLIAMS** was born 13 Aug 1960.

+   17 F   iv. **Pamela Sue WILLIAMS** was born 25 Aug 1962.

    18 F   v. **Dana Leigh WILLIAMS** was born 23 Oct 1964.

              Dana married **Tom FOSTER** on 26 Sep 1992. Tom was born 8 Sep 1956.

    19 F   vi. **Candice WILLIAMS** was born 17 Jul 1967.

6. **George WILLIAMS** (Leatha Carrie) was born 15 May 2002.

George married **Alice LLOYD** on 7 Aug 1964 in Glendale.

They had the following children:

    20 M   i. **William WILLIAMS** was born 1 Jul 1965 in Marshall Co.

21　F　ii.　**Terry WILLIAMS** was born 7 Sep 1966 in Marshall Co., WV.

22　F　iii.　**Becki WILLIAMS** was born 6 Oct 1967.

23　F　iv.　**Jody WILLIAMS** was born 18 Oct 1968.

24　F　v.　**Amy WILLIAMS** was born 28 Apr 1970.

7.　**Hazel WILLIAMS** (Leatha Carrie) was born 1 Nov 1935 in McKeefree, Marshall Co., WV.

Hazel married **Alfred E. SMITH** "Al" on 1 Aug 1953 in St. John's, Benwood. Al was born 6 Sep 1928.

They had the following children:

25　F　i.　**Teresa SMITH** was born 8 Apr 1955.

+　26　M　ii.　**Dennis SMITH** was born 10 May 1956.

+　27　F　iii.　**Paula J. SMITH** was born 19 Nov 1957.

+　28　F　iv.　**Mary Margaret SMITH** was born 18 Mar 1959.

+　29　M　v.　**Patrick Allen SMITH** was born 5 Sep 1961.

+　30　F　vi.　**Elizabeth SMITH** was born 31 Oct 1965.

+　31　F　vii.　**Bridget Marie SMITH** was born 17 Sep 1973.

Third Generation

11.　**Mary TRACY** (Agnes WILLIAMS, Leatha Carrie) was born 15 Apr 1955.

Mary married **HAMILTON**.

They had the following children:

+　32　F　i.　**Carol HAMILTON** was born 15 Oct 1976.

+　33　F　ii.　**Alta HAMILTON** was born 28 Apr 1978.

34　M　iii.　**Gerald HAMILTON** "Eddie" was born 1 Dec 1980.

13. **Alta TRACY** (Agnes WILLIAMS, Leatha Carrie) was born 26 Apr 1963. She died 16 Jun 2000.

Alta married **Borford BLEDSOE Jr.**.

They had the following children:

+   35 M   i. **Borford BLEDSOE III** was born 23 Nov 1981.

+   36 F   ii. **Geneva BLEDSOE** was born 18 Jun 1983.

+   37 F   iii. **Amanda D. BLEDSOE** was born 25 Jun 1984.

14. **Carla Jo WILLIAMS** (Carl WILLIAMS, Leatha Carrie) was born 7 Jan 1957.

Carla was not married (1) to **James ZINK**.

They had the following child:

+   38 M   i. **Carl Edward ZINK** was born 20 Feb 1977.

Carla also married (2) **Dennis WYCKOFF**. The marriage ended in divorce.

They had the following child:

+   39 M   ii. **Matthew Ray WYCKOFF** was born 4 Jul 1981.

15. **Patricia Anne WILLIAMS** (Carl WILLIAMS, Leatha Carrie) was born 27 Feb 1958.

Patricia married **James DAUGHTERY** on 2 Sep 1979. James was born 4 Feb 1957.

They had the following children:

     40 M   i. **Joshua Neil DAUGHTERY** was born 14 Dec 1984.

     41 M   ii. **Shane Taylor DAUGHTERY** was born 3 Jul 1986.

16. **Christy Lynn WILLIAMS** (Carl WILLIAMS, Leatha Carrie) was born 13 Aug 1960.

Christy married **Steven MEHL**. The marriage ended in divorce. Steven was born 21 Apr 1957.

They had the following children:

+ 42 F i. **Allison MEHL** was born 18 Dec 1981.

  43 M ii. **Steven MEHL** was born 30 Nov 1985.

  44 M iii. **Gino MEHL** was born 22 Jul 1987.

17. **Pamela Sue WILLIAMS** (Carl WILLIAMS, Leatha Carrie) was born 25 Aug 1962.

Pamela married **Samuel BUDREVICH** on 12 Sep 1987. Samuel was born 18 Sep 1961.

They had the following children:

  45 M i. **Frank BUDREVICH** was born 11 Jun 1989.

  46 F ii. **Samantha BUDREVICH** was born 16 Aug 1990.

20. **William Williams** (George WILLIAMS, Leatha Carrie) was born 1 Jul 1965.

Bill married (1) **Lori COX** Sep 1984.

They had the following children:

  47 F i. **Breann WILLIAMS** was born 16 Jun 1985.

Bill had the following child:

  48 M ii. **Kyle WILLIAMS** was born 1 Jul 1990.

Bill also married (2) **Salina STIMON** 23 Jan 2001.

They had the following child:

  49 F iii. **Kailynn WILLIAMS** was born 1 Jul 2002.

21. **Terry WILLIAMS** (George WILLIAMS, Leatha Carrie) was born 7 Sep 1966 in Marshall Co., WV.

Terry married **William BLACK** 29 Oct 1988.

They had the following children:

  50 F i. **Sarah BLACK** was born 17 Nov 1986.

51   M   ii.   **Ryan BLACK** was born 1 Oct 1990.

22. **Becki WILLIAMS** (George WILLIAMS, Leatha Carrie) was born 6 Oct 1967.

  Becki had the following child:

  52   M   i.   **Cody WILLIAMS** was born 28 Dec 1994.

23. **Jody WILLIAMS** (George WILLIAMS, Leatha Carrie) was born 18 Oct 1968.

  Jody had the following child:

  53   F   i.   **Amanda WILLIAMS** was born 18 May 1984.

  Jody married **Courtney BLOCK** 15 Sep 1988.

  54   F   ii.   **Danielle BLOCK** was born 12 Jan 1987. She died 21 May 2005 in a plane crash with her father, **Courtney BLOCK.**

24. **Amy WILLIAMS** (George WILLIAMS, Leatha Carrie) was born 28 Apr 1970.

  Amy married **Roger MCDONALD** 25 May 1988.

  They had the following child:

  55   F   i.   **Cheyann WILLIAMS** was born 22 Jun 1989.

26. **Dennis SMITH** (Hazel WILLIAMS, Leatha Carrie) was born 10 May 1956.

  Dennis married (1) **Terry FISHER**. The marriage ended in divorce.

  Dennis was also not married (2) to **Tamarra BRUCE**.

  They had the following children:

  56   F   i.   **Tiffany Nicole SMITH** was born 5 Nov 1990.

  57   F   ii.   **Tanya Danielle SMITH** was born 15 Apr 1993.

27. **Paula J. SMITH** "Beanie" (Hazel WILLIAMS, Leatha Carrie) was born 19 Nov 1957.

  Beanie was not married (1) to **James SCARFPIN**.

They had the following child:

   58 M   i. **James E. SMITH** was born 2 Jan 1976.

Beanie was also not married (2) to **Patrick DUGAN**.

They had the following child:

   59 M   ii. **Andrew A. SMITH** was born 7 Jul 1978.

28. **Mary Margaret SMITH** (Hazel WILLIAMS, Leatha Carrie) was born 18 Mar 1959.

Mary married **Joseph RATLIFF** "Joe".

They had the following child:

   60 F   i. **Dawn RATLIFF**.

           Dawn married **Trey ALLEN** on 7 Aug 2004.

29. **Patrick Allen SMITH** (Hazel WILLIAMS, Leatha Carrie) was born 5 Sep 1961.

Patrick married (1) **Sandy ULLOM**. The marriage ended in divorce.

They had the following children:

   61 F   i. **Heather SMITH** was born 1 Jul 1980.

   62 F   ii. **Heidi SMITH** was born 1 Jul 1980.

Patrick was also not married (2) to **Pam NEY**.

They had the following child:

   63 M   iii. **Patrick Samuel SMITH**.

30. **Elizabeth SMITH** "Lizzie" (Hazel WILLIAMS, Leatha Carrie) was born 31 Oct 1965.

Lizzie was not married to **Aaron BRAK**.

They had the following child:

+   64 F   i. **Megan SMITH** was born 8 Oct 1986.

31. **Bridget Marie SMITH** (Hazel WILLIAMS, Leatha Carrie) was born 17 Sep 1973.

Bridget married **Maurice Delshawn JORDAN** on 1 Feb 1994. The marriage ended in divorce.

They had the following children:

    65 F   i.   **Mia Marshea JORDAN** was born 4 Mar 1994.

    66 M   ii.   **Malik Delshawn JORDAN** was born 11 Feb 1995.

Fourth Generation

32. **Carol HAMILTON** (Mary TRACY, Agnes WILLIAMS, Leatha Carrie) was born 15 Oct 1976.

Carol was not married to **Jeffrey HUTCHISON**.

They had the following children:

    67 F   i.   **Tiffany HAMILTON** was born 11 Apr 1995.

    68 F   ii.   **Mia HUTCHISON** was born 19 Dec 1997.

    69 M iii.   **Jeffrey HUTCHISON** was born 26 Apr 1998.

33. **Alta HAMILTON** (Mary TRACY, Agnes WILLIAMS, Leatha Carrie) was born 28 Apr 1978.

Alta married (1) **Brian MCMAHON** on 3 Jul 2000.

They had the following child:

    70 F   i.   **Kyli MCMAHON** was born 19 Jul 2005.

35. **Borford BLEDSOE III** (Alta TRACY, Agnes WILLIAMS, Leatha Carrie) was born 23 Nov 1981.

He had the following child:

    71 F   i.   **Tanien BLEDSOE** was born 22 Aug 2002.

36. **Geneva BLEDSOE** (Alta TRACY, Agnes WILLIAMS, Leatha Carrie) was born 18 Jun 1983.

She had the following child:

    72 F   i.   **Kyky BLEDSOE** was born 4 Aug 2003.

37. **Amanda D. BLEDSOE** (Alta TRACY, Agnes WILLIAMS, Leatha Carrie) was born 25 Jun 1984.

She had the following child:

   73 F   i. **Ureanna BLEDSOE** was born 27 May 2005.

38. **Carl Edward ZINK** (Carla Jo WILLIAMS, Carl WILLIAMS, Leatha Carrie) was born 20 Feb 1977.

Carl married **Kristy GODFREY** on 14 Nov 1998. Kristy was born 10 Feb 1977.

They had the following children:

   74 F   i. **Carliegh Joanne ZINK** was born 13 Dec 1998.

   75 F   ii. **Maelynn Paige ZINK** was born 19 Nov 2001.

   76 M iii. **James Briar ZINK** was born 19 Feb 2004.

39. **Matthew Ray WYCKOFF** (Carla Jo WILLIAMS, Carl WILLIAMS, Leatha Carrie) was born 4 Jul 1981.

Matthew was not married to **Nicole YOCUM**. Nicole was born 20 Nov 1981.

They had the following children:

   77 F   i. **Hannah Raylene WYCKOFF** was born 3 Mar 2002.

   78 F   ii. **Aubrey Renee WYCKOFF** was born 15 Nov 2004.

42. **Allison MEHL** (Christy Lynn WILLIAMS, Carl WILLIAMS, Leatha Carrie) was born 18 Dec 1981.

Allison married **Jason COLLETIE** on 12 Sep 2004. Jason was born 28 Jan 1979.

They had the following child:

   79 M   i. **Matthew COLLETIE** was born 21 Dec 2004.

53. **Amanda WILLIAMS** (Jody BLOCK, George WILLIAMS, Leatha Carrie) was born 18 May 1984.

Amanda married **Clayton ANDERSON**.

They had the following child:

   80 F   i. **Paige ANDERSON** was born 25 Mar 2000.

   81 F   ii. **Grace ANDERSON** was born 29 Dec 2002.

55. **Megan SMITH** (Elizabeth SMITH, Hazel WILLIAMS, Leatha Carrie) was born 8 Oct 1986.

Megan was not married to **Ricardo M. SUGGS**.

They had the following child:

   82 M   i. **Deante A. SUGGS** was born 8 Feb 2005.

Descendants of

Walter and Gertrude Hamilton Hardman

First Generation

1. **Walter Worthington HARDMAN**[11] was born 15 May 1904 in Fall Run, Braxton Co., WV. He died 20 Apr 1970 and was buried in Sunset Memorial, Clarksburg, WV.

   Walter married **Gertrude HAMILTON** "Gertie", daughter of George HAMILTON and Mary Jane CRITCHFIELD, on ~1928. Gertie was born 3 Oct 1902. She died 28 Sep 1988 and was buried in Sunset Memorial, Clarksburg, WV.

   They had the following children:

   +   2 F   i.   **Naoma HARDMAN** was born 3 Oct 1929.

   +   3 F   ii. **Nina HARDMAN** was born 19 Jul 1934 and died 17 Jul 1999.

   +   4 M   iii. **Walter Noel HARDMAN** was born 9 Oct 1936.

   +   5 M   iv. **Norman Russell HARDMAN** was born 22 Aug 1941.

   +   6 M   v.   **Nelson HARDMAN** was born 15 Sep 1944.

Second Generation

2. **Naoma HARDMAN** (Walter Worthington) was born 3 Oct 1929 in Harrison Co., Clarksburg, WV.

   Naoma married **Harold BORAM**, son of Grant M BORAM and Leora Bell DUNLAP, on 22 Sep 1956. Harold was born 7 Aug 1930.

   They had the following children:

   +   7 F   i.   **Laura BORAM** was born 3 Nov 1967.

   +   8 M   ii. **Brent BORAM** was born 30 Mar 1969.

3. **Nina HARDMAN** (Walter Worthington) was born 19 Jul 1934 in Flemington, WV. She died 17 Jul 1999 and was buried 20 Jul 1999.

Nina married **Lenard PASTERNAK**.

They had the following child:

> 9 M i. **Edmond PASTERNAK** was born 20 Oct 1960 in Clarksburg, WV.
>
> > Edmond married **Tammy UNKNOWN**.

Nina also married **Terry FITZPATRICK**.

4. **Walter Noel HARDMAN** (Walter Worthington) was born 9 Oct 1936 in Gypsy, WV.

Walter married **Carolyn CORNELL**. Carolyn was born 7 Nov 1944.

They had the following children:

> 10 F i. **Stephanie J. HARDMAN** was born 10 Sep 1967 in WV.
>
> 11 M ii. **Steven N. HARDMAN** was born 20 Jan 1975 in WV.

5. **Norman Russell HARDMAN** (Walter Worthington) was born 22 Aug 1941 in Gypsy, WV.

Norman married **Shirley LEWIS** on 7 Aug 1962. The marriage ended in divorce. Shirley was born 23 Oct 1942. She died 9 Jan 2004 and was buried in Sunset Memorial, Clarksburg, WV.

They had the following children:

> 12 F i. **Belinda HARDMAN**.
>
> 13 F ii. **Robin HARDMAN**.
>
> 14 M iii. **Jay HARDMAN**.
>
> 15 M iv. **Jaimie HARDMAN**.

Norman also married **Sandy YOHO** on 2 Jul 1983. Sandy was born 4 Aug 1948.

6. **Nelson HARDMAN** (Walter Worthington) was born 15 Sep 1944 in Harrison Co., Clarksburg, WV.

Nelson married **Nancy BENNETT** on 13 Sep 1969. Nancy was born 29 Dec 1944.

They had the following children:

    16 M   i. **Neil HARDMAN** was born 9 May 1973.

    17 F   ii. **Tracy HARDMAN** was born 3 May 1977.

                Tracy married **Corky ATHA**.

    18 F   iii. **Terry HARDMAN** was born 28 Mar 1979.

Third Generation

7. **Laura BORAM** (Naoma HARDMAN, Walter Worthington) was born 3 Nov 1967 in Wheeling, WV.

Laura married **Greg RAFA** on 27 Jun 1992. Greg was born 30 Jun 1968.

They had the following children:

    19 M   i. **Ryan RAFA** was born 20 May 1994 in Wheeling, WV.

    20 F   ii. **Megan RAFA** was born 18 Jul 1996 in Wheeling, WV.

8. **Brent BORAM** (Naoma HARDMAN, Walter Worthington) was born 30 Mar 1969 in Wheeling, WV.

Brent married **Amy PEGG**. Amy was born 10 Nov 1968.

They had the following children:

    21 F   i. **Abbey BORAM** was born 1 Oct 1992 in Wheeling, WV.

    22 F   ii. **Jenna BORAM** was born 4 Jun 1996 in Wheeling, WV.

    23 M   iii. **Garrett BORAM** was born 14 Apr 2000 in Wheeling, WV.

Descendants of

Retta Hardman Bildstien

Edward and Retta Dale Hardman Bildstien

First Generation

1. **Retta Dale HARDMAN**[12] was born 10 Nov 1910 in Fall Run, Braxton Co., West Virginia. She died 5 Oct 1977 in Glen Burnie, Maryland.

   She had the following children:

      2 F   i. **Oleta HARDMAN** was born 31 May 1928 in Fall Run, Braxton Co., West Virginia.

                    Oleta married **George Edward CARTER**. George died 13 May 1992.

   +   3 M ii. **Irwin HARDMAN** was born 28 Feb 1930.

   Retta also married **Edward BILDSTIEN** about 1955.

Second Generation

Irwin and Carol Criswell Hardman Family

3. **Irwin HARDMAN** (Retta Dale) was born 28 Feb 1930.

   Irwin married **Carol CRISWELL** on 30 Mar 1951.

   They had the following children:

   +   4   F   i.   **Dale HARDMAN** was born 4 Sep 1952.

   +   5   F   ii.   **Deborah HARDMAN** was born 8 Jun 1955.

   +   6   M   iii.   **Brett HARDMAN** was born 8 Jun 1958.

Third Generation

4. **Dale HARDMAN** (Irwin, Retta Dale) was born 4 Sep 1952.

   Dale married **Vincent DERUBBA** on 16 Oct 1988.

   They had the following children:

      7   F   i.   **Christine DERUBBA** was born 30 Sep 1990.

      8   M   ii.   **Matthew DERUBBA** was born 28 Aug 1991.

5. **Deborah HARDMAN** (Irwin, Retta Dale) was born 8 Jun 1955.

Deborah married **Samuel ELMO** on 15 Jul 1978.

They had the following children:

    9 F   i. **Alison ELMO** was born 1 Aug 1984.

    10 M   ii. **Trevor ELMO** was born 3 Jul 1986.

    11 M iii. **Jason ELMO** was born 5 Jun 1989.

6. **Brett HARDMAN** (Irwin, Retta Dale) was born 8 Jun 1958.

Brett married **Robin GARDNER** on 4 Jun 1989.

They had the following children:

    12 M   i. **Brandon HARDMAN** was born 13 Sep 1991.

    13 M   ii. **Colton HARDMAN** was born 1 Oct 1994.

Descendants of

Joshua Roe

First Generation

1. **Joshua ROE**[13] was born ~1755 in England. He died Nov 1805 in Fleming Co. Ky.

   Joshua married **Athaliah GODDARD**.

   They had the following children:

   +   2   M   i.   **Edward Roe** was born 15 Sep 1790 and died 24 Jul 1880.

        3   M   ii.   **Isham Roe.**

        4   M   iii.   **Joshua Roe.**

        5   F   iv.   **Nancy Roe.**

        6   F   v.   **Ariel Roe.**

Second Generation

2. **Edward Roe** (Joshua) was born 15 Sep 1790 in Baltimore, Md. He died 24 Jul 1880 in Lewis County, Ky. and was buried in Stone Family Cemetery, Lewis County, Ky.

   Roe married **Athaliah Ellender LITTLETON** "Eleanor" on 29 Oct 1812 in Fleming County, Ky.

   They had the following children:

        7   F   i.   **Nancy ROE.**

        8   F   ii.   **Mary Ann ROE** "Polly".

   +   9   M   iii.   **Isam Morris ROE** was born 17 Dec 1817 and died 23 Aug 1878.

      10   F   iv.   **Violet ROE.**

      11   F   v.   **Athaliah Ellen ROE** "Eleanor".

      12   M   vi.   **John Littleton ROE.**

      13   F   vii.   **Mary ROE.**

      14   M   viii.   **Sidney ROE.**

15 F ix. **Leanner ROE.**

16 M x. **James Harrison ROE.**

17 F xi. **Malinda ROE.**

Edward also married **Rebecca BURRIS** on 12 Oct 1838 in Court House, Vanceburg, Lewis County, Ky.

They had the following children:

18 M xii. **William ROE.**

19 M xiii. **Morgan ROE.**

20 F xiv. **Angeline ROE.**

21 M xv. **Edward ROE.**

22 M xvi. **Fielding ROE.**

23 F xvii. **Elizabeth ROE.**

24 F xviii. **Rebecca ROE.**

Third Generation

9. **Isam Morris ROE** (Edward, Joshua) was born 17 Dec 1817 in Fleming County, Ky. He died 23 Aug 1878 and was buried in Stone Family Cemetery, Vanceburg, Ky.

Isam married **Eleanor Harrison GILBERT** on 25 Mar 1841 in Carter County, Ky.

They had the following children:

+ 25 M i. **John ROE** was born ~1842 and died 6 Apr 1881.

26 F ii. **Lottie ROE.**

27 F iii. **Sarah ROE** "Sally".

28 F iv. **Martha Ellen ROE.**

29 F v. **Rachel ROE.**

30 M vi. **James Edward ROE.**

31 M vii. **William Isam ROE.**

32 M viii. **Samuel Henry ROE.**

33 F ix. **Georgia ROE.**

34 M x. **Charles Wesley ROE** "Wes".

35 M xi. **Robert Jackson ROE.**

36 M xii. **Thomas Fielding ROE.**

37 M xiii. **Harrison ROE** "Henry".

38 F xiv. **Violet ROE.**

Fourth Generation

25. **John ROE** (Isam Morris, Edward, Joshua) was born ~1842 in Latona, Jasper, Il. He died 6 Apr 1881 in South Muddy Cemetery, Jasper, Il.

John married **Terrese Ann TABER** "Creesie" on 6 Nov 1863 in Sarah Taber's, Carter County, Ky.

They had the following children:

39 M i. **Isom Morris ROE.**

+ 40 M ii. **Hezekiah ROE** was born 21 Mar 1867 and died 16 Apr 1953.

41 M iii. **William F. ROE.**

42 M iv. **George Edward ROE.**

43 F v. **Sarah Ellen ROE.**

44 M vi. **Charles W. ROE.**

Fifth Generation

40. **Hezekiah ROE** "Carr" (John, Isam Morris, Edward, Joshua) was born 21 Mar 1867 in Carter County, Ky. He died 16 Apr 1953 and was buried in Wilburn Cemetery, Carter County, Ky.

Carr married **Luicy MADDIX** on 4 Nov 1896 in Carter County, Ky.

They had the following children:

45	M	i.	**John Charles ROE.**
46	F	ii.	**Crecy ROE.**
47	M	iii.	**William F. ROE.**
+ 48	M	iv.	**Lafayette ROE** was born 27 Jul 1904 and died 27 Sep 1935.
49	F	v.	**Ina ROE.**
50	F	vi.	**Nellie M. ROE.**
51	F	vii.	**Frances ROE.**

Sixth Generation

48. **Lafayette ROE** "Lathe" (Hezekiah, John, Isam Morris, Edward, Joshua) was born 27 Jul 1904 in Carter County, Ky. He died 27 Sep 1935 and was buried in Wilburn Cemetery, Carter County, Ky.

Lathe married **Pearl SCOTT**.

They had the following children:

52	F	i.	**Alwilda ROE** "Billy".
53	M	ii.	**Clifton ROE.**
54	M	iii.	**Willis ROE** "James William". He married **Edith Sharon HARDMAN.** They were divorced.
55	F	iv.	**Jacqueline ROE** "Jackie".

Life Sketch of the John Stout Family

1 http://www.rootsweb.com/`hcpd/norman/STOUT.1.

2 reticent@pacbell.net. This information was emailed to me from a 'cousin' and Stout descendant.

[4] Price, William, *History of Pocahontas County,* 189, 192. Excerpts of this book was sent to me by Emma Snider.

[5] *The Book of Discipline of the United Methodist Church.* (Nashville: The Methodist Publishing House, 2000), 9-11.

[6] Price, William, *History of Pocahontas County,* 188, 195.

[7] Ibid., 194-195

[8] *The Book of Discipline of the United Methodist Church*, (Nashville: The Methodist Publishing House, 2000). 11

[9] Price, William, *History of Pocahontas County,* 189, 191.

10 Copies of these were sent to me by Emma Snider.

11 The copy of this will was sent to me by Emma Snider.

Life Sketch of the Leonard Boyer I Family

12 The copy of this will was sent to me by Emma Snider.

13 The copy of this deed was sent to me by Emma Snider.

Life Sketch of the Henry McWhorter Family

14 McWhorter, Minnie S., *The History of the Henry McWhorter Family of New Jersey and West Virginia,* (Charleston: Charleston Printing Company, 1948), 4.

15 Ibid., 8.

16 Ibid., 25

17 Ibid., 4.

18 Ibid., 6.

19 17 Ibid., 4.

[20] Withers, Alexander, *Chronicles of Border Warfare,* (Parsons, West Virginia: McClain Printing Co. 1895). 410.

Life Sketch of the Thomas De Lowther Family

21 Rootweb's WorldConnect Project: Gary Lewis Family Tree, www.worldconnect.rootsweb.com.

22 Lowther, Minnie Kendall, *History of Ritchie County*, (Wheeling: Wheeling News Litho. Co., 1911), 6.

23 Ibid., 5.

24 Vaughan, Sheryl, www. boards.ancestry.com.

[25] Lowther, Minnie Kendall. *History of Ritchie County,* (Wheeling: Wheeling News Litho. Co. 1911). 6

26 Ibid., 7.

27 Ibid., 8.

28 Ibid., 8.

29 Ibid., 8.

30 Withers, *Chronicles of Border Warfare*, 312, 313, 376, 377.

31 Ibid., 127.

32 Lowther, Minnie Kendall, *The History of Ritchie County*, 8.

33 Gilchrist, Joy and others, *Hacker's Creek Journal*, Vol. XII, Iss 2-3, (Hacker's Creek Pioneer Descendants: A Historical and Genealogical Society of Lewis Co., WV) 161.

34 Lowther, Minnie. History of Ritchie County, 1.

35 Ibid., 9.

36 Ibid., 16.

Life Sketch of the Nicholas Hardman Family

37 Gilchrist, Joy etal, *Hacker's Creek Journal*, Vol. XII, Issue 1, 49.

38 Withers, Alexander, *Chronicles of Border Warfare*, (Cincinnati: The Robert Clarke Company, 1895), 408-9.

39 Gilchrist, Joy et al, *Hacker's Creek Journal*, 50.

40 *The Book of Discipline of the United Methodist*, 13.

Hardesty's History of West Virginia, 81
41 Bassett, Ancell H., *A Concise History of the Methodist Protestant Church*, (Pittsburgh: J. Robison, 1882) 106.

42 Gilchrist, Joy etal, *Hacker's Creek Journal*, 50.

Generations of the John Stout Family

1   Herald F. Stout, *Stout and Allied Families*, Vol.1,1. I received excerpts of this book from a John Stout descendant, reticent@pacbell.net.

2   www.rootsweb.com/hcpd/norman/STOUT.1.

3   Ibid.

4   Ibid.

5   Herald F. Stout, *Stout and Allied Families*,159.

6   www.rootsweb.com/hcpd/norman/STOUT.1.

7   Ibid.

8   Herald F. Stout, *Stout and Allied Families*, 40.

9   Ibid., 85.

10   The sources from www.rootsweb.com/hcpd/norman/STOUT.1 and reticient@pacbell.net do not agree. I used both dates.

13   I accepted the year of 1811 since the first child was born 22 Oct 1814. Don Norman file has 1816.

14   Does he belong?. There are two sons with the same name who apparently grew to adulthood because both married. Could this be one person, a discrepancy in birth date, who married twice?

15 Mary Edith Bowyer Mayse shared this information from the family Bible. She was the daughter of Mary Catora Stout Bowyer.

16 Christie, the great granddaughter of George Washington Stout, shared her research with me for the book.

17 Christie Stout/Other Family Members at Stout Reunion

18 Mary Catora Stout Bowyer's descendants continue in the Bowyer, Hardman and Mayse families.

19 This information was obtained from William C. Dennison, her husband, at the Falls Mill reunion in July, 1995.

20 This was in a letter from Warder and Virgie Stout's daughter, Mavis Jean.

Generations of the Felix Grimes Family

1 Price, William, *History of Pocahontas County*, 188-194.

2 E-mail received from Lawrence Reger, ancestor of Ellen Virginia Bowyer Watson.

3 Age calculated from Pocahontas County (West) Virginia 1850 Census .

4 Jane was the mother of our great grandfather, Charles Osbourne Bowyer.

5 Our lineage within the Stout family comes through the marriage of Mary Catora Stout to Hugh Raymond Bowyer. She was the daughter of Mary Matilda Bowyer, Catharine's daughter.

6 Price, William, *History Of Pocahontas County*, p. 194. Catharine was the second wife of Leonard (Leonidas) Bowyer and the mother of our great grandmother, Mary Matilda Bowyer. She was a first cousin of his first wife, Nancy Jane Grimes.

Generations of the Leonard Bowyer Family

1 Will of Leonard Boyer I. The copy of the will was received from Emma Riffle Snider.

2 William Price, *History of Pocahontas Co.* Includes information from Census 1870, Gilmer Co., 1880 Braxton Co., Microfilm from AFLI catalogue. The research was done by Emma Snider.

3 Copy of field Check by W. P. Cochran received from Emma Snider.

4 Pocahontas Co., (W)V, 1850. In the census Leonard is married to Catherine and Charles Osbourne is listed as ten months old.

5 Census of Gilmer County WV 1870 and 1880. Nancy is named in her father's will and listed as living with her brother, Leonard, in 1870 with her age as 59. In the 1880 census her age is listed as 70 and living with Leonard.

6 Lawrence Reger e-mail of his research with this information noted on it. He sent the marriages of Pocahontas Co., (W)V 1850. Annonated on the bottom were his notes with the date of Leonard and Jane's marriage.

7 Pocahontas Co., (W)V, census of 1850.

8 William Price, *History of Pocahontas Co.*, 194.

9 This was a census of Highland Co., VA done June 2, 1860 and has Mary Matilda as seven years old.

10 Pocahontas Co., (W)V, 1850. This census lists Catharine as 25 y/o, which would make her birth year 1825. The e-mail from Lawrence Reger has it as 1822.

11 E-mail from Christie Stout. From a census of Braxton Co., WV.

12 Research of Emma Snider.

13 Research of Emma Snider. Emma got this information from some papers with which Rebecca was trying to get an Army pension for herself and her children. Emma believes that some of the dates may be wrong.

14 Lawrence Reger, Ellen Virginia Bowyer Watson. This is Lawrence's ancestral grandmother.

15   The information received from Emma Snider was in agreement with Mr. Reger's.

16   The Will of Leonard Bowyer I. 1860 census of Highland Co. Va.

17   Emma says that Jonathan II was born of a previous marriage of Jonathan I.

18   Charles Osbourne Bowyer's Will.

19   Her gravestone. The cemetery marker in the K & P Cemetery has her name spelled as Merry, however, the census of 1880 has it spelled Mary. This was called to my attention by Georgia Grey Hardman Coffey, descendant.

20   1870 census of Gilmer Co. WV. George Allen is listed as 19 y/o.

21   Emma Snider obtained this information from one of the children, Roxie Moneypenny Dowler Butler who was still living in Ravenna, Ohio.

22   Their children were given to Emma by people who should know but there is no documentation.

23   Emma Snider, Emory and Alberta Spaur Bowyer children. The source is Emma Riffle Snider their great great granddaughter.

24   Emma Snider, Olive Jane Bowyer Spaur and descendants. Emma was her granddaughter.

25   Catora Stout Bowyer kept the family Bible. The George Dencil Hardman I Family Bible was kept by his daughter, Hazel Bowyer Hardman. My Aunt Edith Mayse, his daughter, also shared information.

26   Great Uncle Cicero was burned to death in an accident and preceded his father in death.

27   Emma Snider obtained her information from family sources.

28   Emma Snider and Denzil Stilwell. Mrs. Snider found her work from family and census records. Mr. Stilwell e-mailed the information concerning her son, Roy Charles, and his wife Barbara Berry to me. Barbara was Hazel Bowyer's, our mother, best friend and the aunt of Mr. Stilwell's wife, Ellen.

29   His will, 1870 and 1880 censuses of Gilmer Co., WV and living ancestors.

30   The source for this family was Emma Riffle Snider, their child.

31   Emma Riffle Snider, a sister.

32   Our Bowyer lineage continues through Hazel's marriage to George Dencil Hardman.

33   Interviewed my aunt Edith, who was my namesake, for this information. Funeral records for Uncle Paul, Anna Raye and Aunt Edith.

34   I used the Hugh Raymond Bowyer family Bible and my sister's, Coleta Dare Hardman Thompson, record of birth dates and anniversaries for this family.

35   Coleta Dare Hardman Thompson's birthday book.

Generations of the Henry McWhorter Family

1   McWhorter, Minnie S., *History of the Henry McWhorter Family of New Jersey and New York*, 121.

2   Ibid., 121-122.

3   Ibid., 141.

4   Ibid., 16.

5   Ibid., 142.

Generations of the Thomas De Lowther Family

1   worldconnect.rootsweb.com, Gary Lewis Family Tree. Joan, daughter of Hugh and Matilda Detilliol Lowther. The date in the Gary Lewis Family Tree is 1331, which would have made Matilda only thirteen years old. It would have been possible for her to have a child at this age, however, the marriage date is 1338 seven years

after the 1331 date of birth. That too may have been possible, I just prefer the date of 1341 in relation to the dates of birth of her brothers.

2   worldconnect.rootsweb.com, Gary Lewis Family Tree. John Lowther, son of Hugh and Margaret Quale Lowther. I surmised his birth date was wrong as received on the printout since Hugh would have only been seven years old if he had been born in 1347. I entered it as 1367.

3   Ibid. I put the children in their birth order, which differed from the printout I received.

4   Lowther, Minnie Kendall, *History of Ritchie County*, 7. In her book she names only five sons but states that only part of the names of this family were at her command.

5   www.rootsweb.com/hcpd/norman/LOWTHER.

6   Research of Jinny Collins by e-mail and review of her comments/information on the message board at www.rootsweb.com for the Colonel's family. She has been to England to do research on him, our common ancestor.

7   worldconnect.rootsweb.com, Gary Lewis Family Tree. This source was used for the Lowther lineage from Thomas De Lowther (1199) through William Lowther, Jr. (1720). Minnie Lowther's book did not have the daughters.

8   Lowther, Minnie S., *History of Ritchie County*, 16.

9   McWhorter, Minnie S. *History of the Henry McWhorter Family of New Jersey and New York*, 141.

10   Lowther, Minnie S. *History of Ritchie County* 1911,16-17.

11   McWhorter, Minnie S., *History of the Henry McWhorter Family of New Jersey and New York*, 1948, 142.

12   Ibid., 17.

13   Our Lowther lineage continues through the marriage of Bessie Maude Lowther and John William Hardman George Dencil Hardman I's parents.

14   County Clerk's Office, Braxton County Courthouse, #4, p. 144. I have a copy of this certificate obtained and recorded 3 Sept 1982 by their daughter, Lora Hardman Cutright Queen.

15   This information was gleaned from the surviving members of the family. Obituaries, children and as we remembered them.

16   Minnie S. McWhorter, *History of the Henry McWhorter Family of New Jersey and New York*, 144. A letter from my first cousin, Phyllis Cutright McComas, states that her mother, Lora Arvilla Hardman Cutright Queen, said that grandma told her she was 26 years old when she married. The marriage license says they were married in 1899 if she was 26 years old this would make her birth year 1873

.

Generations of the Nicholas Hardman Family

1 Joy Gilchrist etal, Hackers Creek Journal, p. 55.

2   Ibid., 49,The author notes that information obtained from Paul Hardman's manuscript can be found in some genealogy notebooks submitted to WVU by Mrs. Eloise Bosson Hardman.

3   Ibid., 55. Three more children were found in 1880 census.

4   There is an unnamed child born on this date to Perry and Malinda. When repairing the roof on the homestead on Fall Run, WV I found a piece of tin roof with this name on it and an address of Burnsville, WV. The homestead was built in late 1800's and Perry Andrew owned a hardware in Burnsville.

5 Joy Gilchrist and others, *Hackers Creek Journal*, 54.

6 *Hardesty's History of West Virginia*, 81. Two more children were found in 1900 census. His second marriage was found from the 1920 census.

7 The 1880 census has her as nine y/o which means she was born in either 1873 or 1872 depending on when the census was made that year.

8 McWhorter, Minnie S. History of the Henry McWhorter Family of New Jersey and West Virginia, 142.

9 Information was obtained from my father, George Dencil Hardman I and myself.

10 McWhorter, Minnie S., History of the Henry McWhorter Family of New Jersey and West Virginia, 144.

11 His children are from my memory, I hope, in the correct birth order.

12 McWhorter, Minnie S., History of the Henry McWhorter Family of New Jersey and West Virginia, 1948, 147.

13 Aunt Lora entered his death in the McWhorter book in her handwriting.

14 Their children are from my childhood memory and I hope in the correct birth order. They resided in Despard section of Clarksburg, WV.

15 George D. Hardman I Family Bible.

16 The information for the descendants of George Dencil Hardman II was obtained from his daughter, Georgia Grey Hardman Coffey.

17 This information was obtained from my sister, Marjorie Carol Hardman Burke.

18 This information was received from my sister, Marjorie Carol Hardman Burke.

19 This information was obtained from her son, Robert Edward Thompson.

20 This information was obtained from his son, Robert Edward Thompson.

21 He was the informant.

22 This information was obtained from her husband, Robert Edward Thompson.

23 This is my family.

24 This information was obtained from my sister, Marjorie, William's children and myself.

25 This is my family.

26 This information was obtained from her.

Generations of the Orla Cutright, Sr. Family

1   Minnie S. McWhorter, *History of the Henry MCWhorter Family*, p. 147, 2 Feb 2002. The information for Lora Arvilla Cutright and her descendants were on p 147 and supplemented through letters and conversations with her daughter, Phyllis Cutright McComas and a marriage certificate for her second marriage.

2   Parkersburg News-Sentinel, October, 2001.

"Cousins" of George D. Hardman I

1 This information was given to me in a personal interview with Irene and her family.

2 This information was sent to me by Lawrence Reger her great grandson.

3 This information was sent to me by Verl Dyer and through personal interviews with family member. Jan Hagler Cole gave me the information on Susan Barnett from the Latter Day Saints Library. It was confirmed to be true by Verl Dyer. At a Falls Mill Reunion her descendants came looking for their cousins according to Verl. Delbert Bowyer date of death from his obituary sent to me by Emma Snider.

4 This information was received from his descendant, Jan Hagler Cole. This family was lost to the Braxton County descendants. Jan and I found each other on the internet.

5 This information was sent to me by John Sholes. Roy Sholes gave me the information on his wife, Barbara Lee.

6 This information was given to me in a personal interview with Marbie Lowther Tonkin.

7 This is the brother of our descendant John D. Hardman. They were sons of Peterman, son of Nicholas. The information was obtained from Rebecca Hardman, his descendant and Hacker'sCreek Journal, Vol. 12.

8 This information was sent to me by Eileen Hardman, his daughter.

[9] This family information is from a personal interview with Ron Marsh.

[10] This information is from a personal interview with Hazel Williams Smith, her family, surviving spouses and children.

[11] This information was sent to me by Naoma Hardman Boram the oldest child and Nelson Hardman.

[12] This information was given to me by her children.

[13] Rootweb.com These are the ancestors of the children of 'James William' Roe and Edith Sharon Hardman West.

www.ingramcontent.com/pod-product-compliance
Lightning Source LLC
Chambersburg PA
CBHW030253290526
45785CB00001B/71